African-American
  Poets: Volume I
African-American
  Poets: Volume II
Albert Camus
Aldous Huxley
Alfred, Lord Tennyson
Alice Walker
American Women
  Poets: 1650–1950
Arthur Miller
Asian-American
  Writers
The Bible
The Brontës
Carson McCullers
Charles Dickens
Christopher Marlowe
Contemporary Poets
C.S. Lewis
Dante Aligheri
David Mamet
Derek Walcott
Don DeLillo
Doris Lessing
Edgar Allan Poe
Émile Zola
Emily Dickinson
Ernest Hemingway
Eudora Welty
Eugene O'Neill
F. Scott Fitzgerald
Flannery O'Connor
Franz Kafka
Fyodor Dostoevsky
Gabriel García
  Márquez
Geoffrey Chaucer
George Eliot
George Orwell

G.K. Chesterton
Gwendolyn Brooks
Hans Christian
  Andersen
Henry David Thoreau
Herman Melville
Hermann Hesse
H.G. Wells
Hispanic-American
  Writers
Homer
Honoré de Balzac
Jamaica Kincaid
James Joyce
Jane Austen
Jay Wright
J.D. Salinger
Jean-Paul Sartre
John Donne and
  the 17th-Century
  Metaphysical Poets
John Irving
John Keats
John Milton
John Steinbeck
Jorge Luis Borges
José Saramago
Joseph Conrad
Joyce Carol Oates
J.R.R. Tolkien
Julio Cortázar
Kate Chopin
Langston Hughes
Leo Tolstoy
Marcel Proust
Margaret Atwood
Mark Twain
Mary Wollstonecraft
  Shelley
Maya Angelou

Miguel de Cervantes
Milan Kundera
Nathaniel Hawthorne
Norman Mailer
Octavio Paz
Paul Auster
Philip Roth
Ralph Waldo Emerson
Ray Bradbury
Richard Wright
Robert Browning
Robert Frost
Robert Hayden
Robert Louis
  Stevenson
Salman Rushdie
Sinclair Lewis
Stephen Crane
Stephen King
Sylvia Plath
Tennessee Williams
Thomas Hardy
Thomas Pynchon
Tom Wolfe
Toni Morrison
Tony Kushner
Truman Capote
T.S. Eliot
Walt Whitman
W.E.B. Du Bois
William Blake
William Faulkner
William Gaddis
William Shakespeare
William Wordsworth
Zora Neale Hurston

Bloom's Modern Critical Views

JAMAICA KINCAID
New Edition

Edited and with an introduction by
Harold Bloom
Sterling Professor of the Humanities
Yale University

BLOOM'S
LITERARY CRITICISM
An imprint of Infobase Publishing

Bloom's Literary Criticism
An imprint of Infobase Publishing
132 West 31st Street
New York, NY 10001

Library of Congress Cataloging-in-Publication Data
Jamaica Kincaid / edited and with an introduction by Harold Bloom. – Updated ed.
    p. cm. – (Bloom's modern critical views)
 Includes bibliographical references and index.
 ISBN 978-0-7910-9812-7
 1. Kincaid, Jamaica–Criticism and interpretation. I. Bloom, Harold. II. Title. III. Series.

PR9275.A583K565 2008
813'.54–dc22

2007037660

Bloom's Literary Criticism books are available at special discounts when purchased in bulk quantities for businesses, associations, institutions, or sales promotions. Please call our Special Sales Department in New York at (212) 967-8800 or (800) 322-8755.

You can find Bloom's Literary Criticism on the World Wide Web at
http://www.chelseahouse.com

Contributing Editor: Pamela Loos
Cover designed by Takeshi Takahashi
Cover photo Taro Yamasaki/Time & Life Pictures/Getty Images
Printed in the United States of America
Bang EJB 10 9 8 7 6 5 4 3 2 1

This book is printed on acid-free paper.

All links and Web addresses were checked and verified to be correct at the time of publication. Because of the dynamic nature of the Web, some addresses and links may have changed since publication and may no longer be valid.

Contents

Editor's Note

My Introduction praises Jamaica Kincaid's prose poetry and her skill at fantasia, which places me at odds with all the contributors to this volume, who value her primarily upon an ideological basis.

It is difficult for me to distinguish clearly between the dozen essayists, and I am too old not to speak my mind. Their targets are the usual suspects: colonialism, maternalism, racism, economic exploitation. All the essayists are virtuous, and I respect their moral intensity. Here they are: this is how and why Jamaica Kincaid is now esteemed.

HAROLD BLOOM

Introduction

Most of the published criticism of Jamaica Kincaid has stressed her political and social concerns, somewhat at the expense of her literary qualities. This is inevitable at this time, but fashions change, and Kincaid will not always be esteemed primarily upon ideological grounds. Her second book, *Annie John* (1985), so far remains her best (in my judgment), but this writer is likely to go beyond her earlier work. "Girl" (1984) is one of her briefest stories; I have commented upon it elsewhere and return to it here both because of my affection for its prose and also because it qualifies the critical emphases upon her writing. Ideologues insist that Kincaid has broken with all Western canonical standards, which they associate with such patriarchal malefactors as Shakespeare, Milton, and Dante. Were this true, Kincaid's audience would consist of academic feminists and postcolonial rebels. Since her public is rather larger than that, it is likely that Kincaid's fictions, however original, extend canonical traditions even while attempting to subvert them, which is one of the oldest and most prevalent of literary procedures. Here is my favorite paragraph from "Girl":

> This is how you grow okra—far from the house, because okra tree harbors red ants; when you are growing dasheen, make sure it gets plenty of water or else it makes your throat itch when you are eating it; this is how you sweep a corner; this is how you sweep a whole house; this is how you sweep a yard; this is how you smile to someone you don't like too much; this is how you

smile to someone you don't like at all; this is how you smile to
someone you like completely; this is how you set a table for tea;
this is how you set a table for dinner; this is how you set a table
for dinner with an important guest; this is how you set a table for
lunch; this is how you set a table for breakfast; this is how you
behave in the presence of men who don't know you very well, and
this way they won't recognize immediately the slut I have warned
you against becoming; be sure to wash every day, even if it is with
you own spit; don't squat down to play marbles—you are not
a boy, you know; don't pick people's flowers—you might catch
something; don't throw stones at blackbirds, because it might not
be a blackbird at all . . .

The fantasy narratives we associate with the literature of childhood frequently
have employed a prose poetry akin to Kincaid's highly evocative chant. The
girl's voice, speaking to itself, repeats the oppressive mother's litany of
admonitions, with the rhythms of repetition shrewdly working to protest
the mother's authority. This mode of travesty is fundamental to much of
children's literature, whenever the relatively helpless child has to sustain
impositions and injunctions. Kincaid's style here is highly individual, but
it recalls many narratives in which a young girl at once submits to and yet
undermines parental codes of behavior. In some ways, Twain's Huck Finn
provides a large analogue, since he adopts the language of the adult world
while keeping firmly to a stance all his own. Kincaid's intricate blend of
overt submission and implicit defiance repeats (with great skill) immemorial
Western modes in which a child's voice wins out over the stale continuities
of adult authority.

Kincaid's fierce protest against "touristic" values has its own value and
integrity, but would not engage much of her readership if it were not allied to
a considerable art of storytelling, and to a prose poetry capable of sustained
eloquence. Passionate sincerity, like ideological correctness, is not in itself
a *literary* virtue. Fortunately, Kincaid transcends many critical accounts of
her achievement to date. She is a stylist and a visionary, and imaginatively is
essentially a fantasist. So far, her best work has emerged from recollections
of childhood and of her complex relationship to her mother. Her recent
meditations upon gardening have implicit in them a new development in her
work, which her admirers, common readers and critics together, are likely to
welcome.

MOIRA FERGUSON

A Small Place:
Glossing Annie John's Rebellion

Free is how you is from the start, an' when it look different you got to move, just move, an' when you movin' say that it is a natural freedom that make you move.
—George Lamming, quoted in C. L. R. James,
"The Making of the Caribbean People," p. 189

In *Annie John* and *A Small Place* Jamaica Kincaid intertwines discussions of gender relations with colonial and postcolonial rebellion. *Annie John* (1985) narrates eight stories, about Annie John's childhood and burgeoning womanhood from ten to seventeen years of age on the island of Antigua in the eastern Caribbean, a British Crown colony at the time.[1] In *A Small Place* (1988) Jamaica Kincaid's political expose glosses and intertextualizes *Annie John*;[2] it represents a version of Annie John's "revisionary struggle" as Jamaica Kincaid reexamines conflicts that Annie John intimated but could not identify.

Annie John opens on Antigua roughly a year after the first major race riots, precipitated by discrimination against Caribbean immigrants, erupted in London in 1958. In contrast to events at the metropolitan center, Antigua seems peaceful, at least on the surface. Jamaica Kincaid is open about the fact that *Annie John* has a personal dimension and has stated that the feelings in

From *Colonialism and Gender Relations from Mary Wollstonecraft to Jamaica Kincaid: East Caribbean Connections.* ©1993 by Columbia University Press.

it are autobiographical.[3] Written as a polemic, *A Small Place* betrays no such ambiguity about its autobiographical content.

Both texts extend the discussion of Antigua since Jamaica Kincaid was born Elaine Potter Richardson in St. Johns, Antigua, in 1949. Her father worked as a carpenter and cabinetmaker; her mother was a homemaker and a well-known political activist. At seventeen Elaine Richardson left Antigua for the United States and eventually became a staff writer for the *New Yorker* as Jamaica Kincaid.[4]

Annie John records a maturing girl's experiences growing up in an artisanal family similar to Jamaica Kincaid's, in the midst of the seemingly paradisal world of Antigua. Annie John, however, quirkily obsesses on death. This fascination that Annie John initially expresses marks certain subterranean debates as she struggles with adolescence and colonial reality. In partial response to her rebellious nature and as her mother tries to encourage a more independent existence, Annie John succeeds well in school but refuses to bow to authority. Continually negotiating contradictory positions from the center to the margins and back, sometimes occupying both spots simultaneously, she fuses sexual and cultural innocence with a finely honed bravado and self-justifying duplicities.

GENDER RELATIONS

Annie John sublimates feelings of abandonment into conflicted bitterness toward her mother, her dislike magnifying as she mentally augments the gap between them. In her torment she envisions her mother as a manipulative tyrant, characterizing her as a crocodile one moment and in the next as the prey of murderous snakes—overlapping projections of her frustration. The nurturing of hatred, a fear of alienation, and a craving to return to intimate bonding plague her by turn. She secretly harbors a self-conception so monstrous that she has induced a desire for separation in her mother; this negative self-image further indicates that she projects a growing self-hatred. In another sense Annie John displaces onto her mother an antagonistic representation of her agonized feelings of rejection that in turn engender psychic fragmentation. Since her birth she has lived in her mother's shadow and now that she has to fend for herself in her own spotlight, as it were, she seeks shade, assuming she cannot live up to her mother's level of competence; since she cannot conceptualize her mother's cultural construction, she ceaselessly tries to fashion a subjectivity in opposition. All of this she internalizes.

When Annie John reads aloud to her classmates about idyllic times spent with her mother vacationing on Rat Island as a small child, she alters the story to hide current mother–daughter disaffection. She confides her pain to the reader: "I placed the old days' version before my classmates because, I thought, I couldn't bear to show my mother in a bad light before people who hardly knew her. But the real truth was that I couldn't bear to have anyone see how deep in disfavor I was with my mother" (p. 29). Notably, the paradisal story involves water and simple childhood pleasures as if she were not only retelling a favorite story but imagining, too, a return to primal, undifferentiated harmony.[5] In Hélène Cixous's terms she desires her mother's milk.[6]

Deliberately shunning and depriving herself of a female model, fixating on her mother as treacherous, she molds herself into an exciting, desirable subject who obeys and disobeys at will. Her unconscious battle with social conditioning, an already constructed subjectivity, explains much of the subsequent tension. In an extensive account of the fight between herself and her mother over dominance and autonomy, symbolized by marbles, the issue emerges as palpably gender-specific when her mother tells her, "I am so glad you are not one of those girls who like to play marbles" (p. 61). She is trying to create a lady-like daughter. In direct defiance Annie John stays behind after school and arranges to play with the dirty, unruly, nameless Red Girl who punches, then kisses her in an adolescent sexual merry-go-round. She admires the Red Girl's nonconformity and her apparent ability to act as she pleases; she constitutes an alter ego of sorts, certainly a projection of who Annie John would like to be if only to anger her mother.[7] Annie John eventually succeeds in becoming a champion marbles player against express maternal wishes, a thinly veiled metaphor for personal power and successful experimentation.

Annie John secretes her marbles under the bed away from her mother's prying eyes and, by faking homework assignments, she meets clandestinely with the Red Girl. To please herself and trick her mother, she steals money to buy seductive gifts for her friend: "multi-colored grosgrain ribbon or a pair of ring combs studded with rhinestones, or a pair of artificial rosebuds suitable to wear at the waist of a nice dress . . . I simply loved giving her these things . . . it was a pleasure to see they [the parents] didn't know everything" (p. 64).

Playing marbles is a self-directed, symbolic apprenticeship at a time when she already loathes being apprenticed to a seamstress picked out by her mother.[8] Disobeying and abandoning her mother emotionally—a qualified revenge, a victory over surveillance—she becomes an artist in her prowess at marbles and in her appreciation of their appearance. At one level the marbles are embryos of the breasts all her adolescent female friends covet, but they are also beautiful orbs of defiance that proliferate; they have to be concealed, are exchangeable and always desirable. At another level marbles resemble the stolen library books Annie John conceals, treasures that signify rebellion against constraining gender roles, a personal power gained by outwitting authority, and an obsession with knowledge that rivals her previous obsession with death. By stowing books and marbles away she breaks from the adult world and begins to build an alternate way of knowing and doing. Declining to be a gracious object, a lady for the community to admire, or even mother's helper around the house, she constructs herself against the cultural grain through subterfuge. She will not and cannot renounce desire and self-determination.

At other points Annie John edges toward even more overt intimations of subversion, agony, and sexuality. As early as chapter 2, tellingly entitled "The Circling Hand," the twelve-year-old describes her relationship with her parents and their relationship with each other. She recalls old events that wounded her parents: accounts of her mother arguing with her father (Annie John's grandfather), then leaving the childhood home in Dominica, of Annie John's own father waking up in bed with his grandmother dead beside him. Annie John also notes how she once came home from church to discover her parents "lying in their bed" (p. 30). To announce her presence, she aggressively rattles knives and forks, vociferously denying how much this scene affects her. Nevertheless, she obsesses on her mother's hand in a sex- and death-related fantasy that unduly fascinates her; she imagines the hand that caresses her father's back to be that of a skeleton.

These inchoate emotions, stemming from unconscious jealousy, even a buried matricidal wish, explode in a painful remark to her mother as she arranges the cutlery just after the scene. Her mother "looked at me, . . . and walked away. From the back, she looked small and funny. She carried her hands limp at her sides. I was sure I could never let those hands touch me again; I was sure I could never let her kiss me again. All that was finished" (pp. 31–32). Minutes later she disrupts a weekly arrangement. She declines a quiet father–daughter harmony they enjoy on their Sunday walk together: "On our walk, my father tried to hold my hand, but I pulled myself away from him, doing it in such a way that he would think I felt too big for that now" (p. 32). She masks and compensates for her anger and insecurity by designating proximity as her mother's privilege. Parental sexuality bothers the adolescent child; her entry into adolescence and the foreign feelings this generates transform the stirrers of these feelings into "alien parents."[9] The next day she figuratively transfers her overweening maternal love to her friend Gwen, whom she has met at school: "At the end of the day, Gwen and I were in love, and so we walked home arm in arm together. When I got home, my mother greeted me with the customary kiss and inquiries. I told her about my day, going out of my way to provide pleasing details, leaving out, of course, any mention at all of Gwen and my overpowering feelings for her" (p. 33).

Eventually Annie John becomes severely ill. Feeling deprived of maternal care she forgoes all sustenance, akin to stressing self-sufficiency and denial. Yet her refusal affirms her impotence, keeps sexual growth at bay, and attracts hyperattentiveness as she becomes temporarily anorexic.[10] During this prolonged, cryptic illness she experiences unfamiliar sensations after she becomes drenched in bed. As her parents bathe Annie John and change her bedclothes, her distressed father, dressed in his underwear, holds her in his lap:

> Through the folds of my nightie, I could feel the hair on his legs, and as I moved my legs back and forth against his the hair on his legs made a swoosh, swoosh sound, like a brush being rubbed against wood. A funny feeling went through me that I liked and was frightened of at the same time, and I shuddered. At this, my father, thinking I was cold, hugged me even closer. It dawned on me then that my father, except for when he was sick, slept in no clothes at all, for he would never sleep in clothes he had worn the day before. I do not know why that lodged in my mind, but it did. (pp. 112–13)

Masturbatory fantasy and the involuntary sexual arousal for her father coexist with a regression to infantilism, a reenactment of pre-oedipal immersion in amniotic fluid; water is the primary signifier. By inscribing Annie John's psychic watershed in the title of the chapter, "The Long Rain," Kincaid provides a dense, elemental metaphor to represent the terrifying feelings that threaten to engulf Annie. Illness accentuates her longing for motherly attention. To put the case more forcibly, grief has engendered sickness because she equates separation with annihilation. In the earlier Rat Island episode, when she can no longer discern her swimming mother, "a huge black space then opened up in front of me" (p. 43). Anguish blots out the light, conveying a temporary abdication from life. Thus during her illness she recapitulates a primal scene in which water, womblike, surrounds her and engages the undivided attention not only of her mother but also (unwomblike) of her father. This pre-oedipal merging encompasses a strange form of sexual difference, a means of bonding with both parents, a refusal to allow them as a pair to be separate from her as the one. A bizarre incident symbolically illuminates and further problematizes her inner turmoil. As she lies in bed, family photographs agitate her to such a degree that she feels compelled to wash them, both "the creases in Aunt Mary's veil" and "the dirt from the front of my father's trousers" (p. 120). Meaning slides metonymically from washing to a sexual sign; purity dissolves the possibility of birth.[11] She then lays the saturated photographs to rest in a perfumed bed of talcum powder, a miniature erotic grotto. The performance of this purification-obliteration ritual soaks her nightgown and sheets. She has enveloped herself in a primal reprise, rubbing out faces that speak the life of family members: "None of the people in the [ironic] wedding picture, except for me, had any face left. In the picture of my mother and father, I had erased them from the waist down" (p. 120). Immersion has become self-definition as she metonymically recites herself in the security of the womb. In and with this water she can gain freedom. She creates a path to communication and love. Effacing her father's sexuality, she can reclaim oneness with her mother. This revocation, however, can never transpire because she already exists in the symbolic order.

She continues: "In the picture of me wearing my confirmation dress, I had erased all of myself except for my shoes" (p. 120). These particular shoes specify a tense altercation between Annie John and her mother. For the ceremony in which she would be received as an adult into the Methodist church, she selected shoes pronounced too risqué by her mother; they sported cut-out sides that exposed the flesh of Annie John's feet, marks of the virginity that her mother sought to protect. Thus she operates in a state of nonclosure, of confusion, even. Her public, religious induction acknowledges imminent adulthood while the reversion to infantilism infusing her sickness signals a refusal of that very acknowledgment. So in the photos her shoes emphatically remain.

An earlier incident throws further light on Annie John's complex relationship to developing sexuality. After a harmless and unexpected conversation with a boy on the way home from school, her mother denounces her as a slut:

> The word "slut" (in patois) was repeated over and over, until suddenly I felt as if I were drowning in a well but instead of the well being filled with water it was filled with the word "slut," and it was pouring in through my eyes, my ears, my nostrils, my mouth. As if to save myself, I turned to her and said, "Well, like father like son, like mother like daughter." (p. 102)

Her mother's accusation threatening Annie John's already fragile identity, her sense of "moral" equality, the word *slut* suffuses her senses. Once again, as in the ocean story and her illness, water scripts betrayal. The seeming irrationality of the mother's charge suggests some overwhelming fear, a link to the mother's adolescent argument with her father—perhaps concerning sexual freedom—her subsequent departure from home and giving birth. In other words the incident might be explained by the fact that Annie John's mother is drawing on personal shame. This hypothesis would also explain why Annie John recollects this particular memory upon seeing her parents in bed. An intimidating sexuality becomes the womb's fluid, her body's fluid.

She halts this frightening transformation with words that claim a threatening sexuality as parental heritage. Her father's sexual popularity is pointedly included. They engage each other in emotional pain, then retreat to cope individually with the serious aspersions Annie John has cast:

> At that, everything stopped. The whole earth fell silent. The two black things joined together in the middle of the room separated, hers going to her, mine coming back to me. I looked at my mother. She seemed tired and old and broken. Seeing that, I felt happy and sad at the same time. I soon decided that happy was better, and I was just about to enjoy this feeling when she said, "Until this moment, in my whole life I knew without a doubt that, without any exception, I loved you best," and then she turned her back and started again to prepare the green figs for cooking. (pp. 102–3)

This hurtful statement and the issue of the shoes claim the daughter's right to be as sexually independent as her parents; they defy her mother's warped pronouncement. As markers of the mobility she lacks at the moment, they concurrently pinpoint a dread of the adult world and a means of reentry.

At this point another odd break occurs in the text. When her parent's friend Mr. Nigel, the fisherman, visits her sick bed and laughs at a remark she makes, that laughter spontaneously threatens to engulf her. This complex eruption signals that a gap is opening up: Abject passivity and even degradation are transforming into their opposite, a moment of liberation, her laughter an overmiming, a ridiculing of what she feels they have done to her. She is dissolving her trancelike state through a vivid connection with the everyday world of sight and smell. The invitation to laugh back/with the fisherman secures relief, offers a vital safety valve that has remained beyond her grasp. This feeling of self-disappearance is accompanied by memories of Mr. Nigel's domestic happiness. Desperately, she leaps on him, fells him to the ground, and garrulously pours out thoughts that crowd her head. Not long after this, grandmother Ma Chess comes:

> [She] settled in on the floor at the foot of my bed, eating and sleeping there, and soon I grew to count on her smells and the sound her breath made as it went in and out of her body. Sometimes at night, when I would feel that I was locked up in the warm falling soot and could not find my way out, Ma Chess would come into my bed with me and stay until I was myself—whatever that had come to be by then—again. I would lie on my side, curled up like a little comma, and Ma Chess would lie

next to me, curled up like a bigger comma, into which I fit. In the daytime, while my mother attended my father, keeping him company as he ate, Ma Chess fed me my food, coaxing me to take mouthful after mouthful. She bathed me and changed my clothes and sheets and did all the other things that my mother used to do. (pp. 125–26)

Annie John has changed herself into a sign of language without voice. This and her grandmother's obeah practices and "ancestral presence" locate her in a historically perilous border area between speech and magic.[12] Note, too, since obeah has been a source of deep contention between slaves and slaveowners, Annie John is using insurrectionary tools to recover and vanquish the likes of her school teacher, Miss Edwards. Through her grandmother Annie John accepts the intervention of an aboriginal world, part of the identity she has fought for. Ma Chess's success affirms the old ways and denies the validity of paternal disapproval of obeah. After this the illness mysteriously vanishes, coinciding with the cessation of the rain. In her first trip outside Annie John establishes her reemergence in the symbolic order:

The sounds I heard didn't pass through me, forming a giant, angry funnel. The things I saw stayed in their places. My mother sat me down under a tree, and I watched a boy she had paid sixpence climb up a coconut tree to get me some coconuts. My mother looked at my pinched, washed-out face and said: "Poor Little Miss, you look so sad." Just at that moment, I was not feeling sad at all. I was feeling how much I never wanted to see a boy climb a coconut tree again . . . how much I never wanted to see the sun shine day in, day out again, how much I never wanted to see my mother bent over a pot cooking me something that she felt would do me good when I ate it, how much I never wanted to feel her long, bony fingers against my cheek again, how much I never wanted to hear her voice in my ear again, how much I longed to be in a place where nobody knew a thing about me and liked me for just that reason, how much the whole world into which I was born had become an unbearable burden and I wished I could reduce it to some small thing that I could hold underwater until it died. (pp. 127–28)

Through physical illness Annie John has navigated to a place where she can start over without feeling stifled. She transcends a shying from independence, now aware that without a sense of autonomy she will die. Having externalized her distaste for the fantasy and hypocrisy of her world, she recommences a slow, lopsided dance into adulthood. In order to live, she apprehends from this point on that consciously or not, she has to abandon the island to dispel its power over her.

Her return to school points to her reinforced, dual position in the world as insider and outsider. As if play-acting, she dresses quaintly, beating an inward retreat, while enjoying lavish undue attention through eccentric behavior; ontologically dislocated, she buttons up her developing person to hide the mismatch of her physical, cultural, and psychic subject-positions. With this self-imposed outsider status Annie John rejects maternal definition, or rather refashions a sense of pride in her own terms.

Kincaid's inscription of Annie John as a conflicted adolescent operating in a series of psychodramas is further complicated by Annie John's resistance to yet another externally imposed construction of herself as a colonial subject. In response Annie John tries to contextualize pre-1834 colonial life in terms of her own experiences; she revivifies the past by rendering it part of the present. Leaving aside quarrels with her mother, she attributes her smothered emotions to the consequences of imperial relationships, not always consciously realized. She refuses to accept assumed epistemological "realities," nonsensical formulations of a happy colonial world. Despite teachers' efforts to render her a subject who "works by herself," she revolts.[13]

A book entitled *Roman Britain*, we learn, is a customary school prize as well as an inside joke to anyone who stands outside metropolitan indoctrination: Romans, after all, colonized the British who are still attempting to condition Antiguans to accept imperial ideology. In addition students are reading *A History of the West Indies*, chronicling the colonizer's hagiographical version of Caribbean history, generally unchallenged by the students.[14] Annie John, on the other hand, manifests her awareness of cultural contradictions, refuses to be silenced, and tries to counter the complicities of colonialism and its aftermath. She stresses personal affection for Ruth, "the minister's daughter [who] was such a dunce and came from England and had yellow hair" (p. 73), separate from her political response:

> Perhaps she wanted to be in England, where no one would remind her constantly of the terrible things her ancestors had done; perhaps she had felt even worse when her father was a missionary in Africa. I could see how Ruth felt from looking at her face. Her ancestors had been the masters, while ours had been the slaves. She had such a lot to be ashamed of, and by being with us every day she was always being reminded. We could look everybody in the eye, for our ancestors had done nothing wrong except just sit somewhere, defenseless. Of course, sometimes, what with our teachers and our books, it was hard for us to tell

on which side we really now belonged—with the masters or the slaves—for it was all history, it was all in the past, and everybody behaved differently now; all of us celebrated Queen Victoria's birthday, even though she had been dead a long time. But we, the descendants of the slaves, knew quite well what had really happened. (p. 76)

It is no coincidence that Ruth's dunce cap appears to Annie John's conflictual gaze—mocking yet sympathetic—as a regal crown, a synthesis of stupidity and power, not unlike the teacher, Miss Edwards.

Under the picture of a chained-up Columbus in the history text, Annie John has derisively written: "The Great Man Can No Longer Just Get Up and Go." Literally and metaphorically she punctures-punctuates Anglo-Saxon historical reality, attuned to the fact that the Italian adventurer symbolizes all those who have limited, diluted, and even tried to dissolve the political and cultural life of African-Caribbeans.[15] She refuses to sound herself through a white middle-class imaginary. The history lesson that teaches the date of Columbus's "discoveries," we are led to conclude, is neither authentic, nor "all in the past" (p. 76). Since fictions in this culture, she has learned, are called and taught as facts, she plays around with the,"facts" and defaces white culture, or rather revises it to bring it more in line with historical events.[16]

Annie John resists received imperial interpretations and a prescribed subject position, however, and functions as the singular representative of historical maroons, slave rebels whose name derives from the Spanish term *cimarron*—wild or untamed. She declines to be mentally manacled by Miss Edwards, whose name conjures up Edward VIII, a king who recently abdicated from a life of duty to a country bent on territorial acquisition. Later the characterization of Miss Edwards as a "bellowing dragon" (to Annie John's knight, presumably) duly underscores the ethnocentric history lessons (p. 78). Annie John battles Miss Edwards's defense of a holy ground that her pupil, proud of a lineage that includes many insurrectionists, rejects with disdain.

Annie John's defiance stems not only from the exercise of power as an adolescent teetering between childhood and adulthood but also from a calculated political rebellion that she attempts to name: her resistance identifies lies about the colonial past, a distorted present, and an unpredictable future. She disrupts the "veneer of family harmony," the advantages of a traditional education.[17] Although she is doubly suppressed and branded as a tough-minded girl and as an ignorant and presumptuous colonized object in the eyes of colonial gazers like Miss Edwards, she refuses obliteration in either sphere.

The choices of other white protagonists differ drastically. Fanny Price refuses to marry Henry Crawford, but in the play-acting episode she conforms to Sir Thomas's values: she does not break the "dead silence" that greet Sir Thomas's account of Antigua. Antoinette personally withdraws in order to cope with post-emancipation resentment and disorder but she is manipulated into marriage with Rochester. She is unable to ally with the black community, and although she identifies with Tia and Christophine emotionally, suicide is the only choice or recourse she can imagine to defeat Rochester and gain agency.[18]

The episode's symbolic significance is finely encapsulated in the punishment the authoritarian Miss Edwards metes out to Annie John. The pupil is commanded to write out *Paradise Lost*.[19] Having located herself on the edge of naughtiness—nuanced opposition to European invasion of the region—she has surrendered primal innocence. Paradise slips away as she recognizes its limitations. We never learn what happens afterward; this indeterminate closure underscores the multiple lost paradises emblemized by Columbus's presence in the Caribbean.

Not by chance the Columbus incident is associated with an earlier escapade in Annie John's life. While Miss Edwards stares at Annie John's deliberate textual defacement, the student flashes back to memories of herself and her friends dancing "on the tombstones of people who had been buried there before slavery was abolished, in 1833." There they would "sit and sing bad songs, use forbidden words, and of course, show each other various parts of our bodies. [Some] would walk up and down on the large tombstones showing off their legs" (pp. 80–81). A ringleader in these exploits, Annie John thus links Columbus and the white student's unforgotten, plantocratic forerunners to historical memory and her self-confident reclamation of unnamed ancestors. The reverberation within her present situation of these earlier audacious acts recalls the narrator's ongoing struggle for personal freedom and political integrity. It stresses, too, the consistency and dialectic of oppression and rebellion.

This episode, which recapitulates the students' wild dance on the graves of slaves, is compounded by telling references to Queen Victoria's birthday, the Union Jack, the presence of Methodist missionaries, and *Jane Eyre*. In identifying with *Jane Eyre*, with whom Annie John has one name (loosely) in common, she betrays certain gaps in her insights about colonial Antigua.[20] For the time being—though this state of affairs changes—Kincaid appears to accept Jane Eyre's struggle with the disruptive presence of the white creole. Hence Annie John accepts this received reading; she does not always see beyond an educational system that trivializes the cultural context of colonized countries. That young Antoinette Cosway (later Bertha Rochester and Jane Eyre's "rival") is a character—the madwoman in the attic, whose "type" would be historically well-known in Antigua—remains unstated. Annie John desires and identifies with Jane Eyre's status as an independent female, a solitary, fearless subject who visits Brussels, a cold place and the home of colonizers—the antithesis of Antigua, familiar and despised.

Annie John covets Jane Eyre's voluntary exile, her ability to challenge authority. She craves something akin to what appears to her as Jane Eyre's self-crafted autonomy. In ironic reversal Eyre is the exotic outsider and feisty heroine whose gender painfully impedes her.

In the chain of colonial signifiers also appears the name of Enid Blyton, a popular British writer of children's stories. Blyton's presence insinuates something about Annie John's experiences as a black pupil in a colonized society. Long before the writing of *Annie John*, controversy had arisen in Britain over Blyton's ethnocentric texts. In *Here Comes Noddy*, for example, three nasty "golliwogs" mug "poor, little" Noddy.[21] In 1977 Bob Dixon in *Catching Them Young: Sex, Race and Class in Children's Fiction* was one of many British critics to object to Blyton's racist characterizations.[22] Miss Edwards's hagiographical depiction of Columbus as a metropolitan hero bears a second-cousin resemblance to Noddy, pompous white hero of internationally known British children's fiction; the adulation accorded Blyton's characters—like the reverence in which Columbus has been held for centuries—is legend. Blyton's texts were an inevitable component of the storybook repertoire of thousands of British children growing up in the thirties, forties, and fifties. This Blytonian intertextualizing reminds readers of subtle but insistent metropolitan-colonial propaganda about African-Caribbean culture.

Thus Annie John's revolt is indicated through chronological discontinuities that suggest the ubiquity of oppression and indirect revolt in response to colonial lies. Moreover when new information about Annie John in the form of a stream-of-consciousness flashback is introduced in the final chapter as she embarks on her journey to London, these reminiscences enable a rounding out of Annie John's character; its presence through space, time, and place provides some context for what the reader, has been invited to see: a young woman claiming agency for herself. The building of Annie John's narrative through association complements the form: sections follow no consistent chronology; rather they track the narrator's circuitous coming to terms with her environment and her final exit. Through cumulative impressions and anecdotes governed by an informing intelligence, Annie John faces down narcissistic colonial myths.

After her metamorphosis following rain and resolution, a postlapsarian Annie John walks to the jetty with her parents. This time the topos of water represents purification of a different sort. She literally will throw herself into deliberate departure (at the jetty-jeté). Having gained a form of freedom, of temporary transcendent agency, she says goodbye and sails for cold London.

Since *Annie John*, Jamaica Kincaid has published another text that permits us to see *Annie John* from enhanced vantage points, especially how colonization constructed Annie John's particular self. Put differently, Jamaica Kincaid recontextualizes in *A Small Place* crucial experiences in Annie John's life. Reasons for Annie John's barely disguised repression, her sense of being trapped within a "First World" modality, for example, become palpably obvious as Kincaid deliberately strips away colonial complicities. The question that inevitably arises about author–narrator and fiction–history relationships is intricate, fraught with the danger of essentialist oppositions. Let me put it this way: In *Annie John* the narrator in "her own" voice plays a large part in conveying what is going on; in *A Small Place* the author forthrightly presents a point of view that demands some mediation. Thus the polemical perspective in *A Small Place* complements and enriches the play of signification in *Annie John*. Kincaid exemplifies her own social conditioning through specifying the constitution of Annie John as an individual. At the same time the many suppressed voices in *A Small Place*—past colonists and present exploiters, for example—convey diverse perspectives. Moreover, the narrator of Annie John and Jamaica Kincaid—as she outlines certain experiences in the exposé— have so much undisguisedly in common that the reader is invited to equate them.[23] In that sense Annie John functions as Jamaica Kincaid's avatar. At some points—with respect, say, to understanding parental influence—I avail myself of this invitation.[24]

In *A Small Place* Kincaid denounces Antigua as an island with a legacy of corruption where the mimicking of colonialism has become institutionalized. Part of her diatribe involves identifying the Union Jack and celebrations of Queen Victoria's birthday as corrosive signposts of colonizers, techniques for reinforcing ideological subjection. As such, what lurks suggestively in the innuendos and interstices of Annie John are given body and validated through the later narrative.

Additionally, *A Small Place* reilluminates Annie John's father as a glamorous cricketer, a man loved by women long after relationships end. Annie John's mother emerges in a much more focal and public role as a feisty activist who challenges the Antiguan premier himself: "It so happens that in Antigua my mother is fairly notorious for her political opinions" (p. 50). In the earlier text Mrs. John appeared in various guises, often oppositionally to Annie John, so that the adolescent could gradually come to terms with herself, to become, in effect, a writer; she also had to be the mother who extends unconditional love to her daughter. In *A Small Place*, then, the photograph-washing scene in which Annie John sublimates a tumultuous complex of love, anger, and sexual desire takes on a sharper focus. So does her detestation for Columbus. In *A Small Place* tourists are a collective Columbus, new colonists, brash cultural invaders. They are enjoined to forgo

customary mindlessness, to accept some responsibility for halting ongoing
deterioration. Mediated compassion for someone like blonde Ruth has no
place in this uncompromising text. Contemporary prime minister Vere Bird's
hegemonic dynasty is post-British collaboration at its worst; the corruption
of this administration, Jamaica Kincaid takes pains to point out, originates
in a colonizing ethic. *A Small Place* permits us to read Annie John's turmoil
as adolescent confusion that often sprang from what she felt but could not
name—insecurity, as well as repulsion and fury at being treated as a latter-day
colonial object. Yet this is not to deny the intricacy of the reader's position
in the trap of fiction-exposé: we move through various forms and stages of
identifying, with Annie John to viewing Annie John at a greater distance,
as an interpellated subject in realpolitik. We see multiple intersecting
textualities, "the process of producing [texts] through the transformation of
other texts,"[25] that help to explain an often invisible, tyrannical world order,
the "planned epistemic violence of imperialism."[26]

     To put this matter another way, *Annie John* foretells the mature,
radical politic of *A Small Place*. At one level *A Small Place* is *Annie John*,
part 2. Kincaid's disclosures validate Annie John's dimly felt sense of being
indoctrinated and condescended to. Earlier disquiet becomes withering
sarcasm. In yet one more sense Annie John problematizes *A Small Place*,
enables us to see that no last word exists. Together the texts help to
reconceptualize contemporary definitions of female sexuality, motherhood,
and race/gender intersections through the gaze of an African-Caribbean
woman:[27] "A full literary reinscription cannot easily flourish in the imperialist
fracture or discontinuity, covered over by an alien legal system masquerading
as Law as such, an alien ideology established as only Truth, and a set of
human sciences busy establishing the 'native' as self-consolidating other."[28]

     As the main topos of *A Small Place*, colonialism marks Kincaid's candid
characterizations of Horatio Nelson, Sir Francis Drake, and other renowned
heroes of British naval history as "English maritime criminals" (p. 24). In
A Small Place the slippery, dissolving paradise of *Annie John* could be only a
fantastic memory of childhood in which a sophisticated yet horrified narrator
pointedly intertwines contemporary abominations with past atrocities:

> You must not wonder what exactly happened to the contents of
> your lavatory when you flushed it. You must not wonder where
> your bath water went when you pulled out the stopper. You must
> not wonder what happened when you brushed your teeth. Oh, it
> might all end up in the water you are thinking of taking a swim
> in; the contents of your lavatory might, just might, graze gently
> against your ankle as you wade carefree in the water, as you see,
> in Antigua, there is no proper sewage-disposal system. But the

Caribbean Sea is very big and the Atlantic Ocean is even bigger;
it would amaze even you to know the number of black slaves this
ocean has swallowed up. When you sit down to eat your delicious
meal, it's better that you don't know that most of what you are
eating came off a plane from Miami. And before it got on a
plane in Miami, who knows where it came from? A good guess
is that it came from a place like Antigua first, where it was grown
dirt-cheap, went to Miami, and came back. There is a world of
something in this, but I can't go into it right now. (pp. 13–14)

Unilaterally excoriating the reigning Antiguan dynasty of Vere Bird,
Kincaid exposes endless vestiges of colonialism. She mocks the idea of a
"British God" (p. 9); she ridicules tourists who think Antiguans are specially
bonded with nature or act as monkeys just out of trees (p. 29). Tourists
themselves are denounced categorically—each one is "an ugly, empty thing,
a stupid thing, a piece of rubbish" (p. 17) who circulates in a malevolent
miniworld. In response Kincaid asserts: "This empire business was all wrong"
(p. 23). Such unabounding ire radiates elsewhere, as in "There is a world of
something in this, but I can't go into it right now" (p. 14) and "Do you even
try to understand why people like me cannot get over the past, cannot forgive
and cannot forget?" (p. 26).

Incontestable denunciation in *A Small Place* has replaced the implicit
jabs of *Annie John*: "We were taught the names of the Kings of England.
In Antigua, the 24th of May was a holiday—Queen Victoria's official
birthday."[29] One of the colonized coerced into ostensible celebration, she
specifies the perniciousness of "bad post-colonial education" (p. 43) and "an
appropriate obsession with slavery." Black teenagers, she argues, "generally
[make] asses of themselves. What surprised me most about them was not
how familiar they were with the rubbish of North America—compared to
the young people of my generation, who were familiar with the rubbish of
England" (pp. 43–44).

In Antigua, people speak of slavery as if it had been a pageant
full of large ships sailing on the blue water, the large ships filled
up with human cargo—their ancestors, they got off, they were
forced to work under conditions that were cruel and inhuman,
they were beaten, they were murdered, they were sold, their
children were taken from them and these separations lasted
forever, there were many other bad things, and then suddenly the
whole thing came to an end in something called emancipation.
Then they speak of emancipation itself as if it happened just the
other day, not over one hundred and fifty years ago. The word

"emancipation" is used so frequently, it is as if it, emancipation, were a contemporary occurrence, something everybody is familiar with. (pp. 54–55)

Not to put a fine point on it, Kincaid holds colonialism responsible for everything noxious that she hints at and intuits in *Annie John*:

> Have you ever wondered why it is that all we seem to have learned from you is how to corrupt our societies and how to be tyrants? You will have to accept that this is mostly your fault.... You imprisoned people. You robbed people. You opened your own banks and you put our money in them. The accounts were in your name. The banks were in your name. There must have been some good people among you, but they stayed home. And that is the point. That is why they are good. They stayed home. But still, when you think about it, you must be a little sad. The people like me, finally, after years and years of agitation, made deeply moving and eloquent speeches against the wrongness of your domination over us, and then finally, after the mutilated bodies of you, your wife, and your children were found in your beautiful and spacious bungalow at the edge of your rubber plantation—found by one of your many house servants (none of it was ever yours; it was never, ever yours)—you say to me, "Well, I wash my hands of all of you, I am leaving now." (pp. 34–36)

Together these texts build a heady opposition to past and present Antigua. *Annie John* and *A Small Place* produce a "strategic formation"; in a limited way these exposes "acquire mass, density, and referential power among themselves and thereafter in the culture at large."[30] They construct themselves as a textual other, as a counterdiscourse to dominant culture and ideology. As an African-Caribbean writer Kincaid speaks to and from the position of the other. Not only does she identify confrontations along race/gender axes, she unmasks "the results of those distortions internalized within our consciousness of ourselves and one another."[31]

Kincaid signals the degeneration of the public library as the transcendent symbol of outsider devastation, the silencing of a cultural institution that has traditionally been one of the sole and free instructors of the people. It has rendered the people voiceless:[32] "But what I see [ironically at a royal procession] is the millions of people, of whom I am just one, made orphans: no motherland, no fatherland, no gods, no mounds of earth for holy ground, no excess of love which might lead to the things that an excess of love sometimes brings, and worst and most painful of all, no tongue" (p. 31).

Library books, which Annie John felt guilty about stealing, are resymbolized as critical cultural items that have been commandeered by an imperial culture to deprive former slaves of self-education. In Marlene Nourbese Philip's words: "Silence welcomes the hungry word."[33] Colonizers and their servants, not Annie John, were and are the thieves who try to cut off, as colonizers of old, the people's tongue.[34] Jamaica Kincaid sounds the voice of the people into the void. A postcolonial narrative and reevaluated site, *A Small Place* demystifies Annie John's bewilderment about unnamed oppositions.

In the novel bearing her name Annie John charts a complex journey into adolescence, a slow initiation into adulthood; she discerns simultaneous oppressions but refuses to "become" a lady or be a tool of surrogate colonizers. Instead she devises a means to Independence and challenges readers to reexamine old models of what autonomy means for women.[35] She tries to mediate so many different representatives of herself that she speaks in several voices, including a silent or a self-silenced voice. Disrespectful in society's eyes, she records a coming to power that demystifies (to herself, at least) colonial and gender alienation, the stifling realities engendered by a predator's legacy. Initially, until the age of twelve, she assimilates wholesale the given "master narratives" about family, education, and culture. Then she backs off to take a closer look and eventually withdraws. She does not know how else to face cultural worlds and hegemonic practices that she cannot reconcile; she has few tools to cope with such a complicated subjectivity. The seemingly neutral zone of rain becomes the sign of social and psychic self-alienation, an agonized splitting from childhood, her last farewell.[36] In declining to internalize the given epistemology of appearance and reality, she forges a unique identity. Struggle, then, is at the core, is the core of *Annie John*. Having forcibly cracked open the hitherto homogenized, gendered, and colonial space, she maintains herself shakily on several planes, her reconciliations restless and incomplete. Fighting on public and private fronts, Annie John negotiates her way through alienation to choice. She sails off to wrestle an elusive subjectivity and chart an adult identity.

Jamaica Kincaid's subsequent jeremiad about Antigua, *A Small Place*, evokes the repressed subtexts of *Annie John* by openly indicting historical domination, recontextualizing earlier hesitant responses to cultural role-playing, and encoding insensitive tourists as updates of Christopher Columbus. The villains of Annie John's adolescent naïveté—particularly her mother—are reconfigured more authentically to include their status as subalterns in Antiguan society; contemporary leadership is forthrightly condemned. Kincaid's recognition that colonialism is to blame for social corruption only slightly mitigates her rage at the present state of affairs. However, at the end of *Annie John* these articulations are barely a whisper. Annie John's surname, resonating with biblical overtones and sexual innuendo, symbolizes the creative potential she has frequently expressed, the beginnings she has recreated with words, her struggle between male and female modalities. Embarking on the journey to London is simultaneously the end of adolescence and the beginning of her future life as a cultural demystifier.

Notes

1. Jamaica Kincaid, *Annie John* (New York: New American Library, 1983), p. 29. All references are to this edition.

2. Jamaica Kincaid, *A Small Place* (London: Virago, 1988). All references are to this edition.

3. Cudjoe, ed., *Caribbean Women Writers*, p. 220.

4. For concentrated biographical information on Jamaica Kincaid, see particularly Cudjoe, ed., *Caribbean Women Writers*, pp. 215–32, and Dance, ed., *Fifty Caribbean Writers*, pp. 255–63. See also Garis, "Through West Indian Eyes."

5. Sigmund Freud discusses the relationship between water and pre-oedipal harmony (*The Interpretation of Dreams*, pp. 434–37).

6. Cixous, "The Laugh of the Medusa," p. 251.

7. For issues of projection and displacement, see Anna Freud, *Ego*, vol. 2, especially ch. 5.

8. This information comes directly from Jamaica Kincaid, who talks about her life in several interviews. See, for example, Perry, "An Interview with Jamaica Kincaid," and Cudjoe, ed., *Caribbean Women Writers*, p. 220 and passim.

9. Sandra Gilbert and Susan Gubar, *The Madwoman in the Attic: Women Writers and the Literary Imagination* (New Haven: Yale University Press, 1979), p. 269.

10. See, for example, Marilyn Lawrence, *The Anorexic Experience* (London: Women's Press, 1984), pp. 32–39 and passim; Suzanne Abraham and Derek Llewellyn-Jones, *Eating Disorders: The Facts* (Oxford University Press, 1984); and Felicia Romeo, *Understanding Anorexia Nervosa* (Springfield, Ill.: Charles Thomas, 1986).

11. See Cora Kaplan, "Language and Gender," in *Sea Changes: Essays on Culture and Feminism* (London: Verso, 1986), especially pp. 78–80.

12. See Averil Mackenzie-Grieve, *The Last Years of the English Slave Trade, Liverpool, 1750–1807* (New York: Cass, 1968), p. 156. For obeah, see also Goveia, *Slave Society*, pp. 245–47, and Cudjoe, ed., *Caribbean Women Writers*, pp. 225–31. The telling phrase comes from Carole Boyce Davies, "Writing Home," p. 65.

13. For the discussion of Annie John's conditioning, her construction of subjectivity, see Louis Althusser, "Ideology and Ideological State Apparatuses," in *Lenin and Other Essays* (New York: Monthly Review, 1970), pp. 127–86.

14. It is conceivable that Jamaica Kincaid is referring to an abridged version of Bryan Edwards's notoriously racist text, *The History, Civil and Commercial of the British Colonies in the West Indies*, 2 vols. (London, 1793). Edwards was a well-known planter and English politician.

15. Todorov talks extensively about Columbus as the signifier of colonial power and the anxieties of the colonizer in *The Conquest of America*, especially pp. 3–50.

16. In a reading at the University of Nebraska at Lincoln, November 9, 1990, Marlene Nourbese Philip stated that "playing around with fiction and fact is a black thing."

17. Valerie Smith in "Black Feminist Theory and the Representation of the 'Other'" in Cheryl Wall, ed., *Changing Our Own Words: Essays on Criticism, Theory, and Writing by Black Women* (New Brunswick, N. J.: Rutgers University Press, 1989), p. 55.

18. James, *The Ladies and the Mammies*.

19. *Paradise Lost* is a clever choice on several fronts. Apart from the references to Milton and the implications of the British literary canon, paradise could also refer to Columbus's "most striking" belief in the earthly paradise. He is looking for this place when he stumbles on the Caribbean (Todorov, *The Conquest of America*, pp. 16–18).

20. Cudjoe, ed., *Caribbean Women Writers*, p. 218.

21. Enid Blyton, *Here Comes Noddy* (London: Sampson Low, Marston and Richards Press, 1951).

22. Bob Dixon, *Catching Them Young: Sex, Race, and Class in Children's Fiction—Political Ideas in Children's Fiction* (London: Pluto, 1977), 2: 56–73. For *Here Comes Noddy*, see particularly Sheila G. Ray, *The Blyton Phenomenon: The Controversy Surrounding the World's Most Successful Children's Writer* (London: Andre Deutsch, 1982), p. 104.

23. Garis, "Through West Indian Eyes," pp. 42–44, 70–91.

24. For my discussion in this section, I am indebted to Gayatri Chakravorty Spivak's discussions in "Draupadi," in *In Other Worlds: Essays on Cultural Politics* (New York: Methuen, 1987), pp. 179–87, and in "Three Women's Texts and a Critique of Imperialism," in *The Feminist Reader: Essays on Gender and the Politics of Literary Criticism*, edited by Catherine Belsey and Jane Moore (New York: Basil Blackwell, 1989), p. 175–95.

25. For an elaboration of this point, see Mary Jacobus, "A Difference of View," in Mary Jacobus, ed., *Women Writers and Writing About Women* (New York: Barnes and Noble Imports, 1979), pp. 10–21. For a valuable discussion of textuality, see Elizabeth Meese, *Crossing the Double Cross: The Practice of Feminist Criticism* (Chapel Hill: University of North Carolina Press, 1986), p. 44.

26. Spivak, "Three Women's texts," p. 187.

27. Barbara Christian, "But What Do We Think We're Doing Anyway: The State of Black Feminist Criticism(s) or My Version of a Little Bit of History," in Wall, ed., *Changing Our Own Words*, p. 73.

28. Spivak, "Three Women's Texts," p. 187.

29. Kincaid, *A Small Place*, p. 30.

30. Said, *Orientalism*, p. 20.

31. Audre Lorde, "Eye to Eye," in *Sister Outsider* (Trumansburg, N.Y.: Crossing Press, 1984), p. 147.

32. In his analysis of Sahagun, Todorov underlines the anxieties generated in imperialists by the fear of the colonized peoples' literacy, *The Conquest of America*, p. 221 and passim. In a slightly different context, Henry Louis Gates, Jr., evaluates the crucial roles of literacy among slaves in *Figures in Black: Words, Signs and the Racial Self* (London: Oxford University Press, 1987).

33. Marlene Nourbese Philips's poem entitled "Discourse on the Logic of Language," in Nasta, ed., *Motherlands*.

34. Goveia, *Slave Society*, pp. 134–36, 156–57, and passim.

35. Donna Perry, "Initiation in Jamaica Kincaid's *Annie John*," in Cudjoe, ed., *Caribbean Women Writers*, p. 253.

36. This argument borrows from Jacques Lacan's ideas about psychosexual development in Jacques Lacan, *Écrits: A Selection*, translated by Alan Sheridan (London: Tavistock, 1977), especially pp. 1–7.

MERLE HODGE

Caribbean Writers and Caribbean Language: A Study of Jamaica Kincaid's Annie John

Caribbean writers operate in a language situation which is both problematic and full of possibility, and the relationship between the Caribbean writer and the language of the people who are the focus of Caribbean literature is an area of study yet to be fully explored by literary critics. In most Caribbean countries the main medium of spoken communication is a Creole language which is the product of contact between European and West African languages. However, in every case the official language, the language of education and the written word, is a European language. The pattern is, by and large, that the Creole spoken in a particular place shares the lexicon of the official language, while in its sound system and its grammatical structure it owes more to Africa than to Europe. The essential features of this underlying grammatical structure are the same across all the Caribbean Creoles.

The Anglophone Caribbean presents not a cut-and-dried bilingual situation of two languages confined to separate compartments, but a spread of variations which can more accurately be likened to a continuum, with Creole at one extreme and Standard English at the other, and a range of nuances between. In speaking situations West Indians produce different admixtures of Creole and the standard which may reflect differences in education, social class, or age, or may give other important information about speakers and the context of communication, such as self-concept, mood, attitude,

From *Winds of Change: The Transforming Voices of Caribbean Women Writers and Scholars*, edited by Adele S. Newson and Linda Strong-Leek. ©1998 by Peter Lang Publishing, Inc., New York.

relationship. Writers may therefore effectively use these nuances of language for the purposes of characterization and the development of theme and plot. The language situation is in itself a resource not available to creative writers in societies where language variety is less complex.

Using this resource, however, is not without its challenges. The language forged out of a people's experience may be the medium which most accurately describes that experience and most faithfully records the worldview of that people. Yet unlike the artist of the oral tradition (storyteller, calypsonian, dub poet) for whom the Creole is the natural medium, the writer of novels and short stories has entered a tradition shaped by the culture of the official language. The Creole is something of an intruder into that tradition.

Moreover, Caribbean writers are themselves the product of an education process which may have alienated them from their first language so that they are not as proficient in it as in the standard language. Or, education may have produced at worst contempt, at best a certain discomfort with the Creole which does not allow one to take it seriously or to see it as having artistic potential. Some Caribbean writers in exile are simply not able to accurately reproduce a Creole language, and in our literary history there can be found some truly disastrous attempts at creating Creole-speaking characters from imperfect memory. (Such disasters are not, however, the exclusive preserve of writers in physical exile.)

Then there is the problem of audience. Who are the targeted readership of the Caribbean writer? And who are the real readership? We cling fondly to the ideological position that our primary audience is our own people. But for the moment it is only a small fraction of "our own people" who read our works. And our people are only a small fraction of the Anglophone world, so that when the revolution comes and Caribbean people turn to consuming Caribbean literature, they will probably still constitute an audience too small to sustain the writer. Our audience, therefore, is the larger English-speaking world, which is to say that we write largely, overwhelmingly, for foreigners. This imposes certain kinds of constraints on the use of our native language, which in turn compromises our relationship with our wished-for primary audience.

Caribbean writers of prose fiction have approached the question of language in a number of different ways, and some writers use more than one approach. The most traditional and most enduring language strategy is to render the speech of Caribbean people realistically in dialogue but to use the standard for the narrative voice. Beginning with the work of Samuel Selvon, there is also a whole tradition of Caribbean fiction in which Creole is used as the medium of both dialogue and narration. There are also Caribbean writers who do not attempt realism but who might simply translate the dialogue of Creole speakers into the standard language, or use an avoidance strategy such as affecting some form of stylization in order to indicate that the language being spoken is different from the standard.

There can be no imposed orthodoxy of language use for the Caribbean writer. The language situation offers writers not only a rich range of expression, but also a variety of options regarding how one responds to this language situation. One of these options is not to engage with the language situation at all. This is the option exercised by Jamaica Kincaid, who has lived outside of the Caribbean and out of earshot of Caribbean language for all of her adult life, having left Antigua at the age of seventeen.

Kincaid's writings contain occasional references to language and language issues which allow us some insight into the level of her awareness of the Caribbean language situation as well as her attitude to it. In a number of places Kincaid refers to the French-lexicon Creole which her mother (who is from Dominica) spoke to her.[1] This Creole remains part of Kincaid's language repertoire, although today she might have only passive competence in it. Kincaid's essay on Antiguan society, *A Small Place*, contains a few reflections on language, most of which are asides, physically enclosed in parentheses, but quite passionate in their tone. In two places she seems to bring into focus the highly developed Caribbean art of open-air verbal confrontation:

> Since we were ruled by the English, we also had their laws. There was a law against using abusive language. Can you imagine such a law among people for whom making a spectacle of yourself through speech is everything? When West Indians went to England, the police there had to get a glossary of bad West Indian words so they could understand whether they were hearing abusive language or not.[2]

and

> Here is this: On a Saturday, at market, two people who, as far as they know, have never met before, collide by accident; this accidental collision leads to an enormous quarrel—a drama, really—in which the two people stand at opposite ends of a street and shout insults at each other at the top of their lungs. (56)

Elsewhere in the essay she speaks of colonialism as having robbed "millions of people" of culture and tradition, and her comment does not seem to indicate a recognition that Caribbean people have a language of their own:

> and worst and most painful of all, no tongue. (For isn't it odd that the only language I have in which to speak of this crime is the language of the criminal who committed the crime? . . .) (31)

In another aside she comments on the English language competence of young Antiguans, again based on the premise that Standard English is their first and only language:

> In Antigua today, most young people seem almost illiterate. On the airwaves, where they work as news personalities, they speak English as if it were their sixth language. . . . What surprised me most about them was . . . how unable they were to answer in a straight-forward way, and in their own native tongue of English. (43–44)

Toward the end of *Annie John*, the adolescent describes her overwhelming feelings of unhappiness and a desire to turn her back on the environment of her growing up: ". . . the world into which I was born had become an unbearable burden" (128).

There is enough in published interviews given by Jamaica Kincaid to establish the closely autobiographical nature of her writing and in particular the intensity of these feelings of alienation from her milieu. In *Annie John* she seems to indicate that part of her act of withdrawal was a deliberately cultivated change in her language: ". . . I acquired a strange accent—at least, no one had ever heard anyone talk that way before—and some other tricks" (129).

In *Lucy*, which takes up where *Annie John* leaves off, the language of the newly arrived West Indian girl working *au pair* in a New York household draws the mistrust of the housemaid who deduces from her speech mannerisms a wider renunciation: "One day the maid who said she did not like me because of the way I talked told me that she was sure I could not dance. She said that I spoke like a nun . . ." (11). The girl has cast off the pronunciation and intonation patterns ("accent") of Antiguan speech and concocted a special dialect that began to set her apart from her speech community even before she physically took her leave of this community.

Yet in the essay *A Small Place* Kincaid's last word on language in her native land is an expression of fondness. In a lyrical passage near the end she reflects on the beauty of Antigua (although her ultimate point is the impression of unrealness), and she sees as part of this beauty the language of Antiguans:

> . . . and the way people there speak English (they break it up) and the way they might be angry with each other and the sound they make when they laugh, all of this is so beautiful, all of this is not real like any other real thing that there is . . . (79)

Perhaps the major achievement of Jamaica Kincaid is the beauty of the language that she herself has created, the diamond-like clarity and precision of her English prose. In appropriating the work of this outstanding writer into Caribbean literary history, we might seek to trace her verbal ability to the stimulating language environment of her childhood, when she functioned in three languages: the French-lexicon Creole of Dominica from her mother, the English-lexicon Creole of Antigua spoken all around her, and the Standard English acquired through formal education and hours of immersion in books. It is quite conceivable that close analysis of Kincaid's language might yield deep affinities and influences attributable to her Creole foundation, but on the surface there is very little that seems to connect her written English to a Caribbean vernacular.

Kincaid's language in *Annie John*, which is set in Antigua, is only minimally sprinkled with Creolisms. In the narration there are certain adverbial set phrases not found in Standard English. For example, "it was her duty to accompany her father up to ground on Saturdays" (68). Or, "the unhappiness of wanting to go to cinema on a Sunday" (85). Standard English would require that the singular countable nouns *ground* and *cinema* be preceded by an article or some other determiner. (Creole has extended the English "irregular" pattern of *to bed*, *to school*, *to church* to a larger group of countable nouns. In this pattern the noun refers to a concept, an abstraction rather than a single item, and therefore cannot in this context strictly be categorized as "countable.") The narrator calls bananas by the name they carry over a large part of the Caribbean, "figs" (68, 101), and once uses "dunce" as an adjective, which is Creole usage: "Ruth sat in the last row, the row reserved for all the dunce girls" (73). The protagonist in one place addresses her mother as "Mamie" (101), and she and her school friends chant in Creole as they dance: "Tee la la la, come go. Tee la la la, come go" (81).

For dialogue, Kincaid does not attempt to reconstruct Creole speech. All discourse is translated into Standard English, with a very few notable exceptions. The rare occurrences of Creole speech are poignant in their isolation and unexpectedness. These flashes of dialogue in Creole seem to come as part and parcel of certain intimate and unprocessed memories, preserved in such detail that the actual language used is indelibly recorded, resisting translation. During a prolonged illness, the young girl wakes up one night in her father's lap and sees her mother changing the bedsheets. Her father explains: "You wet, Little Miss, you wet" (112). What makes the incident memorable to the child is her experience of sexual arousal associated with this physical contact with her father, although the child is unable to account for her own train of thought at the time: "I do not know why that lodged in my mind, but it did" (113).

Recall of another, related incident also pulls up an intact recording of Creole speech. The speaker is one of a pair of fishermen who seem to have been a source of fascination for the young girl and who turn up again in *Lucy*. One of them particularly engages the girl's attention. In both novels, but more explicitly in *Lucy*, the protagonist remembers this man in details and images suggestive of her awakening sexuality. During the same period of illness this man delivers fish to the home and looks in on her:

> As I was thinking of how much he reminded me of my father, the words "You are just like Mr. John" came out of my mouth.
>   He laughed and said, "Now, mind, I don't tell him you say that." (121)

Another piece of Creole emerges during the same recollection of Mr. Earl. It has been preserved as part of a family legend about her great-great-grandfather who was also a fisherman, and whose dying words were: "Dem damn fish" (122). This last utterance is indisputably intended to be Creole because the writer has used the phonetic spelling for "dem." The other two leave room for ambiguity in their interpretation. "You wet, Little Miss, you wet" could be read as English, with "you" as the subject of the sentence and "wet" a verb in the past simple tense. Heard as Creole, however, "wet" is here an adjective, or more precisely a Creole adjectival verb, indicating not an action but a state. "You wet" is formed on the Creole sentence pattern which involves a subject followed by an adjective functioning as the predicate.

The other Creole sentence, "Now, mind, I don't tell him you say that" (121) is punctuated in a curious way. The word "mind" is followed by a comma which makes no sense, and suggests an editorial "correction" by someone reading the sentence as English. The comma separates "mind" from the rest of the sentence, making this word a mere interjection attached to a declarative sentence in the present habitual tense/aspect: "I don't tell him you say that." In the Creole interpretation the sentence is not declarative—it does not give information. "Mind" is a verb in the imperative mood, it gives, or pretends to give, a warning. Then, the meaning of the unmarked verb "say" is perfective, not habitual. The man is playfully threatening to tell her father what she has said, not informing her that he habitually does not tell him something that she habitually says. "Mind" is the main verb, not a spliced-in, nonessential element. The comma, which assumes that the sentence is English, enforces a quite different intonation pattern and a different meaning from the Creole structure. The ambiguous identity of these two sentences has its advantages. They can be recognized as Creole by those who know Creole, and they can equally well pass for English on the page, escaping the notice of the English-speaking reader. That is to say, to the majority of readers they are unobtrusive.

There is overall very little direct speech in *Annie John*, and only one exchange between speakers prolonged enough to be called a conversation (65–66). Direct speech is largely restricted to utterances of one sentence, one phrase or even one word, punctuating at wide intervals the flow of the narrative. Instead, the writer favors reported speech:

> When I got home, my mother asked me for the fish I was to have picked up from Mr. Earl, one of our fishermen, on the way home from school. But in my excitement I had completely forgotten. Trying to think quickly, I said that when I got to the market Mr. Earl told me that they hadn't gone to sea that day because the sea was too rough. "Oh?" said my mother. (12)

One might be tempted to see in the low incidence of direct speech an avoidance strategy, a way around the language of Kincaid's prototypes who would have been mostly Creole speakers, except for the fact that *Lucy*, set in an English-speaking environment, shows the same scarcity of dialogue.

This is simply a feature of Kincaid's narrative style in which the main speaking voice is the voice of the protagonist/narrator, and the main dialogue is with her own, searching self. Kincaid's fictional works are novels of introspection, only one central character is drawn in depth. The other characters are experienced by the narrator, and therefore by the reader, only insofar as their behavior has an impact upon her development. This applies, I think, even to the portrayal of the mother with whom the child is so intensely involved. Our perception of the mother remains quite limited. We gain only a partial view of her. The subject is the girl's journey, her inner life, and there is no attempt at complete and detailed characterization in the case of the other actors in her life story. Not much attention is therefore paid to their individual speaking styles. The predominance of reported speech signifies that the content of her characters' speaking is more important than anything their speech might reveal about them individually. There is no obvious differentiation of characters' language.

The fact is that neither the personal speech patterns of individual characters nor the distinguishing features of Antiguan speech are relevant to the writer's purpose. Certainly the decision (if conscious decision there was) not to attempt realism in creating dialogue for her Creole-speaking characters is a judicious one. An artist cannot successfully use a medium that s/he does not completely control. It is very likely that Kincaid's competence in her native language has succumbed to amnesia induced not only by the passage of time, but possibly also by the deliberate distancing of her adolescent years.

Kincaid's medium is English, a register of English far removed from the Creole end of the continuum. Out of this medium she has produced a distillation so rarefied that to juxtapose with it any vernacular at all would be unwise. Vernaculars are by definition spontaneous, unself-conscious, uncut. The speech of Kincaid's characters even shies away from the more informal, conversational varieties of Standard English, and in *Annie John* all dialogue displays to some extent the fine-tuned precision and educatedness of the narrator's language. There are, for example, sentences such as this one spoken by mother to child: "Until this moment, in my whole life I knew without a doubt that, without any exception, I loved you best" (103).

The novels of Jamaica Kincaid actually sit on a cusp between fiction and essay. They are a genre unto themselves in which both narrator and fictional characters may be said to speak in the reflective style of the essayist. Dialogue in Creole would have set up such a contrast of codes as to create a focus which is not part of the writer's theme. Code-shifting invites attention to issues such as class and cultural difference, issues which are not central to the novel. Creole speech in the context of Kincaid's fiction would simply seem idiosyncratic, distracting, except for Creole speech that is not too obviously another language, such as the snatches of dialogue discussed earlier (*Annie John*, 112, 121).

There is sufficient reference, in *Annie John*, to details of the physical environment and the indigenous culture to ground the novel in a specific place. This is very important, for completely disembodied fiction does not work. But the specificity of Antiguan experience is not in itself a major preoccupation of the writer. *Annie John* is not primarily about collective experience. It is about individual experience, which in the telling expands into universal experience, often approaching the mythological in its dimensions.

Kincaid's is a different kind of writing from that which concerns itself with exploring and affirming the experience of a specific collectivity, a task which has informed a large part of Caribbean writing to date. Yet both kinds of writing rejoin the universal, if the writer achieves truth. Both kinds of writing are valid, and necessary.

Notes

1. Jamaica Kincaid, *Annie John* (New York: Farrar, Straus and Giroux, 1983), 102; *Lucy* (London: Jonathan Cape, 1990), 90. Subsequent references to *Annie John* and *Lucy* are cited by page numbers within the text.

2. Jamaica Kincaid, *A Small Place* (London: Jonathan Cape, 1991), 25. All subsequent references will be indicated within the text.

ANTONIA MACDONALD-SMYTHE

Authorizing the Slut in Jamaica Kincaid's
At the Bottom of the River

> ... prevent yourself from looking, like the slut I know you are so bent on
> becoming; ... and this way they won't recognize immediately the slut I
> have warned you against becoming.
>
> (Kincaid, *At the Bottom of the River* 4)

Jamaica Kincaid, as she has herself established, is no respecter of rules, literary or otherwise. She has, in her countless interviews, detailed the ways in which she has chosen to authorize herself through a change of name and a separation from the small island on which she was born. Kincaid has spoken at length about the process of her becoming a writer at a time when she had no literary models to follow, when she didn't even know that there were West Indians like herself who wrote and published. Her readers have not only been privy to her literary emergence; Kincaid has also provided many accounts of her social adventures in North America as she struggled to establish her own personhood within a landscape where her mother's mores and morality had no scope or relevance. The public persona who is Jamaica Kincaid seems willful and unorthodox.

Key to all her circulating narratives of an emerging, self-invented author is the notion of an empowering transgressiveness. Specifically, these narratives feed into a sustained self-mythologizing which has as its core a nonpenitent and contrary consciousness. This paper argues that, in her first

From *MaComère* 2 (1999). ©1999 by Jacqueline Brice-Finch.

published collection *At the Bottom of the River*, the persona with whom this writer identifies manifests this consciousness through a negotiation between two resisting modes of being: the *jablesse*[1] (she-devil), and the *jamette*[2] (slut). Moreover, this first collection of stories, given its strong autobiographical nature, can be read as the working through of these modalities towards the creation of an authorial self. While this negotiation is an ongoing one and is not limited to this collection, in *At the Bottom of the River* the writer comes to privilege one modality as allowing her greater scope for the expression of an emergent consciousness. The manner in which she arrives at this position and the factors which shape that decision constitute the argument of this essay.

In *At the Bottom of the River* Kincaid invokes the magic of her mother's lore, the power of the folk world and its contradictory rhythms. The powerful presence of obeah as a way of life is one example of the natural accessible magic that is part of the richness of the folk world into which Kincaid has entry. Obeah is presented as a folk practice which manipulates supernatural forces in order to either protect oneself from evil or to achieve evil ends. Thus obeah, accessible and indiscriminate folk magic, becomes a marker both of promise and of danger. For the unknowing, the uninitiated, and the fearful, obeah reduces the folk world to an impenetrable blackness. For the knowing, the initiated, and the brave, obeah illuminates the possibilities of the folk world. The *jablesse*, homed in this magical space, participates in the power of the folk-based world and is a figure who commands both fear and respect. She is both a part of and an outsider to community life.

The story "In the Night" provides a rich delineation of that folk world and its myriad inhabitants. The night soil men who have the task of removing human waste are, like the Kincaid reader, also privy to the flux and flow which constitute community life. In the daytime, the night soil men participate in the dreams and ambitions of their community. They love and are loved; have children; betray their wives with their mistresses; make promises to their children which they do not keep; indulge in small vanities. At night, they are observers and silent participants in another drama, another reality. They witness the nightly perambulations of the *jablesse* who "has removed her kin and is on her way to drink the blood of her secret enemies" (6).[3] They observe the various manipulations of the magical to service the mundane. They are seduced by the *jablesse* whom Kincaid, in a later story, describes as a beautiful woman, "a person who can turn into anything. But you know they aren't real because of their eyes" (9). And in this folk world, the real and the non real occupy the same space. This is emblematized in the ghost of Mr. Gishard— the non real—as it stands under the cedar tree looking at and yearning for the life left behind—the real.

Initially, Kincaid seems comfortable with the real/non real paradox which characterizes this creole space. The self-identification as *jablesse* allows her many creative possibilities. It becomes the occasion to re-arrange the facts of her personal history; it makes a space for an alternative rendering of experience—one which, like the transformative magic of obeah, allows for truth to be identified as other than factual or locatable. Like the blackbird in the story "Girl" which is not really a blackbird, like the beautiful woman who is really a *jablesse*, Kincaid's autobiography, as represented in *At the Bottom of the River*, gestures at a truth which is not absolute and which requires no authentication except that it lies chimerically embedded in her own experiences. Even while self remains the center of narrative interest, it is never a fixed or identifiable self. Rather, it imitates the mother persona who in an unguarded moment, very much like the *jablesse*, "grew plates of metal-colored scales on her back, . . . uncoiled her hair from her head and then removed her hair altogether, . . . taking her head into her large palms, she flattened it so that her eyes . . . sat on the top of her head and spun like two revolving balls" (55). From this vantage point, the *jablesse* is able to view the world from myriad perspectives. Similarly, the mode of *jablesse* allows Kincaid to participate in the folk world inhabited by her mother—a world where she can deploy a fluid, hypnotic prose; a world where the rich melody of mother-tongued words, the inexplicable magic of maternal ways of coming to know are co-opted as the power to alter existing literary forms into new modes of self-representation.

These positives notwithstanding, the solid pervasiveness of the mother's presence, simultaneously reassuring and threatening, is presented as what the persona wants to both participate in and undermine. This paradoxical negotiation is at the heart of Kincaid's narrative enterprise. She has often admitted that her ambiguous relationship with her mother constitutes her inspirational springboard. In an interview with Kay Bonetti, Kincaid insists: "It was the thing I knew. Quite possibly if I had had another kind of life I would not have been moved to write. That was the immediate thing, the immediate oppression, I knew. I wanted to free myself of that" (133). It is her mother for whom Kincaid writes, it is her mother's voice which she attempts to capture in her prose and it is her mother from whom she needs to free herself. Kincaid writes to escape the lure of that *jablesse*. But its insidious power is not so easily negated and the stories in *At the Bottom of the River* shuttle back and forth, seeking a way out, another resolution, an alternative way of being.

The circulating contradictions: the vacillation between joy at belonging and fear of separation—between desire for selfhood and the pain of remembered separation—are captured in the short story "My Mother." The relationship between the mother and daughter is an injurious one, and the child dreams of freeing herself from the tyranny of her mother's love. She wishes her mother dead, yet cannot imagine a world without her mother.

She feels suffocated by the constancy of her mother's devotion and plots self-indulgent escapes from a "climate not suited to [her] nature" (57). In the narrator's growing anger, pits, traps, poisons, strangulation and alternative magic are fantasized as ways to bring about the mother's demise. The child narrator longs to grow her "own bosoms, small mounds at first, leaving a small, soft place between them, where, if ever necessary, [she] could rest [her] own head" (53).

Nonetheless the narrator is cognizant that there is still much she can learn from her mother, particularly the ways in which the mother/mentor's powers can be annexed and extended. Indeed, she dreams of a world where she is bigger and more dominant than her mother. She pretends frailty in order to ascertain the source of the mother's strength. "I sighed occasionally— long soft sighs, the kind of sigh she had long ago taught me could evoke sympathy. In fact, how I really felt was invincible. I was no longer a child but I was not yet a woman" (56). But to become truly invincible, she needs to reconfigure the space wherein the mother and daughter wrestle to assert their selfhood. The folk world, dominated by the *jablesse* and her chameleon magic, is ultimately the mother's milieu and must necessarily be rejected by the narrator/writer as she seeks another site wherein she can sport mastery. To remain in the mother's world is to be forever caught between a "horrible roar . . . [and] a self-pitying whine" (56).

Apprenticed to her mother, having learned how to work her mother's special kind of obeah, the narrator sets about transforming the terms of her location in her mother's oral world. She is as much the initiate as she is the challenger. She is both a child and a woman. She loves her mother, yet she is constantly seeking to destroy her. She glories in her mother's presence, yet yearns to escape into exile.[4] The child imagines herself growing into her mother, yet never achieving the power: "I had grown big but my mother was bigger" (56). "My mother has grown to an enormous height. I have grown to an enormous height also, but my mother's height is three times mine" (58). While the child narrator can never approximate the mother's power, Kincaid achieves a successful annexation because of the tactics of intervention she deploys—her judicious use of the magic of language.

A novice in the *jablesse* world, learning how to make creative use of the magic and power inherent to the folk world, Kincaid can take her place alongside her literary creations. In that spirit, "Wingless" offers an example of how to survive that world. Exploring the ways in which survival in that world depends on submitting to a larger maternal authority, "Wingless" advocates an acceptance of dependence as necessary and inevitable. The story details a life apprenticed to the instructions of others, a life where she is "a defenseless and pitiful child" (23). But the paradox of submission and resistance remains. The inquiry "But how can my limbs that hate be the same limbs that love? How can the same limbs that make me blind make me see? I am defenseless and small" (22) is followed by "My hands, brown on this side, pink on this side, now indiscriminately dangerous, now vagabond and prodigal, now cruel and careless, now without remorse or forgiveness . . ." (27).

"Wingless" offers surrender as a means of survival. In the safety of her mother's presence, the protagonist can survive the co-existence of the fearful and the mysterious. Now keeping a safe distance she can follow the woman she loves, can witness the encounter between *Papa Bois*, ruler of the forest, who "wore clothes made of tree bark and sticks in his ears" (25)[5] and the woman—the *jablesse* who roams the forest and the mountains, the lowlands and the valleys. The child can hear *Papa Bois* say forceful things to the woman, can watch him blow himself up until he looks like a boil, and can remain unafraid. She is safely aligned to the woman who "instead of removing her cutlass from the folds of her big and beautiful skirt and cutting the man in two at the waist, . . . only smiled—a red, red smile [at the man] and like a fly he dropped dead" (25). In this game for dominion, the power of the *jablesse* is uncontested and the frightened child's choice of alignment assures her safe survival. But there can be other negotiations, ones which do not assure the same degree of protection or survival.

The story "Blackness" reiterates the inconstancies of the mother's world—a world where one is erased, annihilated, one's form made formless. However, this story suggests a different strategy for charting the geography of that seemingly immeasurable world—surrender to its boundaryless silence. "Living in the silent voice, I am no longer 'I.' Living in the silent voice, I am at last at peace. Living in the silent voice, I am at last erased" (52). There is power in this surrender because it allows the persona to move towards *claritas* and the blackness which threatened erasure now assumes a lambent potential. There is a suggestion that the power contained in blackness can be accessed by being absorbed into it, even while this absorption means that the creative voice is as yet silent.

Nevertheless, the reader is assured that the voicelessness is only temporary, for the persona is not "one with it" (48) only as yet isolated within it. Indeed, this isolation is at the polar opposite to the earlier community which was loud with voices and indomitable wills which endangered the embryonic Id. Now community wears many conflicting faces, and blackness comes in different ways. In the new world which is marauded by "bands of men . . . [with] guns and cannons" (48), blackness becomes the metonym for colonial conquest. Community, presented then as the antithesis of blackness, evokes the oral rhythms of the world, its beauty, its power, as they were before they were blackened and destroyed by colonial adventures. Community can bring one to voice. It can provide a counternarrative to what Moira Ferguson[6] describes as "linguistic alienation, feelings of loss and censorship that threaten to annihilate . . ." (23).

In "Blackness" the child which the persona has made becomes the writing self, a newly empowered, writing Id who appropriates the power of the monstrous mother. Out of the womb-like blackness comes this child, a powerful, pitiless and unimperiled, still silent self. "Though I have summoned her into a fleeting existence, one that is perilous and subject to the violence of chance, she embraces time as it passes in numbing sameness, bearing in its wake a multitude of great sadnesses" (51). Blackness expands to a space of silence waiting to be filled, a place without boundaries, without limits, a blank space wherein and upon which new narratives can be written. Silence is now bigger than blackness, yet part of it. Silence is also non-threatening and welcoming. Silence is a progression of blackness. There is safety in it.

Silence, safety, blackness, all these constituents of the *jablesse* world notwithstanding, the expansive reality of the folk world is ultimately insufficient to the aspirations of the persona. In her experimentation with the *jablesse* as a mode of being, Kincaid comes to the realization of its limits even while she concedes that it allows for what María Lugones describes as "weaving [which] reveals the possibility and complexity of a pluralistic feminism, a feminism that affirms the plurality in each of us . . . as richness and as central to feminist ontology and epistemology" (390). Indeed, the *jablesse*, once she has taken off her skin, is free to go anywhere, become anything. She is now mysterious and magical. She is intrusive and intimidating. She is beautiful, yet fearsome. But to be all these things she must take her skin off, and it is this act which renders the *jablesse* non real. In taking off her skin she becomes **anything** only because now she is **nothing**; she lacks shape and substance. While the *jablesse* may provoke fear, that fear is deconstructed by classification of the *jablesse* as the mere phantom of the imagination. Similarly the mother's power can be neutralized by the recognition that its range of influence is limited to the yard. It is not real elsewhere. Outside the folk world the *jablesse* ceases to be; the mother's powers cease to matter. Both have limited transferability and in fact depend on the child/narrator for their continuance. It has limited transferability and in fact depends on the child/narrator for its continuance.

Thus, in spite of its potential for playful traveling, the *jablesse* modality remains nonviable; its lack of ontological status confines the *jablesse* to gallivanting in the mountains (9). It is therefore displaced by a more viable alternative—the *jamette*. The *jamette* is as intrusive and intimidating as the *jablesse*; she too can smile a red, red deadly smile, but she is offensively real. Moreover the *jamette* is everything the mother has rejected as a viable mode of survival and is therefore the marker of filial rejection, rebellion and power. Both of and outside the folk world, the *jamette* has wider gallivanting range.

Sluttishness now becomes the familiar in Kincaid's version of magic—her way of conjuring.

And Jamaica Kincaid has indeed become the slut[7] whom the mother warned against becoming. But slut, as I propose to use it here, is more than a dirty, slovenly woman. In becoming a slut, Kincaid both subverts and revises these sociolinguistic conventions. Instead, she styles herself as a woman whose freedom of self expression makes it difficult for her to submit to neat classifications and safe, social categories. Moreover, Kincaid recuperates the notion of freely expressed funk[8] implicit to the slut/*jamette*. Funk stands as the opposite of anesthetized cleanliness; it stands for the healthy dirtiness venerated by the business of living. Funk is freely expressed passions, unreined emotion. Funk has energy and lacks restraint. Funk celebrates self-will. Kincaid's staging of her individualism becomes an expression of her funk, a display of the sluttishness which her mother had once warned against, and the proclamation of self as *jamette*. Funk is something which communities may react to and attempt to curb. Indeed, for Kincaid, the folk community from which she emerges becomes suffocating, repressing the "funk" which must necessarily erupt so that she can come into her own literary personhood.

Kincaid manipulates the freedom of mobility which the jamette gains through a refusal to be confined by social rules and attitudes. The *jamette* gives offense—deliberately. The *jamette*'s tongue has no curb, knows no strictures. She says what she wants, where and whenever she wants. *At the Bottom of the River* is preoccupied with the coming to voice and the legitimizing of that voice. Thus, for Kincaid, the eruption of her funk functions on a psychic as well as on a narrative level. It is both the disruption of social expectations, the glorying in dismantled and discarded social strictures, and a destabilizing of literary conventions. Where previously the word "slut" described a moral or material condition, now Kincaid's reclamation of sluttishness invests it with a freedom to transgress narratively, to disobey literary rules, and to play with generic boundaries. It is these characteristics which Kincaid seems to demonstrate so often in her writing.

Kincaid's story "Girl," the first in the collection *At the Bottom of the River*, tells of the child persona's growth into the slut in spite of the mother's best efforts. "Girl" focuses on the noisy insistence of the mother's speech, its fidelity to cultural practices which reinforce patriarchy, and its ambivalent vernacular locations. This story functions as an evocation of a mother throwing sharp words of counsel at her daughter, warning against becoming the slut:

Wash the white clothes on Monday and put them on the stone heap; wash the color clothes on Tuesday and put them on the clothesline to dry; don't walk barehead in the hot sun; cook pumpkin fritters in very hot sweet oil; soak your little cloths right after you take them off, . . . on Sundays try to walk like a lady . . . ; don't sing benna in Sunday school; you mustn't speak to wharf-rat boys, not even to give direction; don't eat fruits on the street—flies will follow you. (3–4)

Situated in the mother's speech are the rhythms of a domestic life which remains connected to a creole reality even while they simultaneously suggest a colonial-inspired, social world of duty and decorum to which the girl must ultimately submit. The mother's relentless volley of instructions and admonitions leaves no space for the daughter's responses or desire, for it assumes that the girl's destiny, like hers, is to become part of the discourse of provisional domestic independence within patriarchal domination.

The woman whom the mother admonishes the girl into becoming is as much the socially-constructed good woman who knows how to cook, clean and keep a man as she is the successful rebel who can, quietly and undetected, circumvent social mores, who can "spit up in the air if [she] feel[s] like it" but who can "move quick so that it doesn't fall on [her]" (5). Indeed, she is allowed to be a secret slut. Ultimately the advice proffered is geared towards creating what the mother defines as a powerful woman—one who is in control of all spheres, the domestic one within which society has conscribed her, the sexual one where her power is felt but never analyzed, and the social one within which she bounds herself. In contrast, the publicly-recognized slut—the *jamette* whom the girl is admonished against becoming—is dismissed by the mother as a non-viable mode of being. Social constructions of the *jamette* define her as lacking control over both her funk and her material condition. As a recognized slut she is reduced to a woman outside of community, isolated from systems of exchange, the kind of woman whose physical survival is imperiled, "the kind of woman who the baker won't let near the bread" (5), the *jamette* scorned by her community.

While the mother is preaching guerrilla resistance, she is training the child into habits of patriarchal compliance. She teaches the girl how to be a good daughter: "This is how to iron your father's khaki shirt so that it does not have a crease. This is how you iron your father's khaki pants so that they don't have a crease" (4). She teaches her how to be a good wife: "This is how to bully a man; this is how a man bullies you; this is how to love a man, and if this doesn't work there are other ways" (5). Inserted in the text of the mother's instructions are subtle lessons on how to empower one's self within these inevitable social strictures. Her instructions on marital control begin by casting the woman as prime actor and the man as reactive. The paradoxical alignment of patriarchal hegemony and female agency, where the woman is constructed as passive and submissive on one hand and controlling on the other, is at the heart of the mother's discourse; indeed it is very much a part of the *jablesse* world where appearance and reality are constantly warring.

Even while the child's voice is not allowed to interrupt the mother's spiel on good West Indian housekeeping, the absence of that resisting voice must not be read as silence, for Kincaid remains anxious about the pervasive presence of her mother's voice, the ambiguity of its utterances, and its silencing authority. Kincaid, in assuming the role of the *jamette*, gives her tongue the liberty to gallivant into hitherto forbidden arenas. One such space is the mother's mouth where entry thus allows the child persona in "Girl" to become a ventriloquist for the mother's instructing voice. Now it is the child persona who has agency; the act of inserting her tongue into her mother's mouth does not only bring the mother to voice but ultimately establishes the daughter's control over that voice. Such an activity serves to demonstrate the power of both the mother and the child and the battle which ensues because of these power alignments. Moreover, the intrusion of the renegade tongue allows for a radical re-telling of the story "Girl."

The oppressive weight of the mother's words as presented in "Girl" speaks to the magnitude of the battle which the child needs to engage in so as to gain independence and dominion. "Girl" presents the mother's discourse on private sluttishness in order that it can be dismissed as an option. The private slut cannot show off how much of a *jamette* she truly is. Compelled to mask her power, she thus becomes silenced, her transgression undone. Succumbing to middle class hypocrisy results in the co-optation of cunning and resistance to serve bourgeois conformity. But the *jamette* thrives on open and public rebellion. The mother's text preaches covert resistance. Indeed, "Girl" is a story not merely of the speaking mother but of the silent rather than silenced daughter. It is the story of a mother whose voice is mediated and made accessible through the linguistic intervention of a willful, traveling daughter whose unfettered tongue recognizes no restrictions. Nonetheless, intrusive tongues can become coated with responsibilities. And the mother, whose formidability continually surges through Kincaid's narratives, cannot be easily silenced. She still has her own tongue in her mouth, and it is this presence that Kincaid continues both to rely on and react to. Thus, for Kincaid, the metaphoric act of inserting her tongue into her mother's mouth functions both as a way of trammeling the power of the mother's noise and as a means of trying to understand it more fully.

Specifically, in such an activity Kincaid is potentially double-tongued. She can manipulate her mother's tongue and her own. In *Sister Outsider*, Audre Lorde speaks about the necessity of transforming silence into language and action, at the same time warning that doing so involves a process of self-revelation which is often fraught with danger. Kincaid, however, seems to circumvent the danger. While self-revelation is her agenda, she strategically seeks this self-definition through entry into her mother's language and world. With the intrusion of the persona's tongue into her mother's mouth comes the encounter with the mother's resident tongue. This meeting allows the persona to understand the mother, to recognize that beyond the seeming maternal alignment with the dominant hegemonic discourse is an oral tradition embedded in the tongue. When her tongue resides in her mother's mouth Kincaid learns how to knead language into a shape that explains and reflects the folk world of which her mother continues to be part. Access to her mother/tongue teaches Kincaid how to use poetry of the kitchen[9] to give voice to the most complex ideas. From her mother, she can learn that language is the magic which erases former silences and fills out old blanks with new ideas. The magic of the *jablesse* is now reconfigured within this *jamette* modality and the richness of the folk world in which the former thrives becomes a site rich in possibilities for the latter.

Indeed, this folk world has a diversity which allows for the bringing together of both oral and written narratives, the stories of mothers and their daughters. The expansion of the creative terrain available through this *jamette* modality makes for a partial reconfiguration of the term "oral tradition." Emilio Jorge Rodriguez in "Oral Tradition and Recent Caribbean Poetry" provides an insightful discussion on the Caribbean writers' preoccupation with the dynamics of their culture and the linguistic and artistic possibilities it opens up. Rodriguez explains it thus:

> The oral traditions of the Caribbean region are thus not simply receptacles containing the material of culture in static, compilatory, preserved form. They are, rather, streams meandering, or urging, across the landscape of history, merging with the diluting flow of other tributaries, and transforming into broader yet more discrete currents of cultural identity. Identity here is not a past to be evoked, nor an object to be contemplated in tranquillity, but a dynamic quest, as well as the sum of successive encounters and mixings across time. (1)

The dynamism and the mixing which result from these cultural encounters result in an unruliness of this oral world, and it is to this essential energy that Kincaid responds, using it as the context for self-definition and identification. This activity, initiated by the dismantling of old narratives of power, both maternal and colonial, is more than gratuitous rebellion. Further into this process comes a renaming and a redefinition of the world in which she finds herself. Moreover, even while the choice of the mother's tongue has initiated an understanding of its ambivalence, there is no wholesale acceptance of and surrender to its power. Instead the folk community becomes a place framed in departure, conditional returns, and yearning to be there and to be elsewhere. It is a space which cannot confine the *jamette*.

Intent on establishing a location which is attentive to her myriad subject positions, Kincaid demonstrates the *jamette*'s instinctive fear of fixed structures, be these strictures conformity to the canon into which her colonial education forced her or the oral world of her mother. More particularly, the mother's sphere of influence, easily transformable and lacking fixity, is always rendered in terms of power and powerlessness with Kincaid finding herself usually aligned with the powerless, but seeking to become part of the empowered and the powerful.

Jamaica Kincaid is insistent on establishing an identity which is distinctly individualistic. Kincaid begins with the assurance of community—a consequence of letting her tongue reside in her mother's mouth—yet her destination is the establishing of a separate identity. Having rendered traditional constructions inadequate to her self-mythologizing, she is reluctant to abandon them totally, for she needs community and a history of connectedness to root her while she gallivants. In her essay "Rootedness, the Ancestor as Foundation," Morrison argues that the ancestor is always present in black literature: "And these ancestors are not just parents, they are sort of timeless people whose relationships to the characters are benevolent, instructive, and protective, and they provide a certain kind of wisdom" (496). Though she is appreciative of the contribution of the ancestors and for her connectedness to them, Kincaid's self-articulations insist on her development of a voice and spirit which accedes to ancestral wisdom even as it proclaims its independence. It is this tension which characterizes the final story in the collection.[10]

Jamaica Kincaid's vision of what lies at the bottom of the river seems to be a narcissistic image of a self which is constantly threatened with dissolution by a community that assigns her an identity which is a reflection of her mother's. Kincaid's ambivalent response to the legacy of unity between herself and her mother, her triumph in speaking with her mother's voice, and her ever present need to escape that voice, to create an identity which is distinct, loud, and separate, produces a multiplicity of images of selves. These selves, like fractured reflections in water, can only be explicated through art, the form alternating between an oral and a written one.

Kincaid's ongoing autobiographical project is to create a discourse specific to those fractured and conflicting identities—rebel child and devoted daughter—to rescue the image of self, wavering at the bottom of the river. However, instead of trying to write self into community, Kincaid moves in the opposite direction—her project is to write herself as an individual distinct and apart from community. The act of writing becomes a way into self exploration and discovery, the arrival at a personal truth. She explains it thus: "I don't know if this sense of 'here I am, let me tell you about me,' is universal to women, but it's a very West Indian trait. Maybe it's because she's confined to home and family that there's a great love of self as an aesthetic thing among West Indian women" (145). This great love of self assumes a primacy which makes Kincaid's entry into the traditions of the Antiguan folk world provisional. The act of narrating personal history constitutes a rearranging and artistic manipulation of the facts of the life lived so as to unearth the meaning which is core to it. The control suggested by this artistic manipulation establishes a power relationship between Kincaid and her mother which in according dominance to the daughter transforms the *jamette* into a powerful, offense-giving subject rather than the manipulated object of the oral and colonial traditions.

Kincaid's lyrical weaving of poetry and prose, dream and reality, the domestic and the cosmic marks the birth of a literary consciousness intent on exploring the memories of a prelapsarian mother/child idyll which is the site of both empowerment and disempowerment. The exploration of the residue at the bottom of the river of her postcolonial consciousness is the necessary beginning in which Kincaid must situate her own gendered and cultural identities, ones tested against the looming shadow of a problematic and paradoxical maternal presence. This process is continuous, every conclusion unraveling into doubt and new tactics of intervention.

In her title story of the collection, "At the Bottom of the River," these contradictions contouring the maternal tongue move towards yet another resolution. Kincaid sets up a contrasting frame of a lonely man, a man who is so thoroughly interpellated by colonialism that he is oblivious to the creole rhythms of his world. The man cannot conceive of the harmony of a woman and child at play; he has not seen birds in flight; he has not heard the sound of the wind in the trees. This man has held himself aloof from life's turbulent vitality and is now deaf to the singing sounds of the sea. He faces a silent world, a world where the mother's voice has been allowed no intrusion, where the oral tradition has no influence. The near-existential nothingness of his self-inflicted cultural dislocation engenders a Naipaulian futility, a world not of opposites but of absences. "'Sing again. Sing now,' he says in his heart. . . . But again and again he feels the futility in all that. For stretching out before him is a silence so dreadful, a vastness, its length and breadth and depth immeasurable. Nothing" (68).

The next movement introduces the girl who knows and understands her place in the world, who is comfortable with the *jablesse* modality and has come to accept death as part of the circle of life. "Inevitable to life is death and not inevitable to death is life" (72). She recognizes that death brings a partial silence but that in the natural inconstancies of her world love and adoration create a harmony which is continuous, "an extraordinary chain: a hymn sung in rounds" (74). It is that assurance which renders her world paradisial. Content in that understanding and knowledge of love and its relation to life, she is able to assume the carapace of invincibility and certainty. "How much I loved myself and how much I was loved by my mother" (73). This assurance, bequeathed to the child by her mother, makes her solidly impregnable, and the creative potential of that maternal legacy allows for the confident litany of being and of naming: "I was not made up of flesh and blood and muscles and bones and tissue and cells and vital organs but was made up of my will, and over my will I had complete dominion" (79).

But there are other ways of achieving dominion. While separation is inevitable to the event of growing up, Kincaid, at the end of the collection, presents it as neither the lonely patriarch's self-alienation nor the confident *jablesse* child's self placement. Instead separation and individuality reside in a house of one's own—a one room house made of rough boards, with its A-shaped red galvanized roof. This locale celebrates an Antiguan world, and the four windows facing all sides represent an openness to nature, literally and metaphorically gesturing to the wide-lens perspective at which Kincaid has arrived. The native world is made to harmonize with aspects of the learnt story book of European culture—legacies of her father tongue: "There were flowers: yellow and blue irises, red poppies, daffodils, marigolds. They grew as if wild; intertwined. . . ." (76). The much maligned daffodils in *Lucy* here partially constitute the fixity which she sees at the bottom of the river. In the intertextuality of the two experiences, one lived, the other read, one Antiguan, the other European, is the suggestion of a playful, *jamette* consciousness celebrating variety: "And so it was with everything else that lay so still at the bottom of the river. It all lay there not like a picture but like a true thing and a different kind of true thing: one that I had never known before" (76).

Finally, in this story, the Kincaid persona seems to resolve her struggle to claim a voice which, while it carries echoes of her mother's, is not her mother's voice. The self which emerges at the bottom of the river is one which, though clad in the familiar images of maternal connectedness, wears a newness born out of difference as conflicting identities are replaced with multiple ones, each fragile, each as yet unnamed and unreadable:

> I had no name for the thing I had become, so new was it to me, except that I did not exist in pain or pleasure, east or west or north or south, or up or down, or past or present or future, or real or not real. I stood as if I were a prism, many-sided and transparent, refracting or reflecting light as it reached me, light that never could be destroyed. (80)

Interestingly, the language used to describe the process of self revelation carries obvious traces of two linguistic traditions and reflects the presence of both the *jablesse* child and the lonely man. The language of "At the Bottom of the River" reminds us of the fluidity of form which is so much a part of the mother's world of Anancy stories, riddles and word games. It also suggests the father tongue which has interpellated her. Kincaid's prose makes fluent and deliberate use of the poetic language of Milton's lost paradise, and her evocation of the sublime as an expressive context for the self she is about to become is generous and unapologetic.[11] Yet the presence of the mother's voice remains constant. "At the Bottom of the River" returns to the same prosaic structure which dominated "Girl," to what Diane Simmons elsewhere[12] described as an incantatory list. Only here, the voice and the power implicit to the one who names are reassigned to daughter. Common to both stories is the ritualistic naming of domestic certainties and the assurance found in this act of naming, for the comfort of those solid presences brace against the nothingness which the lonely man at the beginning of "At the Bottom of the River" experiences. Ironically, the persona chooses to envisage herself in a house, the domestic structure to which the law of the father has confined women such as her mother, and a space wherein the *jamette* is free to come and go as she pleases. The house can enclose. It also allows for the staging of separateness of mother and daughter.

Where "Girl" had pointed to the mother's choice of strategies useful to the negotiation of an adult and threatening world, "At the Bottom of the River" melds the earlier images so that they reappear as non-threatening, marked by unquestionable truth and beauty. However, underwriting this euphoric construction of a paradisial world are the cautionary postscripts which, while they accede to the constructedness of these concepts, are careful to show how useful these are in giving the girl/artist a temporary frame within which to fix the world and with which to fix herself in that world.

Indeed, Kincaid's construction deliberately leaves the lonely man (whose condition is never relieved by community) suspended in the narrative as the embodiment of the potential threat to this paradise. Once again there is the reiteration that accommodation, in the folk world and elsewhere, is always provisional and continual. The reader is left uncertain as to whether this frequent reiteration constitutes a lamentation of unbelonging or a reminder of the possibilities implicit to this fluidity.

The foregrounding of the I, rather than the communal we, as subject can only occur after the *jamette* daughter has negotiated her way in and out of her mother's mouth. The speech it has provoked in this writer is one which is mindful to filiation, shared community and appreciative audience. The story of the self which Kincaid offers is fluid and inconstant. It is a folk myth which is part of the repertoire of *jablesse* world and therefore confirms her connectedness to that world and to her mother. At the same time, the story of self is a portrait of a *jamette* who is intent on expressing her funk in various forms and forums.

In the Caribbean, the storytelling traditions survive in a variety of forms—folk tales, proverbs, patterns of performance, rhetoric and calypso. These oral traditions inform the structure of *At the Bottom of the River*. Like the calypso, a form which Gordon Rohlehr in "Articulating A Caribbean Aesthetic" describes as "a flexible medium capable of accommodating narrative, social and political protest . . . and celebration [of] an entire and virtually unexplored body of oral literature . . ." (4), the stories which Kincaid offers begin with a play on the infinite shades of possible meanings. Making use of a variety of tones and voices; she creates improvisations which assert and define identities; identities which, even as they are being established, are simultaneously being revised.[13] Now Kincaid's playfulness with form allows her to create a benna song,[14] the type of folk-song which the mother in "Girl" had labeled as the slut's signature tune.

Further, the oral traditions which Jamaica Kincaid puts to creative use serve as both a source of nourishment and as a challenge when the private act of autobiography becomes a public act of story telling—another folk tale. Like folk tales, these issues circulating in her autobiography are repeated, constituting a never-ending narrative which continue to echo in a variety of places, with no discernible beginning, middle, and end, throughout her later works. Moreover, the autobiography offered by this writer never arrives at a conceptual resting place, but instead pauses at sites rich in interventions and transgressions. Identity remains very much a process, and the selves being made within these folk homes are only aspects of a multiple-constructed persona.

The oral tradition, once presented as a unified definitive text which ascribed to women particular roles, is disrupted and transformed through Kincaid's intervention. Autobiography becomes her contribution to the rich lore of the oral tradition which Kincaid has discovered in her gallivanting through her mother's mouth and world. Thus empowered, Kincaid uses the treasures of her mother's world to refashion herself unapologetically, and in turn, respectful of her liberal borrowing, bequeaths a tale about the self to the collection of never-ending stories. And in the tradition of the never-ending story, her narratives of becoming turn back repeatedly on themselves, reappearing in partial, revised forms, in each instance marking the passage to self explication as a labyrinthine process. These never-ending stories about identity formation constitute a serial autobiography which speaks to a fractal and fractious identity, an autobiography which cannot be confined to one specific geography and which, in its constant reiterations, generates a visionary charge which sustains the writer. It is an identity rife with funk.

Kincaid's story "What I Have Been Doing Lately" is a dramatic example of this regenerative, yet transgressive writing process. In it, Kincaid suggests that there is no single definitive text. Instead the text is born through a verbalizing occasion, coming into being through the act of saying and coming undone through silence. The protagonist's decision to go back to the place where she is lying on her bed means that the text does not become extinct so much as it gestates anew as the constraining linearity of narration is once again disrupted. Yet while the narrative repeats itself, it does so with subtle differences. In the echo of a never-ending story, similar to children's word games, the circularity of the tale is displaced in each transformative version, as passivity is replaced by activity. Indeed the narrator takes possession of the tale in a way which mimics Kincaid's commandeering of her mother's text, her stories, her voice.

Interestingly, the tactics of intervention once deployed to establish separation from the mother differ from the strategy of survival now assumed. Permanence seems to reside in the act of writing her world: the mention of a table, a pen, and a lamp to write by, evoking a new room of one's own where the artist will reside, writing her way out of the provisional nature of that paradise. And the mother's voice once again echoes an assertion that paradise is always yet never lost. It is in this conundrum that the images at the bottom of the river reside, for images written in water by definition lack fixity and permanence even while they have a particular truth and a definite beauty: ". . . how bound up I know I am to all that is human endeavor, to all that is past and to all that shall be, to all that shall be lost and leave no trace. I claim these things then—mine—and now feel myself grow solid and complete, my name filling up my mouth" (82).

What Kincaid arrives at here is similar to the position identified by Inderpal Grewal in "Autobiographical Subjects, Diasporic Locations . . ." where she insists that "there can be syncretic, 'immigrant,' cross-cultural, and plural subjectivities, which enable a politics through positions that are . . . intransigent, in process, and contradictory" (234). *At the Bottom of the River* initiates such a process. The narrative perspective has shifted, the discursive strategy less vested in the mythic and the surrealistic, but the fragments remain the same. Reassembled, they reveal Kincaid's desire to name herself as part of a community which begins with mother and child, whose echoes resonate with cultural continuity. Yet, this community, in not allowing her to be the *jamette*, demands her distance.

Mindful of the problematic location of the *jamette* as both part of yet external to folk community, *At the Bottom of the River* reads as a repository of oral histories. Interpretations of the experiences of other members of the oral community exist alongside individualized accounts of the now-speaking subject. Self is defined, in relation to other traditions, through other (primarily written) traditions and ultimately as part of both an oral and a literate tradition. Exploration of an oral past leads to a celebration of all its elements—both the positives and the negatives.

The reality of the colonial education which Kincaid has undergone cannot be dismissed nor the utility of the oral tradition essentialized. The traces of both traditions remain unerasable, and intertextuality becomes a constant characteristic of her discourse. However, becoming double-tongued and double-voiced from her immersion in the mother's oral world, Kincaid as the self-styled *jamette* can now talk back fearlessly to both the mother's oral text and the white literary text to which she has gained educated access. Mindful of what Fanon in *The Wretched of the Earth* described as "a whole body of efforts made by a people in a sphere of thought, to describe, justify and praise the actions through which a people has created itself and keeps its existence" (188), Kincaid uses the act of self-narrative to bring both the individual and the community into narrative existence through the co-optation of the "speakerly" text.[15] In giving primacy to the Antiguan, communal tongue, Kincaid creates her own edition of the talking book, and the speaking black voice which assumes the podium carries the remarkable volume of shared communal experiences, and the untrammeled power of her newly minted words makes it impossible for her fiery speech to be ignored. What is yet to be accommodated is the ambiguity of her location within the oral community. However negotiable, this contested community provides a supportive audience which not only encourages the noise of Kincaid's critical voice but which, by its very presence, transforms the individual literary voice into a black public voice and moves the resulting discourse from rebellious monologue to polyvocal conversation. But the *jamette* may well be unprepared for that responsibility.

Having struggled to create a voice which is not her mother's, having to cope with the recurring power of that maternal voice, its colonial interpellation and its folk inheritance, Kincaid's expressions of her funk find correspondence in what Michael Awkward identifies in *Negotiating Difference* "as the useful manipulation of border crossings." Awkward argues that "location within a geography of difference contributes to strategies of racial, gendered, class, and sexual performance that . . . can be accepted or rejected, in part or in full" (6). *At the Bottom of the River* constantly interrogates the cultural wisdom which the community, as represented by the maternal voice, imparts. Moreover it does so even while it retrieves and reclaims the Afro-Caribbean cultural experience—its songs and music, its stories and language, and all the practices which make up the daily life of people like her mother.

These are the very practices from which Kincaid, the **newly authorized** *jamette*, willfully and publicly[16] exiles herself and from which, given her earlier commandeering of her mother's tongue, she can never escape. Caught between affirmation and critique, between the mother's traditional mythology and the desire to formulate her own myths—myths suitable to a description of her process of self-actualization, Kincaid's version of the speakerly text creates a system of interpretation which expresses her critical dissent. *At the Bottom of the River* becomes her talking book and speaks to what Rachel DuPlessis in *Writing Beyond the Ending* explains as "putting things at their most extreme, [so as] to stand at the impact point of a strong system of interpretation masked as representation and to rehearse one's own colonization or 'iconization' through the materials one's culture considers powerful and primary" (106). This deliberate confrontation—the *jamette's* talking back to dominating forces—brings the oral and the literal into literal and ideological juxtaposition. And into dialogue.

In *Noises in the Blood*, Cooper offers the following position on the relationship between these two forms of representation:

> The history of ideas in the "Anglophone" Caribbean has conventionally been defined as a one-way flow of knowledge from the centred "mother country" to the peripheral colonies. Though the patriarch has long given her illegitimate children flag-independence, the superstition that upper-case Culture is intrinsically foreign does persist. Conversely, the womanist project ... is to reproduce a body of subversive knowledge that originates in centres of consciousness of the historically dehumanised people of the region. (174)

Part of this revisionary project requires, for Cooper, a remapping of the boundaries of margin and center. Oral literature has long been dismissed as the vulgar noises, the rude vernacular speech, of common people and pushed to the margins of literary considerations only because its persistence does not allow it to be ignored or altogether dismissed. Ideologically relegated to a binary which cites Africa as the origin of the vulgar and Europe the producer of its antithesis—the refined, the written text—oral literatures have not been actively considered as part of Afro-Caribbean letters. Kincaid, in her own theoretical endeavors, provides new and radical "centers of consciousness," ones which bring the hitherto disruptive, interfering and vagrant oral text into conversation with the great scribal tradition of English literature, while conceding the limitations of each to speak to her history as self-styled *jamette*.

Finally, in the celebration of the vulgar as defined by Cooper, Kincaid frees herself from the conventions which had sought to contain her, be they colonial or folk. Having allowed her funk to erupt, freely and powerfully,

Kincaid grows beyond the repressive magic of her mother's words and can use the mother's milk and magic to write herself into being. And having now freed her words from servile maternal and colonial ownership, Jamaica Kincaid can let them loose so that, echoing a line out of Hurston's *Their Eyes Were Watching God*, they become "Words walking without masters, walking altogether like harmony in a song" (8). These words will enter various discourse communities, will bear witness, will criticize, will give offense. And thus authorized by the *jamette* which Kincaid has become, the range of her activities will transform the popular West Indian folk accusation "Your tongue too long" into an advantage, abroad if not at home.

Notes

1. A *jablesse* is the French patois word for devil woman (called *diablesse* in Standard French). The *jablesse* is usually constructed as an extremely beautiful woman whose cloven foot indicates the demon she really is. She is usually found at crossroads, her favorite site, from which she lures susceptible males. She is said to be afraid of salt, smoke and crucifixes and in the presence of these transforms herself into a wild animal.

2. The *jamette*, an Eastern Caribbean word which describes a harlot, is also used as a descriptor for people of the lower class whose way of life is a rejection of societal norms. See Richard Allsopp's definition of *jamette* in *Dictionary of Caribbean English Usage* for a fuller explication of the way *jamette* is nuanced.

3. In Caribbean folklore, there are many demons who remove their skins before setting off for nightly mischief. In some islands, folk legend has it that the removal of the skin allows the *soucoyant*/ole higue/Loup garrou/la *jablesse*, or whatever other name she goes by, to enter the house of the unsuspecting. Her traveling can however be curtailed if the abandoned skin is sprinkled with salt. Thus she is denied reentry into human form.

4. Some scenes presented here will resurface in *Annie John* if only to confirm the indomitable presence of the mother and the continuing, seemingly futile struggle to escape that hegemony. The farewell scene in *Annie John* is in *At the Bottom of the River*, written as a paean of reconciliation where the mother/daughter relationship, temporarily suspended in departure, is resurrected in a new place.

5. *Papa Bois* (Father of the Forest) is a West Indian mythological character. It is one representation of the devil and typically appears in human form, but like the *jablesse*, *Papa Bois* has a cloven hoof which betrays him as non-human.

6. See Moira Ferguson's *Jamaica Kincaid: Where the Land Meets the Body* for a detailed analysis of mother/motherland representations in Kincaid's work. Ferguson's intervention locates Kincaid's writing within current postcolonial formulations.

7. I am aware that here my reading of "slut" differs somewhat from the concept of slut as a dissolute immoral woman which is the definition that Diane Simmons privileges in *Jamaica Kincaid*, pg. 75–6. Simmons sees the mother's admonitions as repressing the child's burgeoning sexuality.

8. I am also using "funk" in the sense which African American writers use it. See Toni Morrison's *The Bluest Eye*: "Whenever it erupts, this funk, they try to wipe it away" (58). Funk is also what Valerie Lee in *Granny Midwives and Black Women Writers* describes as "a subversive discursive practice, a destabilizing of what is expected because of an alternative cultural matrix" (54).

9. I am playing with the term which Marshall uses to describe her artistic development in her article "Poets in the Kitchen."

10. While there is a certain chronology to the collection *At the Bottom of the River*, my own reading of the collection disrupts that chronology. I am justifying my decision on the basis that Kincaid's chronology is often accidental. Further, given her much discussed stance on circularity and invented order, the stories in the collection can thus be read as similar to the one told in "What I Have Been Doing Lately."

11. See Diane Simmons, *Jamaica Kincaid* (New York: Twayne Publishers, 1994), for a discussion of the ways in which Kincaid writes back to the English canon and the influence of Milton on her writing.

12. See *Jamaica Kincaid* 24.

13. It is no accident that in the novel *Lucy*, when the eponymous heroine is asked to reveal something of herself, she responds with a calypso on escape and transgression which she offers as the metonym of her character.

14. The benna or benna song according to Allsopp is "A type of two or three-line folk-song repeated over and over; in former times it was considered inappropriate for Sundays, or for children; there was a dance to it" (94).

15. In *The Signifying Monkey*, Henry Louis Gates, Jr. defines the speakerly text as one which has as part of its narrative strategies the literary representation of the speaking voice. Going on to relate the contribution of Zora Neale Hurston to that trope, Gates further clarifies: "speakerly texts privilege the representation of the speaking black voice, of what the Russian Formalist called *skaz* and which Hurston and Reed have defined as 'an oral book, a talking book'" (112).

16. I am referring here to Kincaid's interviews in the North American press and her repeated denials that her writings carry traces of a West Indian literary tradition. This public disavowal of the richness of the oral world from which she emerges notwithstanding, Kincaid does not escape the influence of her mother. That much she is prepared to concede, over and over again.

Works Cited

Awkward, Michael. *Negotiating Difference: Race, Gender and the Politics of Positionality*. Chicago: U of Chicago P, 1995.

Allsopp, Richard. *Dictionary of Caribbean English Usage*. New York: Oxford UP, 1996.

Bonetti, Kay. "An Interview with Jamaica Kincaid." *The Missouri Review* 15.2 (1992): 123–42.

Cooper, Carolyn. *Noises in the Blood: Orality, Gender and the "Vulgar" Body of Jamaican Popular Culture*. Durham, NC: Duke UP, 1995.

DuPlessis, Rachel. *Writing Beyond the Ending: Narrative Strategies of Twentieth Century Women Writers*. Bloomington: Indiana UP, 1985.

Fanon, Franz. *The Wretched of The Earth*. Trans. Constance Farrington. New York: Grove/Atlantic, 1963.

Ferguson, Moira. *Jamaica Kincaid: Where the Land Meets the Body*. Charlottesville and London: UP of Virginia, 1994.

Gates, Henry Louis, Jr. *The Signifying Monkey: A Theory of Afro-American Literary Criticism*. New York: Oxford UP, 1988.

Grewal, Inderpal. "Autobiographical Subjects and Diasporic Locations: *Meatless Days* and *Borderlands*." *Scattered Hegemonies: Postmodernity and Transnational Feminist*

Practices. Eds. Inderpal Grewal and Caren Kaplan. Minneapolis: U of Minnesota P, 1994. 231–54.

Hurston, Zora Neale. *Their Eyes Were Watching God*. Urbana and Chicago: U of Illinois P, 1978 (first published 1937).

Kincaid, Jamaica. *At the Bottom of the River*. New York: Farrar, Strauss and Giroux, 1983.

———. *Annie John*. New York: Farrar, Strauss and Giroux, 1985.

———. *Lucy*. New York: Farrar, Strauss and Giroux, 1990.

Lee, Valerie. *Granny Midwives and Black Women Writers: Double-Dutched Readings*. New York: Routledge, 1996.

Lorde, Audre. *Sister Outsider: Essays and Speeches*. Freedom, CA: The Crossing Press, 1984.

Lugones, María. "Playfulness, 'World'-Traveling and Loving Perception." *Making Face, Making Soul-Haciendo Caras: Creative and Critical Perspectives of Feminists of Color*. Ed. Gloria Anzaldua. San Francisco: Aunte Lute, 1990: 390–402.

Marshall, Paule. *Reena and other Stories*. Old Westbury, NY: The Feminist Press, 1983.

Morrison, Toni. "Rootedness: The Ancestor as Foundation." In *The Woman That I Am*. Ed. D. Soyini Madison. New York: St. Martin's, 1994. 492–97.

Rodriguez, Emilio, Jorge. "Oral Tradition and Recent Caribbean Poetry." *Caribbean Writers: Between Orality and Writing*. Atlanta, GA: Rodopi, 1994. 1–16.

Rohlehr, Gordon. "Articulating A Caribbean Aesthetic: The Revolution in Self-Perception." *My Strangled City and Other Essays*. Trinidad: Longman Trinidad Ltd., 1992.

Simmons, Diane. *Jamaica Kincaid*. New York: Macmillan Library Reference, 1994.

LAURA NIESEN de ABRUNA

Jamaica Kincaid's Writing and the Maternal-Colonial Matrix

Acknowledged as one of the leading women writers from the Caribbean, Jamaica Kincaid was born in 1949 in St. Johns, Antigua. At the age of 19 she left the island for the United States, where she took various jobs before establishing herself as a writer. Kincaid's father was a carpenter and cabinet-maker. Her grandmother was a Carib Indian, and her mother, Annie, is from Dominica. In 1966 Kincaid went to the United States to pursue her education. She attended college for one year, but became alienated before the second year started and dropped out. Soon afterwards she began to submit freelance articles to magazines, two of which were published in *Ms*. With the help of her friend George Trow, she became a contributor to the *New Yorker*. From 1976 to the present, she has been a staff writer for the *New Yorker*, contributing some 80 pieces, a few as letters with her name attached, some unsigned, to the 'Talk of the Town' section, and over 14 short stories. Her first volume of short stories, *At the Bottom of the River*, published in 1978, presented modernist dream visions of life in Antigua. Her best work to date is the coming-of-age novel, *Annie John*, which appeared in 1983. Her collection of short essays on Antigua, *A Small Place*, was published in 1988. Her novel *Lucy* appeared in 1990. Her most recent novel is entitled *The Autobiography of My Mother* (1996) and picks up the theme of the maternal matrix, as Kincaid presents her mother's life in the first person. Kincaid now

From *Caribbean Women Writers: Fiction in English*, edited by Mary Condé and Thorunn Lonsdale. ©1999 by Macmillan Press Ltd.

lives in Vermont with her husband Allen, a music professor at Bennington College, and their two children, Annie and Harold Shawn.

Kincaid is notable for her presentation of women's experience. Jean Rhys was the first or at least the first published among Caribbean women writers to present the mother–daughter matrix as part of the full range of women's experiences in the Caribbean. Like Rhys, Kincaid employs a wide range of modernist and postmodern strategies, such as dreams and associative thinking, as parts of the narrator's strategies of resistance to the dominant culture. In *Lucy*, and in the *New Yorker* stories, in *Annie John*, *A Small Place*, and *The Autobiography of My Mother*, Kincaid puts little distance between herself and the narrator who recounts a portion of her life and analyses its trajectory. The one exception to this is *At the Bottom of the River*, which treats the mother–daughter matrix but always through the literary mediation of dream associations and their language. Kincaid's greatest contribution to the full presentation of female life is her exploration of the mother–daughter bond, and specifically, the effects of the loss of the maternal matrix on the relationship between the mother and daughter. In *Annie John*, as well as in *Lucy* and *The Autobiography of My Mother*, the alienation from the mother becomes a metaphor for the young woman's alienation from an island culture that has been completely dominated by the imperialist power of England. In *Lucy*, this point is made through the narrator's very name. She feels that her mother's teasing explanation of the name 'Lucy' as a diminutive of 'Lucifer' is accurate because it represents her sense of herself as fallen away from a relationship with a kind of god, and at several points in the novel she refers to her vision of her mother as 'godlike.' In most of Kincaid's work, her narrators perceive and present their early, preoedipal relationship with their mothers as a type of Eden from which they have irretrievably fallen away.

Recent critics have found that an emphasis on the personal area of experience, like the mother–daughter relationships in Kincaid's *Lucy* and *The Autobiography of My Mother*, is a characteristic of women's writing in general and of Caribbean women's writing in particular. In their anthology entitled *Her True-True Name*, the Jamaican writers Betty Wilson and Pamela Mordecai have testified to a flowering in the 1980s of women's writing dealing with such concerns as surviving sexism, negotiating mother–daughter relationships, and an interest in relational interaction, or 'bonding'. Most of this literature is concerned with bringing personal and emotional issues into the public and literary arenas. In her anthology of black women writers, *Watchers & Seekers: Creative Writing by Black Women*, Rhonda Cobham argues for the centrality of either bonding or the absence of bonding in the texts of Caribbean women writers, especially in their focus on the emotional interdependence of mothers and daughters, granddaughters and grandmothers, friends, and sisters:

Their perspectives may be critical, nostalgic or celebratory, sentimental or distanced. But repeatedly there emerges a sense of sisterly solidarity with mother figures, whose strengths and frailties assume new significance for daughters now faced with the challenge of raising children and/or achieving artistic recognition in an environment hostile to the idea of female self-fulfillment.[1]

Kincaid focuses intensely in all of her work on the relationship between her narrator and her mother. And there is always a correlation between the political difficulties afflicting the island–'mother' country relationship and the problems affecting the mother–daughter family relationships in these texts. The characters' separation from the mother, or the 'mother' country, evokes extreme anxiety that appears as cultural and psychic alienation. In all of Kincaid's work, it is the absence of the once-affirming mother or an affirming 'mother' country, that causes dislocation and alienation. In both *Annie John* and *Lucy*, the narrators Annie and Lucy experience great tensions in their experiences with their mothers because of the early intensity of the bond and its later complete severance. For Annie, the severance is initiated by her mother and occurs before she leaves the island. For Lucy, the separation seems to be initiated by her and is demonstrated in her habit of not opening the 19 or so letters that arrive from her mother. In both novels, the importance of female bonding is central, and is centred on the narrator's relationship with her mother. In both texts the character's personal alienation is explored first directly and then as a metaphor for the alienation of the daughter-island from the mother-country. The metaphorical exploration offers a criticism of the neocolonial situation that inhibits the lives of both Annie and Lucy. Both women are victims of their environments and both are in states of extreme anger because of this situation. At the end of *Annie John*, Annie can find her own identity; she is able to do this through her identification with her mother and her grandmother, Ma Chess, who fills the maternal role when Annie's mother can no longer cope with Annie's psychological breakdown and physical illness.

In *Lucy*, the narrator is much older, 19 rather than 15, and her relationship with her mother is much less clear to her than it is to Annie. Because Lucy is in the United States working as an au pair, she has no group of female relatives who could form a support group for her. In fact, she seems to long for total anonymity because those who know her harshly evaluated and judged each of her actions. She has a tremendous amount of anger about her relationship with her mother. Again, Lucy feels that the closeness she experienced with her mother was a kind of trap set by their biological connection. As her mother says to her, "'You can run away, but you cannot escape the fact that I am your mother, my blood runs in you, I carried you for nine months' inside me.'"[2] Yet Lucy would die of longing for her mother if she read even one letter.

The most dramatic example of Lucy's anger is her response to her father's death. She thinks of saying to her mother's friend, Maude:

> 'I am not like my mother. She and I are not alike. She should not have married my father. She should not have had children. She should not have thrown away her intelligence. She should not have paid so little attention to mine. She should have ignored someone like you. I am not like her at all.'[3]

She seems to have very few feelings of regret about her father, whom she describes as having behaved very badly, in a way that Antiguan women would have expected. It is with her mother that the conflict continues. Her letter is extremely cold:

> It matched my heart. It amazed even me, but I sent it all the same. In the letter I asked my mother how she could have married a man who would die and leave her in debt even for his own burial. I pointed out the ways she had betrayed herself. I said I believed she had betrayed me also, and that I knew it to be true even if I couldn't find a concrete example right then. I said that she had acted like a saint, but that since I was living in this real world I had really wanted just a mother. I reminded her that my whole upbringing had been devoted to preventing me from becoming a slut; I then gave a brief description of my personal life, offering each detail as evidence that my upbringing had been a failure and that, in fact, life as a slut was quite enjoyable, thank you very much. I would not come home now, I said. I would not come home ever.[4]

Lucy is, of course, in the process of working out her relationship with her mother from the distance of the United States. She sees in Mariah a number of different people, but she often sees Mariah as a sort of substitute for her mother. With Mariah she has the closeness of conversation and intimacy that she could not have experienced with her 'saint-like' mother. It is Mariah who points out to Lucy that she is filled with anger and later suggests, even as her own marriage is falling apart, that Lucy must forgive her mother in order to thaw her cold heart: "Why don't you forgive your mother for whatever it is you feel she has done? Why don't you just go home and tell her you forgive her?"[5] These words allow Lucy to recognize the real source of her anger in the treatment she had received from her mother, which Lucy perceives as a series of betrayals.

The first betrayal is the betrayal of the first child in a family into which other children are born. But the other children were all male children, each of whom would be considered by her parents as potential candidates for the university in England or to study as a doctor or a lawyer. Lucy feels this discrimination stingingly. She seems not to respect her father, an old man who had fathered thirty children and left their mothers. But she could not accept the betrayal by her mother:

> I did not mind my father saying these things about his sons, his own kind, and leaving me out. My father did not know me at all; I did not expect him to imagine a life for me filled with excitement and triumph. But my mother knew me well, as well as she knew herself: I, at the time, even thought of us as identical; and whenever I saw her eyes fill up with tears at the thought of how proud she would be at some deed her sons had accomplished, I felt a sword go through my heart, for there was no accompanying scenario in which she saw me, her only identical offspring, in a remotely similar situation. To myself I then began to call her Mrs. Judas, and I began to plan a separation from her that even then I suspected would never be complete.[6]

Lucy's anger is different from Annie's. Annie's anger comes from her mother's indifference to her once she attains puberty. Lucy's anger comes from her mother's lack of faith in her abilities and talents. Although Mariah points out to Lucy that part of her mother's attitude comes from cultural conditioning, that is something that Lucy is unwilling to accept. For, at this point, and indeed even at the end of the novel, the mother remains a figure who is not an individual, partly conditioned by history, culture, and class. Instead, the mother remains the 'god', as she is referred to so often, or the 'monster', as in the stories collected in the anthology, *At the Bottom of the River*. This is one of the major problems with the novel, since the narrator never moves away from a childlike view of her mother as both superhuman and subhuman. In fact, her response is melodramatic and fixated at the preoedipal level: '. . . for ten of my twenty years, half of my life, I had been mourning the end of a love affair, perhaps the only true love in my whole life I would ever know'.[7] Unfortunately, this statement is made by a 20-year-old narrator who has also claimed that she is breaking the bond she felt with her mother. The intensity of that bond is remarkable, although its sources are not revealed in the text.

According to Lucy, she has never had any love for the men she saw around her either in Antigua or in the United States. The couple with whom she lives, Mariah and Lewis, are moving toward the end of their marriage. Lewis is having an affair with Mariah's best friend, Dinah, and neither Dinah nor Lewis has any feelings of concern for Mariah or her four children. For Lucy, Lewis's behaviour in rejecting his wife Mariah for Dinah comes as no surprise, but as behaviour expected from men:

> A woman like Dinah was not unfamiliar to me, nor was a man like Lewis. Where I came from, it was well known that some women and all men in general could not be trusted in certain areas. My father had perhaps thirty children; he did not know for sure. He would try to make a count but then he would give up after a while. One woman he had children with tried to kill me when I was in my mother's stomach. She had earlier failed to kill my mother. My father had lived with another woman for years and was the father of her three children; she tried to kill my mother and me many times. My mother saw an obeah woman every Friday to prevent these attempts from being successful.[8]

In a situation in which the parental focus is so asymmetrical, the bond between the mother and the daughter will attain great importance.

In both *Annie John* and *Lucy* the process of leaving the mother is complicated by the similar process of leaving an island dominated by British cultural imperialism. Lucy's anger about this is best seen in her reaction to reading a poem about daffodils, probably Wordsworth's. As a ten-year-old on a tropical island, Lucy was forced to memorize and recite a poem about daffodils approved by the Queen Victoria Girls' School. The flowers, which do not grow in the Caribbean, are symbolic of the many ways British culture had been forced on the young women in Antigua. After reciting the poem, Lucy tried to repress all of its lines. She is herself surprised when Mariah's mention of daffodils unleashes strong emotions: 'I had forgotten all of this until Mariah mentioned daffodils, and now I told it to her with such an amount of anger I surprised both of us'.[9] Later, when Mariah again presses the issue of these flowers, Lucy finds that she wants to kill them: 'There was such joy in her voice as she said this, such a music, how could I explain to her the feeling I had about daffodils—that it wasn't exactly daffodils, but that they would do as well as anything else?'[10] Finally, Lucy is able to push this anger into full consciousness as she explains to Mariah, '"Mariah, do you realize that at ten years of age I had to learn by heart a long poem about some flowers I would not see in real life until I was nineteen?"'[11]

In a 'Talk of the Town' article for the *New Yorker* which appeared in 1977, Kincaid, who rejected her British name Richardson, recalled that most of the African-Caribbean people of Antigua worked as carpenters, masons, servants in private homes, seamstresses, fishermen, or dockworkers. She added that, 'A few grew crops and a very small number worked in offices and banks'.[12] When Kincaid was seven, she was herself apprenticed to a seamstress for two afternoons a week. People who worked in offices and banks were white, and the wealthiest ran a country club called the Mill Reef Club. The whites owned the banks and the offices and reserved most of the island's pleasant beaches for themselves. All of these historical and political contexts are important to Kincaid's fiction. Despite her affection for her surrogate family in the United States, Lucy is still the 'Visitor', and she questions the basis of the family's comfortable life. For example, Lucy comments ironically on the connection between the endangered species for which Mariah evinces such concern and her family wealth. And Lucy is offended when Mariah boasts that she has some 'Indian' blood in her: 'How do you get to be the sort of victor who can claim to be the vanquished also?'[13]

Much of Kincaid's distrust of the postcolonial environment went unnoticed by the reviewers of *Annie John* and *Lucy*. Like *Annie John*, *Lucy* was received in many academic circles as a book about mothers and daughters, a popular topic in feminist literary criticism, especially since the late seventies when Nancy Chodorow and Carol Gilligan published their influential studies. In both of Kincaid's novels, female bonding is the primary subject and receives the most narrative attention, whereas within *Annie John*, for example, there are only two direct statements of resentment made about the political situation. One is a comment the narrator makes while observing a classmate, Ruth, who is the child of British missionaries:

> Perhaps she wanted to be in England, where no one would remind her constantly of the terrible things her ancestors had done; perhaps she had felt even worse when her father was a missionary in Africa. I could see how Ruth felt from looking at her face. Her ancestors had been the masters, while ours had been the slaves. She had a lot to be ashamed of. . . . I am quite sure that if the tables had been turned we would have acted quite differently.[14]

Earlier in the novel, while Annie and her friend 'The Red Girl' watch a cruise ship with wealthy passengers go by, she fantasizes that they wreck the ship: 'How we laughed as their cries of joy turned to cries of sorrow'.[15]

A Small Place, published in 1988, makes explicit Kincaid's resentment of the British upper class and forces us to look at *Annie John* and *Lucy* from a different angle. In *A Small Place* Kincaid recites an elegy for an Antigua that no longer exists. The British have ruined much of the island:

And so everywhere they went they turned it into England; and everybody they met they turned English. But no place could ever really be England, and nobody who did not look exactly like them would ever be English, so you can imagine the destruction of people and land that came from that. The English hate each other and they hate England, and the reason is they have no place else to go and nobody else to feel better than.[16]

At the age of seven, Kincaid remembers waiting for hours in the hot sun to see a 'putty-faced princess' from England disappear behind the walls of the governor's house. Later she found that the princess was sent to Antigua to recover from an affair with a married man! In schools and libraries the British found opportunities to distort and erase Antiguan history and to glorify British history in its place. One of the crimes of the colonial era was the violation of the colonized peoples' languages: 'For isn't it odd that the only language I have in which to speak of this crime is the language of the criminal who committed the crime?'[17]

The thematic connection between *Annie John* and *A Small Place* is made clear in an interview with Selwyn Cudjoe in *Callaloo*. In this interview Kincaid discusses her ideas in *A Small Place*, particularly her dislike of colonialism, which she had developed by the age of nine:

When I was nine, I refused to stand up at the refrain of 'God Save Our King.' I hated 'Rule Britannia'; and I used to say that we weren't Britons, we were slaves. I never had any idea why. I just thought that there was no sense to it—'Rule Britannia, Britannia rule the waves, Britons never shall be slaves.' I thought that we weren't Britons and that we were slaves.[18]

Elsewhere in the interview Kincaid indicates the instinctive rebellion she felt against England, despite the omnipresent validation of British culture: 'Everything seemed divine and good only if it was English'.[19] Although Kincaid eschews an overtly political allegiance, there is a close connection between Kincaid's anti-colonialist essays in *A Small Place* and the feelings ascribed to the young narrators of *Annie John* and *Lucy*.

In her review of Jamaica Kincaid's *Lucy*, Nicolette Jones suggests that the 19-year-old narrator is both innocent and wise. In that novel, Lucy is able to see through Mariah's good intentions, but she is also warm enough to care for Mariah and her children; 'It is a significant achievement that Kincaid allows Lucy to expose faults in her friend without undermining her grounds for affection'.[20] In the novel Lucy is both warm and remote;

even in the midst of a love affair, she maintains a detachment from her lover. Jones refers to this as 'the emotional deficiency that will always make her an outsider'.[21]

It is precisely this warmth that is lacking in Kincaid's latest novel, *The Autobiography of My Mother* (1996). In the *New York Times Book Review*, Cathleen Schine claims that this is a 'shocking' book in which the narrator is 'intoxicated with self-hatred', producing a 'truly ugly meditation on life'.[22] The novel starts with the claim 'My mother died at the moment I was born, and so for my whole life there was nothing standing between myself and eternity; at my back was always a bleak, black wind'.[23] Although *The Autobiography of My Mother* is based on the real facts of Kincaid's mother's life, this claim of maternal death is purely fictional, although it is used to explain a psychic crippling. As John Skow says in his review for *Time*, Kincaid's primal theme, repeated well past the point of obsession, has been her abiding resentment of her mother, connected with, but not overriding, her resentment of a cultural imperialism.

Notes

1. R. Cobham and M. Collins (eds), *Watchers & Seekers: Creative Writing by Black Women* (New York: Bedrick, 1988) p. 6.

2. J. Kincaid, *Lucy* (New York: Farrar Straus Giroux, 1990) p. 90.

3. Ibid., p. 123.

4. Ibid., pp. 127–8.

5. Ibid., p. 129.

6. Ibid., pp. 130–1.

7. Ibid., p. 132.

8. Ibid., p. 80.

9. Ibid., pp. 18–19.

10. Ibid., p. 29.

11. Ibid., p. 30.

12. J. Kincaid, 'The Talk of the Town', *New Yorker* (17 October 1977) p. 37.

13. J. Kincaid, *Lucy*, p. 41.

14. J. Kincaid, *Annie John* (New York: New American Library, 1983) p. 76.

15. Ibid., p. 71.

16. J. Kincaid, *A Small Place* (New York: Farrar Straus Giroux, 1988) p. 24.

17. Ibid., p. 31.

18. S. R. Cudjoe, 'Interview with Jamaica Kincaid', *Callaloo*, 12 (1989) p. 397.

19. Ibid., p. 398.

20. N. Jones, 'An Innocent Abroad', Review of *Lucy* by Jamaica Kincaid, *The Sunday Times* (23 June 1991) p. 5.

21. Ibid.

22. C. Schine, 'A World as Cruel as Job's', Review of *The Autobiography of My Mother* by Jamaica Kincaid, *The New York Times Book Review* (4 February 1996) p. 5.

23. J. Kincaid, *The Autobiography of My Mother* (New York: Farrar Straus Giroux, 1996) p. 3.

BIBLIOGRAPHY

Ashcroft, B., G. Griffiths and H. Tiffin. *The Empire Writes Back: Theory and Practice in Post-Colonial Literatures*. London and New York: Routledge, 1989.

Boyce Davies, C. and E. Fido (eds). *Out of the Kumbla: Caribbean Women and Literature*. Trenton, New Jersey: Africa World Press, 1990.

Cobham R. and M. Collins (eds). *Watchers & Seekers: Creative Writing by Black Women*. New York: Bedrick, 1988.

Cudjoe, S.R. 'Interview with Jamaica Kincaid', *Callaloo*, 12 (1989) pp. 396–411.

Cumber-Dance, D. (ed.). *Fifty Caribbean Writers*. New York: Greenwood, 1986.

Davis, T. 'Girl-Child in a Foreign Land', Review of Lucy by Jamaica Kincaid, *New York Times Book Review* (28 October 1990) p. 11.

Ferguson, M. *Jamaica Kincaid: Where the Land Meets the Body*. Charlottesville, VA: UP of Virginia, 1994.

Freeman, S. Review of *At the Bottom of the River* by Jamaica Kincaid. *Ms.* (12 January 1984) pp. 15–16.

Gates Jr. H.L. (ed.). *Reading Black, Reading Feminist: A Critical Anthology*. New York: Meridian, 1990.

James, L. Review of *Lucy* by Jamaica Kincaid in *Wasafiri*, 15 (1992) p. 37.

Jones, N. 'An Innocent Abroad', Review of *Lucy* by Jamaica Kincaid, *Sunday Times* (23 June 1991) p. 5.

Kenney, S. 'Paradise with Snake', Review of *Annie John* by Jamaica Kincaid, *New York Times Book Review* (7 April 1985) p. 6.

Kincaid, J. 'The Talk of the Town', *New Yorker* (17 October 1977) p. 37.

———. *At the Bottom of the River*. New York: Vintage, 1978.

———. *Annie John*. New York: New American Library, 1983.

———. *A Small Place*. New York: Farrar Straus Giroux, 1988.

———. *Lucy*. New York: Farrar Straus Giroux, 1990.

———. *The Autobiography of My Mother*. New York: Farrar Straus Giroux, 1996.

Maguire, G. Review of *At the Bottom of the River* by Jamaica Kincaid, *Horn Book*, 60 (1984) p. 91.

Milton, E. Review of *At the Bottom of the River* by Jamaica Kincaid, *New York Times Book Review* (15 January 1984) p. 22.

Mordecai, P. and B. Wilson (eds). *Her True-True Name: An Anthology of Women's Writing from the Caribbean*. London: Heinemann, 1989.

Niesen de Abruna, L. 'Family Connections: Mother and Mother Country in the Fiction of Jean Rhys and Jamaica Kincaid' in S. Nasta (ed.) *Motherlands: Black Women's Writing from Africa, the Caribbean and South Asia*. New Brunswick, NJ: Rutgers UP, 1991 pp. 257–89.

O'Callaghan, E. 'Feminist Consciousness: European/American Theory, Jamaican Stories', *Journal of Caribbean Studies*, 6:2 (1988) pp. 143–62.

Schine, C. 'A World as Cruel as Job's', Review of *The Autobiography of My Mother* by Jamaica Kincaid, *New York Times Book Review* (4 February 1996) p. 5.

Skow, J. 'Sharper than a Serpent's Pen', Review of *The Autobiography of My Mother* by Jamaica Kincaid, *Time* (5 February 1996).

Spivak, G.C. *In Other Worlds: Essays in Cultural Politics*. New York: Routledge, 1987.

Tyler, A. 'Mothers and Mysteries', *New Republic*, 189 (1983) pp. 32–3.

Wiche, J. Review of *At the Bottom of the River* by Jamaica Kincaid, *Library Journal*, 108 (1983), p. 2262.

K. B. CONAL BYRNE

Under English, Obeah English: Jamaica Kincaid's New Language

The language we are speaking is his before it is mine. How different are the words home, Christ, ale, master, on his lips and on mine! I cannot speak or write these words without unrest of spirit. His language, so familiar and so foreign, will always be for me an acquired speech. I have not made or accepted these words. My voice holds them at bay. My soul frets in the shadow of his language.

—James Joyce, *A Portrait of the Artist as a Young Man*

[T]he only language I have in which to speak of this crime [of enslavement] is the language of the criminal who committed the crime [which] can explain and express the deed only from the criminal's point of view.

—Jamaica Kincaid, *A Small Place*

I. UNDER ENGLISH

There had been several solutions posed for the problem of Irish nationalism at the beginning of this century. Yeats had argued for the revival of an Irish mythology founded upon unreal versions of the Protestant Ascendancy and Irish peasantry. Others, in an attempt to free themselves from the imperialism inherent in the English tongue, suggested a return to Gaelic. And, in line

From *CLA Journal* 43, no. 3 (March 2000). © 2000 by the College Language Association.

with an early Ezra Pound reading of James Joyce, it had also been argued that Ireland free itself of nationalism entirely and move into the more universalist discourse of modernity and modernism.

For Joyce, the issue was certainly language. He felt, however, that even when these various nationalistic movements did focus their arguments on language, their views tended toward nostalgic, impractical proposals. Ireland could not forge for itself a modern nationalism because its nationalistic institutions—the Church, the political parties and ideologies—were as much linguistic constructs and fictions as Joyce's own writing. And without understanding well how to manipulate their language into reality—how to travel the road between rhetoric and substance—the country could not begin. Of course, the language in question was not theirs to begin with.

Joyce chooses in *A Portrait of the Artist as a Young Man* to reinvent the English language for his—and for Stephen Dedalus's, and for Ireland's—own ends. While originally being dominated by the English literary canon, then, Stephen manages ultimately to move beyond it, using words in a private, rebellious manner. Finally, Joyce's protagonist will choose exile. Following Joyce's example, however, Stephen will not abandon Ireland, but create its culture anew precisely by re-forming its language all over again, liberating it from an oppressive stagnancy.

There arise so many similarities between Stephen's youth and that of Annie John that a study simply comparing Joyce to Jamaica Kincaid is merited. For our purposes, Joyce will be used only as a springboard for focusing on the dilemma of imperialist language in *Annie John*. As Joyce might argue, the question of reshaping words into a personal, unoppressive style may be the fundamental impasse of Kincaid's work. After all, and as our epigraphs argue for us, how is Kincaid to write her culture anew using the master's tools and the imperialist tongue?

II. ANNIE JOHN'S MOTHER, ANNIE JOHN

There has been much critical conflict regarding the role of Annie John's mother. Donna Perry, especially, has accentuated the healthy heritage which the mother bestows on Annie John, and the "matrilinear bonding" which empowers Annie "to leave home and create an independent life. . . ."[1] Louis F. Caton has also argued for this crucial bond between mother and daughter. Indeed, as Ma Chess and Annie's mother gather near her bed, Caton maintains that "each member represents a generation with particular beliefs. In spite of their individual cultural convictions, though, the larger familial commonalities produce a single, unified identity at the scene."[2] Infused with such relationships, Annie understands "that the commitment between a daughter and a parent seems to transcend all," and for Caton such a transcendence provides unity and grounding (Caton 138).

By psychoanalytically focusing his study, Murdoch touches upon the more traumatic elements of such a heavy maternal hand. Referring in turn to Edith Clarke's *My Mother Who Fathered Me*, Murdoch speaks of a central paradox of West Indian culture. On the one hand, men are

> the focus of society's power relationships and occupy, in general, positions within it which inculcate concomitant attitudes of social and psychological authority. [. . .] Theirs is also the major responsibility in financial maintenance of the household, and upkeep of the children in or out of wedlock . . .[3]

On the other hand, and acutely in the case of Annie John, a mother's word does carry weight:

> Mother and children co-operate in the small daily duties of the home. [. . .] There is constant companionship, and a constant interdependence. The girl child identifies herself with mother. (Clarke, in Murdoch 328)

During most of his essay, Murdoch delineates the psychological dependence of Annie on her mother. Yet, given these notes about the social structure of Antigua, Annie John's subjection to her mother's identity seems as much social as it does psychological.

Consequently, Annie's repudiation of her mother occurs in this same, dual fashion. In the critical, "primal scene" of Annie's upbringing, she witnesses her mother and father having sex. Her mother had previously been posited, as Murdoch argues, as a maternal phallic figure, the "ultimate repository and embodiment, vis-a-vis Annie, of power and authority" (Murdoch 332). Murdoch insightfully notes the convergence of two forms of betrayal here on the part of Annie's mother. Not only does Annie see her mother sexually overcome by the now authoritative, phallic father, but she is also forced to recognize the racial, cultural difference between herself and her mother: ". . . her hand! It was white and bony as if it had long been dead and had been left out to the elements. It seemed not to be her hand, yet it could only be her hand, so well did I know it."[4] Murdoch maintains that the break between mother and daughter here is decisive; Annie subsequently transfers her interest to Gwen, the Red Girl, and even her father.

However, Annie's break does not seem so definitive. Indeed, each of her acts of severing from her mother can be exposed as the predetermined imitation of a rebellion which her mother, also named Annie John, has already enacted—an imitation, in a sense, of a language her mother has already spoken. It seems, then, that because of the intense and obsessive nature of Annie's relationship with Annie Senior, no language of her own is possible.

Several examples effectively elucidate the point. In what would seem to be a clear rejection of imperialist authority, Annie mars "the picture of Columbus sitting there all locked up in his chains," writing just below the image the words "The Great Man Can No Longer Just Get Up and Go" (*AJ* 78). As we have understood from the explanation preceding this scene, however, Annie takes her words from her aunt, who has described Annie's grandfather as "having a bit of trouble with his limbs," and "not able to go about as he pleased" (*AJ* 78). Annie then sees her mother, who has been reading the letter aloud, turn to her father and tell him, laughing sardonically, "So the great man can no longer just get up and go. How I would love to see his face now!" (*AJ* 78). Annie's own rebellion against Columbus is somewhat deflated, then, since her rebellious language has merely been borrowed from another authoritative source from which she strives to break away. If we understand her rebellion, or her forging her own identity, as fundamentally a linguistic project, she is off to a bad start.

The trunk which Annie's mother preserves for her and the new trunk which Annie will finally request of her father are certainly relevant here. Donna Perry regards the trunk which the mother keeps as a kind of healthy, affirming heirloom, to be passed on to Annie at the appropriate time and to facilitate the formation and maintenance of her own identity:

> Annie Senior goes through the contents [of the trunk], piece by piece, holding up each item and recreating her daughter's past through vivid accounts of its significance. [. . .] Annie's mother creates the myth of Annie for her so that her past becomes as real to her as her present . . . Annie's mother sings her daughter's praises and empowers the child.[5]

This is certainly overoptimistic. Indeed, as Murdoch argues, the trunk is "an indicator of repression and discontent," consolidating in one symbol "the mother's enclosure, containment, limitation, possession and direction of her daughter's life and identity" (Murdoch 330). Rather than the loving transfer of an oral tradition, then, the trunk gives the mother a firm control over her daughter, "based on knowledge which she alone, of the two, possesses" (Murdoch 331).

In what Murdoch celebrates as "the major psychological event of the novel," this symbol seems to be significantly inverted in Annie's desire for her own trunk:

> This demand is the overwhelming, preponderant sign of Annie's desire finally to escape and overcome the ... control that her mother's trunk signifies. Establishing her own life and identity will constitute a sort of rebirth, phoenix-like, from the deathly images and fears of dissolution which had haunted her for so long. (Murdoch 338)

We must contest Murdoch here as well, however. After all, how can Annie's own rebellion and identity be truly "phoenix-like" when it is so obviously determined by and caught up in the forms of rebellion of her mother?

Annie is indeed inculcated with the traditions contained within the trunk—or with the tradition of the trunk itself—so that when she does look to rebel, she must draw upon these same, predetermined, controlling traditions. She has yet to speak a language of her own. In this regard, the trunk is as much an heirloom as it is a coffin; as much a grounding, affirming history, as it is a stifling record of who Annie has been and must become. Moreover, the trunk is implicitly confused with a coffin as Annie's heels bump against it underneath her bed: "At that moment I wanted to see [my mother] lying dead, all withered and in a coffin at my feet" (*AJ* 106). If there is any ground-breaking recognition on Annie's part here, it may be her intermingling the trunk and coffin: the historical record and the obstacle it presents to her own life, respectively.

Even within the rebellious world which Annie creates under her house we see the heavy influence of Annie Senior's hand. Again, what was once a symbol of rebellion for Annie's mother—the trunk—is all too similar to Annie's own hidden collection of objects. More concretely, some objects of Annie Senior's trunk for her daughter—"the first notebook in which [she] wrote," "the sheets for [her] crib and the sheets for [her] first bed, . . . [her] report cards, [her] certificates of merit from school, and [her] certificates of merit from Sunday School" (*AJ* 21)—seem a clear precursor to "the Christmas and birthday cards and old letters from [her] mother's family," and the "neat pile of books" (*AJ* 66) which Annie has defiantly hidden in her private—and yet pre-scripted—underworld. The marbles and stolen library books hidden under the house signify for Moira Ferguson a "rebellion against constraining gender roles, a personal power gained by outwitting authority, and an obsession with knowledge, . . ."[6] These objects merely seem, however, to adhere to the mother's established discourse: indeed, even this intense symbol of rebellion, the marble, was first given to Annie by her mother (*AJ* 55). And in adhering to her mother's "language," much of what seemed acutely rebellious is dulled.

Once we accept this interpretive frame, less overt examples quickly fall into place. More subtle, for example, are the repercussions of Annie Senior's story of "the very long black snake" among a basket of figs she once carried. This tale probably causes an association to be formed in Annie's mind between her mother's death, or the danger thereof, and the serpent (*AJ* 68–70). Soon after hearing this story, Annie begins to menstruate. On the first day of her menstruation, we are told that despite the façade of closeness to her mother which she upholds, she hatefully thinks to herself, "What a serpent!" (*AJ* 52). But this rebellious thought now seems predetermined by the story passed on from the mother.

A moment earlier in the text, we learn that whenever she spoke of her mother to Gwen, Annie would always "turn the corners of [her] mouth down, to show [her] scorn" (*AJ* 51). Even this gesture is scripted by the mother's own disapproving gestures towards Annie: "Now I often saw [my mother]," Annie tells us, "with the corners of her mouth turned down in disapproval of me" (*AJ* 28). Elsewhere, Annie will recognize the gestures that she takes from her mother and consciously copies. Namely, as Gwen and Annie scorn their peers by rolling up their eyes and tossing their hands in the air, Annie grants that the gesture is "an exact copy, of course, of what we had seen our mothers do" (*AJ* 48). As she claims these maternal imitations to have been more or less consciously intended, the unremarked, un-self-conscious imitations seem, in comparison, all the more deeply ingrained in her character. That is, the gestures which she does not recognize to be maternal imitation have become too instinctive for her to recognize and move beyond.

Even Annie's most courageous, identity-forging moments become somehow compromised when seen to be in line with the language of her mother. And perhaps this mark of her mother, her "home," and its discourse is permanent: "It doesn't matter what you do or where you go," Annie Senior tells her daughter finally, "I'll always be your mother and this will always be your home" (*AJ* 147). A moment earlier, Annie herself has recognized something similar: "When I look at things in a certain way . . . I should say that [my parents] made me with their own hands" (*AJ* 133).

III. MOTHER ENGLISH

This reading may be too deterministic. After all, as Murdoch maintains, "Such compulsive repetitions [of the mother's actions] are signs of desire for difference and for independent identity" on Annie's part, an identity "which will be fulfilled ineluctably through repetitions of past events in [Annie's] own particular context" (Murdoch 337). In other terms, Annie's imitating her mother is not circular or deterministic, but instead forms a kind of spiral moving toward a more personal identity which uses the mother's gestures and language to its own ends.

By such a view, however, the mother still provides the basis for Annie's identity, individually liberated or not. And while this may seem an innocuous case-study of mother–daughter bonding, the issue of an imitated maternal language becomes much more urgent in light of the several parallels which are drawn in *Annie John* between Annie Senior and imperial England. For example, during her early infatuation with her mother, Annie remarks her mother's head to be so beautiful as to belong "on a sixpence"—in the place, of course, of the Queen of England (*AJ* 18). Immediately following, the mother is said to wear her hair pinned up around the "crown" of her head. Moreover, the memoirs of Annie's life which her mother contains within the trunk are distinct signs of imperialism: the christening outfit, jewelry "made of gold from British Guiana," certificates of merit from Sunday School (*AJ* 20–21).

Donna Perry overlooks this heavy-handed foreign influence over Annie—carried out, in the case of the trunk at least, by the mother—by calling these objects innocent "symbols of the girl [Annie] was and the woman she would become . . . through her mother's transformative language."[7] However, if the mother, for all her obeah practices, has been equated with imperialist power, and her objects of containment are recognized as signs of imperialism, then the maternal "transformative language" must also be recognized as the oppressive English Word imposed on the colonist's mind. And if Annie John's story is in significant ways an autobiography of Jamaica Kincaid herself, how are we to be sure that the very text in our hands is not another product of imperialism, a frustrated attempt to speak against the master with his own tools?

Ferguson's argument is more hopeful: "Annie John . . . manifests her awareness of cultural contradictions [and] refuses to be silenced"; and again: "Annie John resists received imperial interpretations and a prescribed subject position" (Ferguson 127, 128). However, if Kincaid "denounces Antigua as an island with a legacy of corruption where the mimicking of colonialism has become institutionalized," how would Annie's upbringing be exempt from this kind of ingrained imperialism? (Ferguson 132).

Kincaid herself has spoken of the extent to which English imperialism determined the perception of Antiguans: "England was our source of myth and the source from which we got our sense of reality, our sense of what was meaningful, our sense of what was meaningless."[8] Even this imperialist sense of "what was meaningful" would be held ransom by Kincaid's English instructors until she adopted herself physically to their standards: "[B]efore we were allowed into our classrooms our teachers would inspect us, and children . . . whose hair had not been combed anew would not be allowed to attend class."[9] One must first mimic the colonizers before being permitted to ingest their culture. The especially disturbing point here is that Kincaid's

English identity could not be contrasted to some previous, truer character. Rather, she is indoctrinated so early with English canonical culture that outside of it there is only, as Kincaid tells us, "a hole filled with nothing."[10] Is it conceivable, then, that Annie "deliberately [sites] herself outside the context of the colonizers," and is "a subject in her own right, resisting indoctrination?" (Ferguson 144).

Most obviously in favor of our argument is Annie John's deeply felt connection with Charlotte Brontë and the racist author of children's literature, Enid Blyton. Even Ferguson claims this interest in English literature to betray "certain gaps in [Annie's, and even Kincaid's] insights about colonial Antigua" (Ferguson 130). Beyond an admitted interest in these authors—indeed, she almost proudly claims to have discovered Blyton on her own (*AJ* 51)—Annie is made to read other imperialist works, such as *Roman Britain*, *A History of the West Indies*, and *Paradise Lost*. Focusing on this last work, one can see that it is not difficult to expose precisely how this literature invades—or colonizes—Kincaid's text itself. For example, Annie is "ordered to copy Books I and II of *Paradise Lost*" as punishment for having defamed the image of Columbus. It may be assumed, then, that at some level, at least, she must absorb this very canonical text. Perhaps consequently, Edenic references appear throughout Kincaid's work. For instance, Annie John deeply relates with an image of Satan she notices in the painting "The Young Lucifer," which must refer her back to the text she has been forced to copy out. Given her description of Satan as portrayed in the painting—"his skin was coarse," "his hair was made up of live snakes," he "was wearing a smile . . . one of those smiles that make you know the person is just putting up a good front"—Annie seems to identify physically and emotionally with Satan in his painted and, presumably, literary depiction (*AJ* 94).

Louis Caton pays special attention to Kincaid's creating "an atmosphere of wholeness and innocence reminiscent of the prelapsarian garden of Eden" in her descriptions of Antigua (Caton 130). Caton will even argue that Annie's own understanding of her youthful home as a "paradise" (*AJ* 25) and her regarding her relationship between her and her mother as a "perfect harmony" (*AJ* 27) "implies that the mother–daughter bond arises in a naturally perfect pre-linguistic, pre-oedipal state" (Caton 131). Yet, given her submission to the Christian myth of paradise, these are in fact Edenic terms which canonically dominate Annie—and Kincaid. John Milton and Mother English have colonized even the farthest, purest reaches of Annie's idyllic Antiguan youth.

Even Annie's unconscious daydreams are transplanted from the life of Charlotte Brontë. Namely, since the latter "spent a year or so" in Belgium, Annie chooses this country as her means of moving out from under her mother's wing: "I imagined that it would be a place my mother would find it difficult to travel to" (*AJ* 92). This is troubling, since Annie is essentially averting one symbol of imperialism, her mother, by adopting another, Charlotte Brontë.

The Red Girl provides an even more troubling example. First depicted as anything but colonized, the Red Girl is associated by Annie with the moon, "a red moon" (*AJ* 57), which significantly links her with menstruation, the body, and perhaps a kind of uncolonized, natural purity. Annie is infatuated with these unrestrained elements: the Red Girl smells "as if she had never taken a bath in her whole life," and to Annie it is a "wonderful smell" (*AJ* 57). Without thinking, then—not asking herself "what use the Red Girl could really have for these gifts," and almost instinctively—Annie proceeds to steal money from her mother and purchase for her friend "multicolored grosgrain ribbon, or a pair of ring combs studded with rhinestones, or a pair of artificial rosebuds suitable for wearing at the waist of a nice dress" (*AJ* 64). The gifts seem innocuous, and are more or less innocently dismissed by Annie: "I simply loved giving her things" (*AJ* 64). Yet, why does she give her companion these things in particular? If the untamed character of the Red Girl is precisely what she admires, why would she shower her—indeed, colonize her—with jewelry and adornments for elegant clothing, objects which go exactly against the Red Girl's nature? Is Annie unconsciously attempting to correct that which directly challenges colonialism?

A more linguistic example is Annie's description of the obeah woman, Ma Chess, who comes to her side during Annie's illness. Ma Chess seems to oppose imperialism in a way similar to the Red Girl: her obeah practice is unscientific, and, given her coming and leaving on days "when the steamer was not due in port," her life seems to exist outside of the rigidity of modern time (*AJ* 127). In the description of their closeness, however, Annie strangely colonizes Ma Chess by "punctualization." That is, instead of allowing the obeah woman to move outside the strict realm of language—Annie's educated edified language—she depicts herself "curled up like a little comma, and Ma Chess . . . next to me, curled up like a bigger comma" (*AJ* 126). This choice of description is significant since Ma Chess's history and reality are probably not written and punctuated, but spoken and mythical.

We see a similar occurrence in Teresa de la Parra's *Iphigenia*, particularly in the character of Gregoria. Like Lunero in Carlos Fuentes' *La muerte de Artemio Cruz*, and Felix, the maid of the Moncada family, in Elena Garro's *Recuerdos del porvenir*, the character of Gregoria represents in *Iphigenia* the preservation of a distant, near-mythical era to which the science of this century has put an end. Yet, for de la Parra, it seems, our own age has corrupted humanity less by scientifically dividing up time—and therefore alienating us from our own history, as Octavio Paz argues—than by manipulating language into utilitarian artifice. In contrast, the ageless

Gregoria (she does not know her own age), unbound by the rigor and method of written language, recounts Maria Eugenia's history to her through unadulterated speech. Gregoria embodies the past and directly transfers it to Maria Eugenia, representing for the latter simple, uncomplicated wisdom. What is frustrating, then, is Maria Eugenia's description of Gregoria, which envelops her in the language of the written, concrete, alienating word: she describes her eyes as "parentheses," her winks as "epigrammatic."[11] In this, of course, de la Parra's passage resembles Kincaid's. To use punctuation to describe Gregoria and Ma Chess traps these characters in the same rigid, cold language which they otherwise defy. In a sense, their a-linguistic "otherness" is "punctualized," edified and colonized.

More subtle still is the example of the piece which Annie writes at school. One day on a beach, in the midst of watching her mother swim, Annie sees "three ships going by, and they were filled with people. They must have been celebrating something, for the ships would blow their horns and the people would cheer in response" (*AJ* 43). Immediately after, Annie's mother disappears. While in reality the mother comes ashore again and reassures Annie that "she would never leave [her]" (*AJ* 44), Annie's dream of the incident concludes quite differently: "My mother never came back . . ." (*AJ* 44). In keeping with Murdoch's argument, this dark sort of wish-fulfillment may indeed reflect the associations between death and her parents which the maturing Annie psychologically constructs; this is, of course, an important step in the formation of her own identity. Yet the imagery which Annie latches onto in order to have her mother disappear is interestingly imperialist. The three ships may represent for Annie, and most probably for Kincaid, the expedition of Columbus. In celebration, presumably after having looted the New World, the ships make their way back to Europe. For Annie to place her mother implicitly in those ships as they move away, is to eradicate the greatest obstacle against her maturation in purely colonialist terms. Our argument is subtle here, but importantly suggests how deeply the English, imperialist language may have sunk into Annie's thought.

We have seen, then, that when Annie rebels against her mother, she often does so by using her mother's gestures and words. Our argument here is that the mother, in this regard, may simply represent the English tongue. After all, when Annie defames the image of Columbus, she does so using "Old English lettering" (*AJ* 78). Even in her counter-imperialist thinking, she shows distinct signs of the colonizer's language.

And Annie speaks this language well. She excels at school to the extent that she is "given the responsibility for overseeing the class in the teacher's absence" (*AJ* 49). That is, Annie seems to have become a kind of medium or imperialist prop through which the English teachers can indoctrinate the "natives." This is made clear when Annie responds correctly to a question which another classmate has missed: in this instance, Annie's "exact words" are "repeated over and over again" by those around her (*AJ* 75). Annie dominates Mother English well enough, then, to colonize in turn. She is the quintessential imperialist mouthpiece.

IV. OBEAH ENGLISH

After identifying oppressive, imperialist English as his country's fundamental obstacle to independence and nationalism, Joyce focused on the question of language through self-reflexive texts and there sought to reinvent the Word in his own insurgent style. The nation of Ireland, however, was never abandoned and provided content for Joyce's work throughout his life. In this we may understand that if an artist is to reinvent his own nation, he or she must first recapitulate that nation's cultural project, so to speak. As may be argued through Stephen Dedalus, one's culture may never be entirely abandoned but can be used to re-create itself far beyond itself. For example, Stephen may initially be dominated by—in Seamus Deane's words, "quoted into existence" by—the imperialist traditions of nursery rhymes, Catholic doctrine, and political squabbles. Nonetheless, he will finally come to manipulate these traditions in turn, creating for himself a very personal artistic philosophy. And while Stephen re-creates himself, Joyce re-creates English in narrative chronological breaks, incessant word associations, and parodying streams of consciousness. All along, forming one's individual language is recognized as the most fundamental of political projects. Our aim is to suggest specific techniques by which Kincaid similarly subverts the imperialist tongue, an issue made all the more pertinent since, as we have noted, Annie John's indoctrination in English is said to mirror Kincaid's.

It is tempting to understand Annie's illness in chapter seven, accompanied by torrential rains, as a kind of purification of her language and perhaps the concrete beginning of her own identity. After all, she can no longer hear what her parents say as their "words travel through the air toward [her], but just before they [reach her] ears they . . . fall to the floor, suddenly dead" (*AJ* 109). This ineffective communication is echoed later as Annie tells us, "[I] still couldn't make out what [my mother] was saying, but I could see some of the words as they landed in the air between us. [. . .] They danced around, in and out, as if around a maypole" (*AJ* 116). And if Annie is purifying herself of others' tongues here and forming a personal language in the process, she seems to succeed: upon regaining her health, she has acquired "a strange accent—at least, no one had ever heard anyone talk that way before . . ." (*AJ* 129).

This new way of talking, however, seems only to mimic more exactly the imperialist English from which she should have, through the purification of her illness, escaped. "I would begin my answer," she tells us, "with the words 'Actually' or 'As a matter of fact.' It had the effect of allowing no room for doubt" (*AJ* 129). Her speech is scientific, dominating, and edified, and does not speak at all to an individual's having formed her own identity.

But however instructed her newfound catch-phrases sound, they are spoken differently now. First, Annie has fallen in love with "the sound of the words as they rolled off [her] tongue" (*AJ* 129). As Stephen Dedalus progressed from being a subject of English to its re-creator, so language is no longer forced upon Annie as indoctrination or punishment, but lovingly manipulated by her. This does not mean that she can create her words all anew, of course. Nor does it insinuate that the imperialist words she has been given can be manipulated to describe everything that she, the colonized, feels. On the contrary, she recognizes the ineffable emotions that lie beyond these "other's" words. As she lies on her bed for the last time, for example, she is unable to articulate in these English words her needing to leave her home forever: "[I]f I had been given years to reflect and come up with the words of why I felt this way, I would not have been able to come up with so much as the letter 'A'" (*AJ* 134). In this sense, Annie, and Kincaid, can at best manipulate and subvert the language they have been given in order to approximate the foreign emotions within them. And in this, Kincaid's writing may only be an accentuation of a dilemma we constantly face in our own languages.

Against our first interpretation of *Annie John*, then, we should look now for ways in which Kincaid manages to subvert colonial England from within. Louis Caton, for example, has already suggested that Kincaid infiltrates the canonical genre of the Bildungsroman, along with Joseph Campbell's epic hero monomyth which sometimes accompanies this genre, by inserting into Annie's own Bildungsroman an important episode of initial, loving bonding between her and her mother. Such a bond, Caton argues, is not found in Campbell's conception of the epic sequence of "separation-initiation-return" (Campbell, in Caton 137). In this, Kincaid may be aligned with Joyce's *Portrait* in her insistence that an individual must be infused with his or her culture before attempting to rebel against it or redefine it.

What other literary subversions can we add to this? First, we might remark that some of the imperialist works which Annie must study in school are, in their own way, subversive. *Roman Britain*, as Ferguson points out, is ironic in its implicit nod to England itself as a Roman colony. And *Paradise Lost*—and particularly the first two books of it which Annie must copy out—is, after all, the story of a nearly admirable, indefatigable Satan creating a nation of his own. Moreover, it is Satan's rousing words which, more than anything, have the power to incite his league of demons to action. With this background, Annie, and Kincaid, may have learned of the capacity of language to re-create rather than submit themselves to the stifling imperial Word.

At the level of style, we see that Kincaid moves against Joyce in that her language is straightforward to the extent that it is childishly pure and, in imperialist terms, Edenic. In this sense, Kincaid rebels against the edified, Miltonic language with which she was imbued in her youth and returns to the direct words of young Annie. And yet if the language is often simple, its contents are fragmented and tense. Annie's youth, for example, moves precariously between truth and lies, love and hatred, her mother, Gwen, and the Red Girl, drought and water, English doctors and obeah women, homosexuality and heterosexuality, Annie's own Antiguan identity versus her mother's Dominican one, and so on. This is a crucial move on Kincaid's part in that she manages to fragment and complicate any naive, reductive perception of Antigua. She thereby grants a complex substance to the otherwise two-dimensional categories of "colonized" and "other." Susan Lanser, in her discussion of *A Small Place*,[12] recognizes this move, too, and, of course, when they are defined by others:

> [Kincaid makes] clear the need not to rely on assumptions about national or cultural unity but to confront as subjects of comparison differences within nations and cultures—the differences of race, sex, ethnicity, religion, sexuality, region, and class that in fact get repressed when nations and cultures define themselves.[13]

In this sense, Kincaid may use imperialist words, but only to give Antigua back its profound, contradictory character. Although Annie may describe her childhood as a "paradise," Kincaid presents nothing as simple.

Back at the level of narrative style, we will close by remarking the subversive chronology throughout *Annie John*. Through chapter three of the novel, Kincaid lures us into a nicely linear account of the protagonist's upbringing. Towards the end of chapter four, however, the order of events is complicated: "Soon after, I started to menstruate, and I stopped playing marbles. I never saw the Red Girl again." Chapter four occurs some time before chapter three, then, and significantly informs its events and imagery. For example, as we have already discussed, now that we know the eerie story of the snake in the mother's fruit basket, we have to add weightier, darker meaning to the narrator's having called her mother a "serpent" (*AJ* 52).

The story which the narrator writes about the three ships she sees from the beach and about her panic at her mother's momentary disappearance is also affected. This story is well received by her teacher and classmates and initially stands as a successful first experience with writing on her part, similar to Proust's young narrator writing a letter to his mother in *Swann's Way*. Annie Senior's near-death experience (*AJ* 68–69)—of which we were unaware when we first read the story which the narrator writes at school—affects her deeply, however temporarily (*AJ* 70). This, then, is the intense backdrop against which the previous story has been composed, and changes our reading of it.

There is also the extent to which the Red Girl—whose face is a "red moon" and whose mannerisms are animalistic and natural—informs the narrator's menstruation. That is, only after chapter four are we retroactively able to understand what may have been the narrator's background thoughts in chapter three. Namely, she probably associated the redness of her blood and the perhaps animalistic nature of her menstruation with the Red Girl.

These bits of retroactive information continue to proliferate, as in chapter five: "That happened when I was in the first form. Now here Miss Edward stood" (*AJ* 81). Here, the narrator's mockery of the picture of Columbus not only informs the scene she is presently in—retroactively, again, since we are informed of the scene's history only after we have gone half-way through the scene itself—but also informs the three ships that pass by the shore in the piece the narrator wrote in the beginning of school. At the point of her writing the piece, these ships may not have been an allusion to Columbus, but they have now become so, in our and her mind, by her later study of Columbus's expedition.

Then there is the story of Minieu's near hanging (*AJ* 98–99) and, even more significantly, of Minieu's leading the narrator, naked, to a red anthill (*AJ* 100). Indeed, this last trauma probably affects the book as far back as chapter four, so as to inform and complicate the Red Girl's penchant for pinching the narrator at their meetings. That is, the red ant bites and the Red Girl's pinches become confused in Annie's, and our, minds.

With these delays of meaning, or retroactive bits of information, we become wary and reticent to assign firm significance to any event or symbol. Kincaid tricks us into a childlike, straightforward narrative, only to subtly complicate or destroy it in later stages. Finally, as the narrator walks to the jetty with her parents, a series of memories—all retroactive informers—flood over her. These formative experiences are the real causes or reasons behind the "growing up" we have just read.

Yet we have, inevitably, already assigned to that "growing up" some kind of interpretation or meaning. In this, the past and the present, the narrator's own identity and that of her mother, and our formed interpretations and their subsequent, subtle deconstruction are represented well. As Annie John's present identity is constantly troubled by her mother and past, so our reading is stumped by the constant surfacing of past details lurking in future pages. Form and content nicely join.

This becomes all the more significant in light of Selwyn R. Cudjoe's interview with Kincaid. Speaking of the effect of obeah practices on her own epistemology, Kincaid claims that she was taught "not [to believe] what I saw," and "not [to be] deceived by appearances."[14] Earlier, she tells Cudjoe, "For a while, I lived in utter fear when I was little, of just not being sure that anything I saw was itself"; Cudjoe appropriately responds: "That's the modernist project, isn't it?"[15]

It appears to be Kincaid's literary project, at any rate. That is, by subverting chronology to the point of causing, or teaching, the reader to mistrust every element of the text at first sight is really a means of infusing her work and her audience with a kind of obeah insight. In this, Kincaid creates a text out of her canonical training which counters the authoritative, scientific claim on reality of that very canon. By the novel's end, we learn to mistrust reality, or at least what we think to be causing reality, completely. Less a novel dominated by the imperialist word, then, Kincaid's text may indeed speak a kind of individual and innovative "Obeah English."

Annie's final move is toward Mother England. In light of our first argument, this may have seemed a definitive submission to an imperialist culture and tongue; more concretely, it would have appropriately substituted Mother England for her real mother, Annie John Senior. However, once we begin to notice the subversive nature of some of the texts which Annie reads as a child, along with the irreducibly complicated, fragmented nature of Annie's childhood, and the narrative techniques—or, we may say, "Obeah English"—which bind these elements together, our reading of an oppressed, dominated Annie, or Kincaid, breaks down.

In this sense, the move to England is less of a giving in as it may be a further investigation and challenge on Annie's part of the imperial control over her culture. Kincaid recounts that when she first visited England, or when she first crossed over the "width," the "depth," and the "darkness" which separated her idea of mother England from its reality, she found much of its supposed superiority to be inaccurate.[16] In this sense, the image of England in its colonies rose far above the Mother nation itself. Infiltrating the source of her domination, then, Annie will dismantle its authority.

Moreover, we should remember that Annie moved to London "roughly a year after the first major race riots, precipitated by discrimination against Caribbean immigrants, erupted in London in 1958" (Ferguson 117). Perhaps she went to England to join these protests. This may have been the final stage of her personal decolonization and the formation of her own identity.

Notes

1. Donna Perry, "Initiation in Jamaica Kincaid's *Annie John*," in *Caribbean Women Writers: Essays from the First International Conference*, ed. Selwyn R. Cudjoe (Wellesley: Calaloux, 1990) 247.

2. Louis Caton, "Romantic Struggles: the Bildungsroman and Mother–Daughter Bonding in Jamaica Kincaid's *Annie John*," *MELUS* 21.3 (Fall 1996): 136. Hereafter cited parenthetically in the text.

3. H. Adlai Murdoch, "Severing the (M)other Connection: the Representation of Cultural Identity in Jamaica Kincaid's *Annie John*," *Callaloo* 13.2 (Spring 1990): 328. Hereafter cited parenthetically in the text.

4. Jamaica Kincaid, *Annie John* (New York: Farrar, 1985) 333. Hereafter cited parenthetically in the text as *AJ*, followed by the page number.

5. Perry 248.

6. Moira Ferguson, *Colonialism and Gender Relations from Mary Wollstonecraft to Jamaica Kincaid: East Caribbean Connections* (New York: Columbia UP, 1994) 119. Hereafter cited parenthetically in the text.

7. Perry 248.

8. Jamaica Kincaid, "On Seeing England for the First Time," *Transitions* 51 (1991): 32.

9. Kincaid, "Seeing England" 36.

10. Kincaid, "Seeing England" 36.

11. Teresa de la Parra, *Iphigenia* (Austin: U of Texas P, 1993) 103.

12. See Jamaica Kincaid, *A Small Place* (London: Virago, 1988).

13. Susan Sniader Lanser, "Compared to What? Global Feminism, Comparatism, and the Master's Tools," in *Borderwork: Feminist Engagements with Comparative Literature* (Ithaca: Cornell UP, 1994) 294.

14. Selwyn R. Cudjoe, "Jamaica Kincaid and the Modernist Project: An Interview," *Caribbean Women Writers: Essays from the First International Conference*, ed. Selwyn R. Cudjoe (Wellesley: Calaloux, 1990) 230.

15. Cudjoe 226.

16. Kincaid, "Seeing England" 37, 40.

IRLINE FRANÇOIS

The Daffodil Gap:
Jamaica Kincaid's Lucy

In *Lucy* (1990) Jamaica Kincaid explores the ambiguities, contradictions and the violence of British colonial ideology, its Victorian mores as well as the debilitating legacy of the Plantation system on the mind, body and the memory of her heroine. Kincaid's feisty protagonist scrutinizes the signs of hegemony in the context of emigration. Most significantly, in her representation of Mariah, the well-meaning but naïve white woman, Kincaid exposes the historical gulf which separates white and black feminism. In this paper, I focus primarily on Lucy's dialogue with Mariah. I demonstrate that Lucy's relationship with her employer is often marred because of ideological, cultural and class divisions and because of the heroine's unresolved relationship with her mother. She dismisses Mariah with condescending scorn, not only for her lack of awareness of social and racial inequalities but also for her employer's attempt to intellectualize and universalize women's experiences in a homogenous paradigm. At the same time, however, Lucy remains inexorably drawn to Mariah, in part due to the woman's many acts of generosity and kindness extended to her employee.

Given the fact Jamaica Kincaid grew up in a colonial context completely dominated by the metropolitan dictates inculcated by the mother, her own is viewed as an instrument of patriarchy, a phallic mother. In *Lucy*, the mother–daughter relationship permeates the narrative with a feminine

---

From *MaComère* 4 (2001). © 2001 by Jacqueline Brice-Finch.

potency. The mother figure is made even more potent for she represents the values and structures of the metropolis as well as the feminine mores embodied in the Victorian cult of womanhood from which the daughter desperately seeks to wrest herself. The mother is viewed as an instrument of old patriarchal mores. It is thus in this context that Adrienne Rich's study on mothers and daughters in *Of Woman Born* becomes particularly relevant to Kincaid's *Lucy*.

In her study on motherhood and daughterhood, Adrienne Rich attributes the term *Matrophobia*, or the fear of becoming one's mother, to daughters who see their mothers as having taught a compromise of self-hatred and as having transmitted the restrictions and degradations of a female existence. Rich further explains that it is easier by far to reject a mother outright than to see beyond her the forces acting upon her. Although the mother is hated to the point of matrophobia, there may also be a deep underlying pull toward her, a dread that if one relaxes one's guard, one will identify with her completely. Rich concludes that Matrophobia can be seen as a splitting of the self in the desire to become purged once and for all of our mother's bondage, to become individuated and free. In her search for selfhood, Lucy fights in order to achieve an individuality of her own. And therein lies Lucy's conflict with Mariah who unwittingly recalls both the mother and (by her very appearance, yellow hair and blue eyes), the totalizing values of the "motherland" whose values Lucy must evade.

Mariah, Lucy's beautiful employer, is kind, warm, generous and well-disposed toward Lucy, whom she treats as her protégée rather than as a servant. She is eager to introduce to the young woman many of the pleasures of her world, such as "an early-evening walk in the spring air" (19), a garden full of daffodils (29), spending the night on a train and waking up to breakfast on the train as it moved through "freshly plowed fields" (33) or visiting the large house on the Great Lakes she grew up in (35). As Lucy acknowledges, Mariah's thoughtfulness towards her is conveyed in countless ways: "If she went to a store to buy herself new things, she thought of me and would bring me something also" (110). "She paid me more money than it had been agreed I would earn" (110). She expresses concern for the girl's health and her well-being by taking Lucy to her own gynecologist and reminding her "to make sure I used the things he had given me" (67). As her name suggests, Mariah's many virtues reflect the qualities attributed to a fairy godmother or an adoptive mother, or better yet, to Simone de Beauvoir's "sainted Mother," "the 'mediatrix' between the individual and the cosmos as 'the very incarnation of the Good'" (202–206). Her sense of altruism is duly noted by Lucy in the following words: "Mariah was superior to my mother, for my mother would never come to see that perhaps my needs were more important than her wishes" (64).

Consequently, it is difficult for Lucy not to be seduced by (and thereby give in to) Mariah's disarming disposition, warmth, humanity and extraordinary good will towards her. Paradoxically, Lucy cannot help being enraged (but also intrigued) by her employer's profound naïveté, simplistic world view, complacent ethnocentrism, and lastly (perhaps unforgivably for a young woman in the full throes of rebellion and egotism), Mariah's insistence on placing Lucy's discourse within an intellectual and homogenous cultural paradigm—a discourse which the protagonist categorically refuses to accept.

The conflict between the two women, a conflict to which I refer in this paper as "the daffodil gap," is not based on racial antagonism between a white mistress and the black servant whom she intends to subjugate to her will, as in the consistently trenchant portrayals of Euro-American female characters by African-American women writers.[1] Uniquely, Jamaica Kincaid's narrative is driven by the protagonist's willful impetus to tear herself away from a deeply personal, all-consuming mother/daughter relationship which is metonymic of the colonial condition as a paradigm of the struggle between the self and the other.

Kincaid's relationship to her mother informs this novel whereby the mother becomes the embodiment of old patriarchal mores, as Rich has explained in her study of Matrophobia. To Lucy, Mariah, in her ethereal beauty and generosity, assumes the guise of a god-send, and thus, Lucy risks being consumed by an all-subsuming consecrated (m)Other, like her own beloved/hated, god-like mother who, hitherto, assumed total authority over her life.

Indeed, Jamaica Kincaid's female protagonists are awed and emotionally sustained by their mothers. Accordingly, in *Lucy*, the mother–daughter bond is so tenacious that it withstands anger, hatred, scorn, thousands of miles of distance, separation and emigration. Although Lucy's mother is physically absent from the narrative, she is powerfully evoked. Contours of her mother's life provide the protagonist with a blueprint for her existence. In *Lucy*, Mariah's physical beauty is evoked in contradictory ways, in particular her skin and hair color:

> The yellow light from the sun came in through a window and fell on the pale yellow linoleum tiles of the floor, and on the walls of the kitchen, which were painted yet another shade of pale yellow, and Mariah, with her pale yellow skin and yellow hair, stood still in this almost celestial light, and she looked blessed, no blemish or mark of any kind on her cheek or anywhere else. . . . (27)

> [S]he looked at me, and her blue eyes (which I would have found beautiful even if I hadn't read millions of books in which blue

eyes were always accompanied by the word "beautiful") grew dim
as she slowly closed the lids over them. . . . (39)

Lucy's quasi-erotic gaze may on the surface be related to a Freudian
relationship of transference, where her employer is used as a canvas onto which
she projects her complicated feelings of love and hostility for her, as these
words would attest: "the times I loved Mariah it was because she reminded
me of my mother. The times that I did not love Mariah it was because she
reminded me of my mother" (58). However, a careful examination of this
passage alerts the reader to a range of unsettling, even multiple meanings
in Lucy's choice of words when describing Mariah, meanings which are
based in historical and material grounding. In other words, Lucy's language
is articulated within a vision of colonial domination (i.e. the recognition of
Mariah's "blue eyes" and "yellow hair and skin" as tropes).

In addition to the colonial signifiers attached to Mariah in the text,
Lucy's consciousness is linked to an intricate Caribbean cultural world
view with its singular dynamics of mother–daughter relationships, family
structures, gender, education and religious syncretism. It is this complex
admixture of psychosocial messages, cultural identification and colonial
resistance which I also take into consideration when scrutinizing Lucy's
complicated relationship with Mariah.

As her reactions to Mariah's appreciation of the weather and to her
love of daffodils will demonstrate, Lucy interprets Mariah's benevolent
attentions towards her as an insidious form of conquest, an approach not
as direct and ruthless as British colonialism perhaps, but armed with the
wiles of a *jablesse*,[2] the Caribbean equivalent of a Circean menace bent
on seducing her into a perilous world where she risks abdicating her own
existence. Such a view is illustrated to the reader when Lucy recounts that
as a child she wished:

> If only we had been ruled by the French: they were prettier, much
> happier in appearance, so much more the kind of people I would
> have enjoyed being around. I once had a pen pal on a neighboring
> island, a French island, and even though I could see her island
> from mine, when we sent correspondence to each other it had to
> go to the ruler country, thousands of miles away, before reaching
> its destination. The stamps on her letter were always canceled
> with the French words for liberty, equality, and fraternity; on
> mine there were no such words, only the image of a stony-face,
> sour-mouth woman. (136)

Lucy acquires many years later the political insight that she and her pen pal shared similar political realities (if not sociocultural) except that the dependence of the French neighboring island was presented under a different guise: "I understand the situation better now; I understand that, in spite of those words, my pen pal and I were in the same boat. . . ." (136).

In effect, such a different system of colonization is invoked by Françoise Lionnet who discusses regarding Myriam Warner-Vieyra's novel, *As the Sorcerer Said*, the ambiguous political status of the "French" Caribbean islands of Guadeloupe and Martinique vis-à-vis France:

> . . . a colony means that you're colonized, that's the same as being dominated, controlled, domesticated. Brings to mind whips and kicks up the arse, forced labor, and that's only where the present time are concerned! If we talked about the past, it would take us too far back and we'd have to remember our ancestors, the period of slavery, and everything that entails. No I prefer being "departmentalized," won over, it sounds nicer. It reminds me of Saint-Exupéry's *Little Prince* with the fox who wanted to be tamed. (92)

Lionnet thus concludes:

> It is interesting to note that dependence is presented here under the guise of taming: that is, as a relation of seduction, since being tamed amounts to being taken in, being lured in by one who holds a certain power but who strives to maintain the appearance of a democratic and egalitarian relationship. (92)

Lionnet's insight helps this reader to understand Lucy's complicated often seemingly extreme attitude toward her employer. Lucy keeps Mariah at arm's length in the same manner she keeps away from the mother since she associates love with suffocation, "the millstone around your life's neck" (8). She fears that if she relaxes her guard, she will be subsumed by the power of Mariah's love and thus lose herself. In a similar way, Lucy guards herself from opening her mother's letters from Antigua for "I knew that if I read one, I would die from longing for her" (91). Above all, Lucy is terrified of being (assimilated) transformed into just an "echo" of someone (36). Indeed, she measures herself against this object of attraction.

It starts innocently enough with Mariah's reaction to the weather, specifically the heralding of spring. Mariah says enthusiastically to Lucy:

Have you ever seen daffodils pushing their way up out of the
ground? And when they're in bloom and all massed together,
a breeze comes along and makes them do a curtsy to the lawn
stretching out in front of them? Have you even seen that? When
I see that, I feel so glad to be alive. And I thought, so Mariah is
made to feel alive by some flowers bending in the breeze. How
does a person get to be that way? (17)

Moira Ferguson points out in *Jamaica Kincaid: Where the Land Meets the
Body* that Lucy "cannot fathom how a windy day can make one person
more agitated than someone facing, say, a daily drought. What causes such
priorities? Is it simply that some lives are lived at a trivialized, even perilously
self-indulgent level? Could it be guilt or compensation?" (111).

In contrast, Lucy's attitude towards the weather is due in part to the
fact that she originates from a drought-stricken tropical island where the
months went by in a seemingly mechanical manner which did not seem to be
"influenced by the tilt of the earth at all," a condition which the protagonist
implies is imitative of the miserable, static condition of the people's lives
(86). In an interview in "Talk of the Town" in the *New Yorker*, Kincaid
states: "I had never, in all the time I lived there [in Antigua] heard anyone
say, 'What a beautiful morning'" (37). Xuela echoes similar sentiments in
the *Autobiography of My Mother*: the natives of Dominica "wanted to say,
something not about the weather (that was by now beyond comment), but
about their lives, their disappointments most likely, for joy is so short-lived
there isn't enough time to dwell on its occurrence" (166).

Lucy's reactions demonstrate that the people's lives in her society
are marked primarily by hardship or that they are so shackled by the harsh
conditions of their lives that they are unable to accept the luxury to indulge
in the weather. Her attitude towards the weather mirrors the peasant
mentality of the agricultural Antiguan setting in which she grew up. In
brief, to Lucy, Mariah's leisured, fanciful preoccupation with the vagaries
of the weather seems trivial and, in Moira Ferguson's words, "perilously
self-indulgent" (111).

Nowhere in the narrative is the acute historical and cultural gap
between the two women more accentuated than during the episode in
which Mariah (fully aware of the young woman's aversion to daffodils) takes
Lucy blindfolded to a garden to admire a field of daffodils in bloom. The
protagonist is painfully reminded that as a child she was taught to memorize
(and recite) Wordsworth's poem "Of the Daffodils," which epitomizes
for her a colonial past she abhors. Mariah's "motherly" insistence that, in
spite of the poem, Lucy would share her aesthetic delight in the beauty of
the daffodils reveals the employer's profound historical naïveté. Ferguson

contends, "Mariah cannot comprehend that Lucy's experience of the world induces an oppositional understanding and sites her in a different place" (115). In effect, just as Mariah's class background and position make her assume that aesthetics and politics are separated, in a similar way she had been taught that literature was separate from politics; not so for Lucy. As a young woman whose existence has been defined by British colonization, she knows otherwise. Mariah means well, but in the end, she is incapable of grasping the complicated dynamics of a stultifying colonial education which has forced a young girl to hold in awe a bunch of insignificant "simple" flowers to which she bitterly refers in the text as "some [wretched] flowers I would not see in real life until I was nineteen" (30).

Lucy's violent reaction at her first sight of daffodils might seem disproportionate to Mariah's intentions if we do not place it firmly within the dialectic of colonial discourse and Lucy's personal trajectory. The protagonist's rage is motivated partly out of disappointment. She feels utterly cheated that the "idea" (read: ideal) of those "simple" flowers which her British colonial education has taught her to hold in awe does not live up to the reality of the moment.

Indeed, Lucy is scarred by the politics of "learning by heart," to use Helen Tiffin's word (918).[3] She has come to associate the color yellow (i.e., the color of the daffodils and Mariah's pale yellow skin and hair color) as the symbols of oppression. Elaine Savory Fido, in her study pertaining to "The Politics of Colours and the Politics of Writing in Jean Rhys' Fiction," argues that our sense of the meaning of colour is very subjective and/or cultural or religiously defined (3). She further demonstrates that Jean Rhys, as a white Creole, born in Dominica in an oppressive minority, made her long to be black and to cross over into a world she perceived as warm and joyous and rich in feeling, i.e. the world of African culture (colour-wise). And even though Rhys left for England as a young woman and thus her writing was all done in the context of an England she disliked and did not feel she belonged in, she consistently used in her work the strong colours of landscape in the tropics such as red, blue, green, purple, but ever favours yellow (4).

Although an exploration of the significance of the color yellow in Jean Rhys's writing lies outside the scope of this study, we do know that the color yellow in Jamaica Kincaid's work in general, and specifically in *Lucy*, is attached to powerful subjective meanings. Again, Ferguson's comments are useful: "[For Lucy,] the color yellow is [linked] with painful memories of her mother that interact with pernicious colonial signs. Yellow is the jaundiced marker of white cultural identity" (112).

In other words, the color yellow also reminds Lucy of the totalizing values, history and structures of the homeland from which she seeks to purge herself in order to become individuated and free (Rich 236). At the beginning of the novel, Lucy tells us that she dreams of being chased by Lewis, Mariah's husband, on a road so yellow it looked as if it were paved with cornmeal (i.e. the road to conformity or, worse, colonial assimilation) (14). The color yellow also suggests drabness, domination, corruption, decay and artificiality. In *Annie John*, Ruth, the only white girl in Annie's class, is described to us as "a dunce and came from England and had yellow hair" (73). In the *Autobiography of My Mother*, Xuela associates her father's skin (of jaundiced yellow) with the color of domination, "the color of corruption: gold, copper, ore" and describes her husband's skin as the color of decay, of "a bad-luck cockroach in its pupa stage" (186, 146). Finally, in *Lucy*, Mariah is one of the "six yellow-haired heads of various sizes that were bunched as if they were a bouquet of flowers tied together by an unseen string" (a bouquet of daffodils?) (12). In her revealing essay "Biography of a Dress," Jamaica Kincaid offers disturbing evidence linking the color yellow with painful memories of her childhood and mother as well as with pernicious colonial signs (Ferguson 112):

> My mother was always eager for me to eat in one form (a porridge) or another (as fongie, the starchy part of my midday meal) because it was cheap and therefore easily available ... and because she was taught that foods bearing the colors yellow, green or orange were particularly rich in vitamins and so boiled cornmeal would be particularly good for me.... Whenever I saw this bowl of trembling yellow substance before me I would grow still and silent.... (93–94)

She was also forced to wear

> a yellow poplin dress as the same shade of yellow as boiled cornmeal that her mother had sewn together the various parts with species of birds she had never seen (swan) and species of flowers she had never seen (tulip) and species of animals she had never seen (bear) in real life, only in a picture in a book. My mother made this dress from the picture of such a girl at two years old—a girl whose skin was the color of cream in the process of spoiling, whose hair was the texture of silk and the color of flax, a girl whose eyes gleamed like blue jewels in a crown, *perhaps created a desire in my mother to try and make the daughter she already had look like that.* (96–97, italics mine)

Similarly, then Lucy reacts with anger to Mariah's efforts to inspire her with daffodils and other signifiers of the West.

It is surely Lucy's personal background of domination by her mother and by the British "motherland" which makes her define the world in a binary paradigm of masters and slaves. Upon boarding a train, during her trip to the Great Lakes region with Mariah and her children, she notices that

> the other people sitting down to eat dinner all looked like Mariah's relatives; the people waiting on them all looked like mine. The people who looked like my relatives were all older men and very dignified, as if they were just emerging from a church after Sunday service. On closer observation, they were not all like my relatives; they only looked like them. My relatives always gave backchat. Mariah did not seem to notice what she had in common with the other diners, or what I had in common with the waiters. (32)

For the first time in the narrative, Lucy is consciously aware of her "racial" visibility, as the only black person seated in the first-class car with Mariah and of her subservient status as the employee who tends to the needs of another woman's children. She is also sensitive to the cultural differences between the "dignified" African-American servers on the train and her West Indian relatives who engage in "backchat" (i.e. informal repartee). Mariah is not aware of the contradictions embedded in Lucy's description because she takes her privileged position of class and race as the norm. Mariah belongs to a world of over-stimulation and addiction to aesthetic sensation, to use Patricia Williams's notion, which enables her to merely derive an aesthetic pleasure at the view of freshly plowed fields, devoid of connotative meanings (3). To Lucy, on the other hand, who comes from an agricultural society with a history of slavery, the view of "fresh-turned earth" is evocative of domination and a bitter reminder of the forced labor involved in ploughing plantation acreage (memories of material hardship she has vowed to forget).

It is also important to add that, on a subliminal level, Lucy's anger is motivated by the fear that her employer's delight at the view of the plowed fields is tinged with the history of ownership over the people who toil the land—and by extension, possession of her. Thereby, the reader is reminded that Lucy's greatest fear is to be possessed and that her life is a relentless pursuit of a *récupération de soi*, to extricate herself from both physical and emotional entanglement since she associates love with a millstone around one's neck. In the same light, Mariah's' affection for Gus, her childhood manservant, for example, is also judged suspect by Lucy:

> the way Mariah spoke his name it was as if he belonged to her deeply, like a memory. And, of course, he was a part of her past,

her childhood: he was there apparently, when she took her first
steps; she had caught her first fish in a boat with him; they had
been in a storm on the lake and their survival was a miracle, and
so on. Still, he was a real person, and I thought Mariah should
have long separated the person Gus standing in front of her in
the present from all the things that he had meant to her in the
past. (33–34)

Lucy implies that Gus occupies the confines of Mariah's imagination
in an idealized manner. She resents the fact that Mariah's image of Gus
remains subsumed by nostalgia so that he is denied agency or an identity of
his own making. Moreover, Lucy interprets Gus's position as a subaltern as
he is subjected to the whims of a complacent, privileged class among which a
servant is often patronized, depersonalized and reduced into an object whose
functional value is attached to the employer's needs and emotions. He is not
a person in his own right.

One the most telling episodes in the narratives highlighting Mariah's
incapacity to understand the process of history in anything but superficial terms
involves the incident in which she boasts of her Indian ancestry to Lucy:

I was looking forward to telling you that I have Indian blood,
that the reason I'm so good at catching fish and hunting birds
and roasting corn and doing all sorts of things is that I have
Indian blood. But now, I don't know why, I feel I shouldn't tell
you that. I feel you will take it the wrong way. (39–40)

In her desperate attempt to win Lucy's affection for the absolution of collective
and historical guilt, Mariah appropriates an idealized image of the "Indian"
(and obliterates their social and political reality). Her ignorance blithely
perpetuates the dangerous myth of the "Indian" as a nostalgic, mummified
character of a glorious past whose relevance is merely worthy of "museum
mustiness." As John R. Gillis writes in *Commemorations*: "Women and
minorities often serve as *symbols* of a 'lost' past, nostalgically perceived and
romantically constructed, but their actual lives are most readily forgotten"
(10, italics mine).

At this juncture of our reading, based on Lucy's detailed observations
about her employer, we have been able to draw certain insights of social
relevance from Mariah's upbringing and her life as a young woman offering us
a theoretical profile, allowing us to see "how she got to be that way" and how
Lucy, by aiming her intellect at her employer sharpens her understanding of
the world around her. Mariah was born into a closed, wealthy Midwestern
Anglo-American social circle of high self-regard with names like "Peters,

Smith, Jones and Richards," a circle which nevertheless offered itself as universal, which has afforded her to effortlessly maintain an untested core of idealism, in her view of human relationships (64). It is a world Patricia Williams describes substantively as "a prison of indulgences, an addiction of sensation, a dissolution of the self through over-stimulation," a world Lucy pierces and dissects intellectually (3). Mariah's life is hemmed in by traditions such as long, leisurely summers spent in the ancestral house on the Great Lakes attended by a manservant from Sweden onboard "who had always done things for her family" (33). It is surely those advantages of both spare time and money which allow Lucy's employer to freely engage herself in lofty ecological deeds such as saving the marshlands and then writing and illustrating a "book on these vanishing things and giving any money made to an organization devoted to saving them" (72).

Mariah's acts of freedom are inscribed within her position of class and race privilege in the United States. She is thus the quintessential flower girl of the 1960s, who "wore her yellow hair long and unkempt and did not shave her legs or underarms, as a symbol of something, and was not a virgin and had not been for a long time" (80). Her liberal code of conduct does not serve as a moral judgment since Mariah's gendered identity or "value" rests upon the unstated premise of her wealth and family name and not her sexual purity.

Mariah's married life recalls Beauvoirism, but not the bourgeois feminist radicalism espoused in Simone de Beauvoir's *The Second Sex* with the potential for intellectual and social transformation for white Western women of the middle and upper-classes; rather, the woman's traditional world is evocative of Beauvoir's description of the image of the middle/upper-class woman who seeks feminine fulfillment according to the values of True Womanhood,[4] that is by focusing on the harmonious decor of her house, such as the delicate art of flower arrangement, for the consecration of the romantic dream. Mariah revels in her status as Lewis's "perfect" wife and of the "sainted Mother" of four beautiful blonde daughters. Lastly, perhaps most significantly, she represents de Beauvoir's "aging woman" who dreads the passing of youth as a warning of sexual and social decline. As Lucy notes, Mariah kept saying, "'I am forty years old'—alternating between surprise and foreboding" (46).

In one instance, Mariah confides to Lucy during one of their customary tête-à-têtes in the kitchen that she and Lewis "have such bad sex" (113). Still like Flaubert's heroine Emma Bovary, she is unable or reluctant to disassociate the physical act from a romantic ideal and tells Lucy with candor during one of her sexual escapades "that if you liked being with someone in that particular way, then you must be in love with him" (70). She is therefore devastated when her husband, "the only man she had ever loved," betrays her with her best friend (81). Lucy, on the other hand who has been raised in a cultural matrix where girls are implicitly taught to accept men with their concupiscent disposition, is hardly surprised to discover that Lewis is behaving no differently than the men in Antigua by having an affair with Mariah's friend. Thus, she reacts with customary scorn and cynicism delivered almost as a sermon:

> "Your situation is an everyday thing. Men behave in this way all the time. The ones who do not behave in this way are the exceptions to the rule.... [W]here I came from, ... a man like Lewis would not have been a surprise; his behavior would not have cast a pall over any woman's life. It was expected. Everybody knew that men have no morals, that they do not know how to behave, that they do not know how to treat other people. It was why men like laws so much; it was why they had to invent such things—they need a guide.... This was something I knew; why didn't Mariah know it also?" (142)

Lucy's "knowledge" of male–female relationships is based on a West Indian cultural context molded by the personal experiences of the women around her, including her mother's friend Sylvie and specifically her mother's experience. She saw the world through her mother, for "it was from her own experience that she spoke" (48). Thus, in coming to understand the precariousness of Mariah's position, Lucy is just beginning to learn and embrace relationships and opportunities as she never has before.

Edith Clarke, in her study of family structures and relationships, points out that in the West Indian family "mother and children co-operate in the small daily duties in the home.... They are continually together. There is constant companionship, and a constant interdependence. The girl child identifies herself with the mother" (158). In Kincaid's *Annie John*, daily life, for example, is completely centered around her mother: "My mother and I often took a bath together," shopped and ate together. "I spent the day following my mother around and observing the way she did everything" (14–15). The complete interdependence between mother and child in the West Indies (especially the female child) has also been explained by Trinidadian novelist and sociologist, Merle Hodge, in her study *The Shadow of the Whip* as a pattern inherited from the legacy of slavery in the region.

> The whole humiliation of slavery meant ... [that] the function of fatherhood was limited to fertilizing the female. Gone was the status of head of the family, for there was no family, no living in a unit with wife and children.... Women became mother and

father to the race. And it is this concentration of moral authority in the person of the woman that has influenced relations between men and women of African descent in the Caribbean. [The father's] role is not clearly defined and not binding. . . . [T]he strongest influence in the home is usually female. (115)

Other sociologists, notably Barbara Bush in her recent study entitled *Slave Women in Caribbean Society 1650–1838*, caution against the structural readings of Afro-Caribbean family life as recapitulations of slave family life and stress instead the vagaries of the post-emancipation Caribbean agrarian system:

> Since emancipation changes in the economic and social infrastructure of West Indian societies have occurred which have had important ramifications on the black family structure. For instance, the de-emphasis of the father role amongst some segments of society, which has often been cited in support of matrifocal theories of black family organization rather than being a direct result of the weakening of the father role during the days of slavery, is far more plausibly the result of the migrant labour systems which developed after slavery ended. (84–85)

Lucy's father may have been, in Kincaid's own words, a "sort of typical West Indian man, I mean they have children, but they never seem to connect themselves with these children" (Cudjoe 219). Hence, the news of her father's passing is received by Lucy with detachment. In retrospect, his death presents Lucy with another opportunity to berate her mother's lack of discernment and emphasize her father's irresponsibility: "I wrote to my mother a [cold] letter. . . . In the letter I asked my mother how she could have married a man who would die and leave her in debt even for his own burial" (127). It is easy to discern through Lucy's tirade the lack of respect she felt for him. Yet, in spite of her recriminations against male irresponsibility or their presumed libidinous disposition, male dominance in the Caribbean does not only profoundly affect filial relationships and male–female relations but also the society at large. An examination of the social and historical background of gender relations in the Caribbean is crucial in understanding Lucy's "psychic landscape" regarding issues of male–female relations and female sexuality.

Lucy has been raised strictly under Victorian colonial rule within a social context in which there was much cultural violence directed toward women based on popular attitudes toward their sexuality and their bodies. These attitudes were a combination of "Victorian ideology and Christian missionary zeal . . . aimed at producing women as good wives and mothers.

Cultural and psychic violence in general, such as racist images of self-deprecation were compounded for women in particular through forced repression of their sexuality" (Katrak 171). Indeed, an implicit aspect of the official education system was devoted to remolding West Indian black girls into "ladies" elevated to middle-class society. As Evelyn Brooks Higginbotham reminds us in *African-American Women's History and the Metalanguage of Race*, "Ladies were not merely women; they represented a class, a differentiated status within the generic category of 'women'" (261). It is a social undertaking which Xuela in *The Autobiography of My Mother* sarcastically derides "as a combination of elaborate fabrications, a collection of externals, facial arrangements, and body parts, distortions, lies and empty effort" (159). In *Annie John*, the protagonist tells us with considerable irony that she could "not resist making farting-like noises each time [she] had to practice a curtsy . . . [or] seemed unable to resist eating from the bowl of plums which . . ." the piano teacher, a shriveled-up old spinster from Lancashire, England ". . . had placed on the piano purely for decoration" (28).

Still, no matter how racist or contradictory the colonial grooming may have been to many women, West Indian mothers internalized those aspirations and strove to inculcate those values attributed to the Cult of True Womanhood, for they held the belief that it was the only acceptable way for their daughters to secure social mobility. For example, during the summer Annie John turned twelve, her mother sent her "to someone to teach all about manners and how to meet and greet important people in the world" and would give her lessons in becoming a lady (28). Those notions held by Mrs. John, according to Helen Pyne Timothy, embody a dichotomous Caribbean mentality dictated by a rigid society where women are caught trying to reconcile the values of two world views:

> The Caribbean mother who is bent on seeing her daughter rise from the lower classes to the middle ranks must not only teach her useful housekeeping tasks, cleanliness, good manners, and practical knowledge of her environment but also European norms and the need to desist in the practice of African ones. . . . Thus, in the mother's perception, Christianity, Sunday school, good manners (the ability to curtsy) and piano lessons are all essential to her daughter's acceptability and respectability. (240)

Under colonial rule females are strictly called to conform to a binary moral paradigm based on Victorian sexual duality: "lady" and "slut." For example, in Kincaid's story "Girl" from *At the Bottom of the River*, the mother repeats a list of sexual warnings at her daughter:

On Sundays try to walk like a lady and not like the slut you are
so bent on becoming; this is how to hem a dress when you see
the hem coming down and so to prevent yourself from looking
like the slut I know you are so bent on becoming; ... this is how
to behave in the presence of men who don't know you very well,
and this way they won't recognize immediately the slut I have
warned you against becoming. (3–4)

The abusive tirade directed at the daughter in *At the Bottom of the River*
underscores the fact that the protagonist's mother, raised under the weight
of constant assaults upon black female sexuality, has internalized the racist
notion that a rampant sexuality is inherent to people of African descent.
The mother has also been taught to believe that a woman's body belongs to
the respectable male who, one day, will marry her daughter and insure her
class and social standing. She is thus convinced that it is her responsibility to
keep her daughter sexually untouched so she can better her chances on the
marriage market (Niesen de Abruna 281).

In "Severing the (M)Other Connection: The Representation of
Cultural Identity in Jamaica Kincaid's *Annie John*," H. Adlai Murdoch is
attentive to the nature of the Caribbean family, whose paradoxical form has
implications for Lucy's recognition of and identification with a maternal
power structure.

West Indian men enjoy much greater social and sexual
freedom than do West Indian women. They are the focus of
society's power relationships and occupy, in general, positions
within it which inculcate concomitant attitudes of social and
psychological authority. They maintain sometimes numerous and
contemporaneous extra-familial sexual relationships, a luxury
that women certainly are not afforded by them. ... West Indian
men, in other words, are allowed by society to indulge in libidinal
pleasures; tacit recognition is given to their overwhelming
dominant role in all social relationships. (328)

The dominant social position of men which Murdoch describes is
particularly onerous for woman in a Caribbean colonial context since it
severely restricts their economic opportunities for social advancement. In
1962 V.S. Naipaul reflects with scorn in *The Middle Passage* that the West
Indian community in which he grew up was a "philistine" society for the fact
Trinidadians (read: men) could only aspire to become doctors or lawyers since
those two occupations conferred prestige and social mobility (57). In *Lucy*,
marriage and nursing are assigned by the mother as the only two vocations

accessible to the protagonist due to her cultural conditioning. Marriage is presented as the ultimate goal of every woman's life since, in part, it bestowed the privileges of social mobility, status, and financial security. As Lucy states, "When my mother married my father, he was an old man and she a young woman. This suited them both. She had someone who would leave her alone yet not cause her to lose face in front of other women; he had someone who would take care of him in his dotage" (81).

Lucy paints a portrait of marriage as a pragmatic arrangement in which there is an exchange of service between two parties. Nursing, the other respectable position, is presented to the protagonist by her mother as the vocation relegated to unmarried women, the "ones left on the shelf":

> A nurse ... was a woman my mother respected to her face but had many bad things to say about behind her back. They were: she should never find a man; no man would have her; she carried herself like a strongbox, and from the look on her face a man couldn't find a reason to break in; she had lived alone for so long it was too late to start with a man now. But among the last things my mother had said to me, just before I left, was "Oh I can just see you in your nurse's uniform. I shall be very proud of you." And I could only guess which nurse's uniform she meant—the uniform made of cloth or the one made of circumstances. (93)

The aforementioned citation is important in revealing the contradictions of British colonial rule of the Victorian Cult of True Womanhood. Lucy's mother is torn by her desire to instill in her daughter the values of self-reliance and economic independence while, at the same time, she has internalized the denigrating values of her society about unmarried women.

What Mariah's marital woes and her own experiences allow Lucy to see is that, since the status of marriage confers both social and economic privilege, women are often pushed to extreme measures to secure the ultimate prize. Such a tumultuous situation incites an atmosphere of suspicion, intense rivalry and violence amongst women for the attention of men. In effect, Lucy evokes with ease incidents of death and mayhem which surrounded her life as a child: "My father had lived with another woman for years and was the father of her three children; she tried to kill my mother and me many times" (80). She also recalls, as a girl-child, eavesdropping on her mother's friend, Sylvie, narrating the incident in which she became disfigured as a result of a "big quarrel with another woman . . . over which of the two of them a man they both loved should live with" (24). Thus, Lucy will defy such precedents established through the Cult of Womanhood's demands for feminine purity and submission and through her own mother's role in perpetuating these demands. And in her defiance against these Victorian mores, Lucy will begin to liberate herself from Antigua's distinctly Victorian colonial history.

Emigrating to the United States has enabled Lucy to realize many of her objectives. Leaving Mariah's employment at the end of the novel, she is able to secure herself a room of her own. A new job has given her the financial independence and the personal solitude she has always craved. By seizing power over her life, Lucy no longer feels the weight of history, and more importantly, the burden of her mother's love. Moreover, although the ending of the novel does not indicate a rapprochement of minds and ideas between Lucy and Mariah, during the course of a year, the protagonist has begun to soften her uncompromising dogmatic social vision and is able to bond with her former employer on a human level. As Lucy explains, when Mariah gives her a journal of her own, "she reminded me . . . [in] the way that I had come to love, she spoke of women, journals, and, of course, history" (163). Finally, Lucy acknowledges the uniqueness of her relationship with Mariah, instead of emphasizing Mariah's likeness to her mother or her undifferentiated role as a privileged white woman. It is perhaps at this juncture, Kincaid evinces, that a true dialogue can now begin between the two women.

Notes

1. As Chikwenye Okonjo Ogunyemi writes in "Womanism: The Dynamics of the Contemporary Black Female Novel in English" *Signs* 11.11 (1985): 63–80: "What could be more damaging than Margaret Walker's portrait in *Jubilee* of Big Missy as the hard matriarch or of her daughter, the lily-livered Miss Lilian, in the contrasting stereotype of the fragile, docile woman? Big Missy, for her diabolical treatment of her black slaves, . . . Paule Marshall's [devastating] . . . portrait of the white woman in *Brown Girl, Brownstones* and even more trenchant in the *Chosen Place, the Timeless People*," or Alice Walker's obnoxious portrayal of the mayor's wife and her contemptible treatment of Sophia in *The Color Purple*? (70–71).

2. According to Caribbean myths, a *jablesse* is a beautiful enchantress who removes her skin at night to go drink the blood of her enemies.

3. As Helen Tiffin notes in "Cold Hearts and (Foreign) Tongues," "Through Wordsworth's poem the politics of aesthetics has already been absorbed into Lucy's heart; she is dressed in it, but she has also eaten it, internalized it. Consequently where Mariah sees only "beautiful flowers" Lucy feels "sorrow and bitterness" (918).

4. The attributes of the Cult of True Womanhood by which a woman judges herself and was judged by others around her were divided into four cardinal virtues: piety, purity, submissiveness and domesticity. Religion, or piety, was the core of a woman's virtue. Remolding women to these images was integral to the colonial government's idea of a "civilized social order." For further reading, see Barbara Welter, "The Cult of True Womanhood: 1820–1860," *American Quarterly* 18 (1966): 151–174; and Hilary McD. Beckles. *Centering Woman: Gender Discourse in Caribbean Slave Society*, Kingston: Ian Randles Publishers, 1999.

Works Cited

Bush, Barbara. *Slave Women in Caribbean Society 1650–1838*. Bloomington: Indiana UP, 1990.

Clarke, Edith. *My Mother who Fathered Me*. London: Allen, 1972.

Cudjoe, Selwyn R. "Jamaica Kincaid and the Modernist Project: An Interview." *Caribbean Women Writers*. Amherst: U of Massachusetts P, 1990. 215–232.

de Beauvoir, Simone. *The Second Sex*. Trans. and ed. H.M. Parshley. London: J. Cape, 1953.

Ferguson, Moira. *Jamaica Kincaid: Where the Land Meets the Body*. Charlottesville and London: UP of Virginia, 1994.

Fido, Elaine Savory. "The Politics of Colour and the Politics of Writing in Jean Rhys' Fiction." *Jean Rhys Review* 4.2 (1991): 3–12.

Gillis, John. *Commemorations: The Politics of National Identity*. New Jersey: Princeton UP, 1994.

Hodge, Merle. *The Shadow of the Whip*. "Is Massa Day Dead? Black Moods in the Caribbean." Ed. Orde Coombs. New York: Anchor, 1974.

Higginbotham, Evelyn Brooks. "African-American Women's History and the Metalanguage of Race." *Signs* 17 (1992): 251–274.

Katrak, Ketu H. "Decolonizing Culture: Toward a Theory of Post-Colonial Texts." *Modern Fiction Studies* 35.1 (Spring 1989): 157–179.

Kincaid, Jamaica. *Annie John*. New York: Farrar Straus Giroux, 1985.

———. *At the Bottom of the River*. New York: Vintage, 1983.

———. *Lucy*. New York: Farrar Straus Giroux, 1990.

———. *The Autobiography of My Mother*. New York: Farrar Straus Giroux, 1996.

Lionnet, Françoise. *Postcolonial Representations*. Ithaca and London: Cornell UP, 1995.

Murdoch, Adlai H. "Severing the (M)Other Connection: The Representation of Cultural Identity in Jamaica Kincaid's *Annie John*." *Callaloo* 13.2 (1990): 326–340.

Niesen de Abruna, Laura. "Family Connections: Mother and Mother Country in the Fiction of Jean Rhys and Jamaica Kincaid." *Motherlands*. Ed. Susheila Nasta. Rutgers UP, 1991. 257–289.

Ogunyemi, Chikwenye Okonjo. "Womanism: The Dynamics of the Contemporary Black Female Novel in English." *Signs* 11.11 (1985): 63–80.

Pyne Timothy, Helen. "Adolescent Rebellion and Gender Relations in *At The Bottom of the River* and *Annie John*." Caribbean Women Writers. Ed. Selwyn Cudjoe. Amherst UP, 1990. 233–242.

Rich, Adrienne. *Of Woman Born: Motherhood as Experience and Institution*. New York: Norton, 1976.

Tiffin, Helen. "Cold Hearts and (Foreign) Tongues: Recitation and the Reclamation of the Female Body in the Works of Erna Brodber & Jamaica Kincaid." *Callaloo* 16.4 (1993): 909–21.

Welter, Barbara. "The Cult of True Womanhood: 1820–1860." *American Quarterly* 18 (1966): 151–174.

Williams, Patricia. "The White Blackbird: A Life of the Painter Margaret Sargent by her Granddaughter." *The Women's Review of Books* 8.8 (May 1996): 1–4.

RAMÓN E. SOTO-CRESPO

Death and the Diaspora Writer: Hybridity and Mourning in the Work of Jamaica Kincaid

> It was that time of day when all you have lost is heaviest in your mind: your mother, if you have lost her; your home, if you have lost it; the voices of people who might have loved you or who you only wish had loved you; the places in which something good, something you cannot forget, happened to you.
>
> Jamaica Kincaid, *The Autobiography of My Mother*

Throughout her work, Jamaica Kincaid mourns the loss of not only individuals close to her but also larger, more abstract entities such as "home" and "the places in which something good, something you cannot forget, happened to you." Mourning the homeland is one way for the diaspora writer to maintain a connection with it; this mode of connectivity, I will argue, represents less nostalgia than an inherently political style of transcultural association. The diaspora writer remains distinct from the exile writer in that her diasporic status stems from migration patterns that characterize whole populations, often as a result of colonization. Since dislocation is a topic central to diaspora narratives, those narratives require that cross-cultural connections be made. Mourning functions as one strategy for making such connections, and Kincaid writes about mourning in such a way as to suggest that it is less a psychological phase to be superseded than a political condition of existence. In the process, she alters, or gives new and unexpected nuances

From *Contemporary Literature* 43, no. 2 (Summer 2002). © 2002 by the Board of Regents of the University of Wisconsin System.

to, conventional narrative genres such as memoir and traditional cultural practices such as mourning.

In this essay, I will examine the ways in which Kincaid's *My Garden* (*Book*) connects to apparently unrelated issues from her previous books. In the process, I will attempt to clarify postcolonial theories of hybridity by showing their origins in the history of gardening. Kincaid's brother, Devon Drew, whose death from AIDS she mourns in her memoir *My Brother*, was a gardener, and his fate is part of the intertwined histories of horticulture and colonialism. In *My Brother*, Kincaid analogizes AIDS, the multisymptom illness spreading throughout her brother's body, with the spread of colonialism in the West Indies, an analogy she develops by suggesting that her brother's subaltern body becomes bereft of life in postcolonial Antigua, just as the West Indies were depleted of their flora during colonization. These parallels are augmented by considering the motif of the garden as imperial trope, the garden as paradise, Kincaid's own gardens, the Caribbean slave garden as a site of resistance, the garden as graveyard, and hence the garden as a place of mourning. In *My Garden* (*Book*), Kincaid meditates on the idea that the gardener's death is usually followed by the death of his or her garden—an idea she develops in her short story "Ovando," where she allegorizes the conquest of the West Indies as the first stage in an indigenous garden's death. She pursues this connection in *My Brother*, where she mourns the death of the queer subaltern and explores the significance of this death for a postcolonial (yet neocolonized) West Indies.

*   *   *

In 1999, Kincaid published *My Garden* (*Book*), a series of long essays about gardens that is different in style and subject matter from her previous books. In earlier works Kincaid fictionalized both her own childhood (*Annie John*, 1983) and the life of her half-Carib mother (*The Autobiography of My Mother*, 1996), while in *My Brother* (1997) she memorialized the life of her youngest sibling. By contrast, *My Garden* (*Book*) appears to deal with seasons, plants, and flowers; in fact, it concerns history, cultural institutions, and imperial conquest. The book is divided into three parts: the first is centered on the garden as a place for personal introspection; the second deals with the garden as an imperial form; and the third with the garden in relation to travel writing. *My Garden* (*Book*) narrates its author's adventures in attempting to grow a garden in Vermont, where she now resides. Kincaid tells us about the different kinds of plants cultivated in her garden, the nurseries from which she purchased them, and how the garden became a time-consuming, if not endless, enterprise. She also tells us about the history of gardens, different types of garden books, and the astonishing number of garden catalogues.

She reveals how her passion for gardens led her to travel to England, where she visited Gertrude Jekyll's gardens; to France, where she spent time contemplating Claude Monet's gardens; and to China, where she visited the imperial gardens of the Orient.

My Garden (Book) conveys a sensitivity and an introspective melancholy rarely found in garden handbooks but evident in a long literary tradition linking gardens and reveries in the West. This sentiment of melancholy pervades Kincaid's oeuvre, and it prompts me to read *My Garden (Book)* as a text that connects mourning with historical resistance. If Kincaid's work has usually been read as emphasizing the loss of childhood innocence, *My Garden (Book)* approaches the theme of mourning in a broader context of imperialism and history.[1] What this new book makes clear is that for the diaspora writer mourning can function as a form of political resistance. Resistance is not just a textual enterprise in *My Garden (Book)*, because Kincaid connects the garden to the development of imperial institutions and to the memory of slave resistance found in Caribbean history. While she talks about her own literal gardening habits, gardening is also allegorical in that it evokes the garden's historical and institutional underside— specifically, the West Indian slaves' garden plots on the plantations. In the Caribbean, the garden is, in part, a site of alterity and wildness, because one purpose the garden plots served was to grow poisonous seeds used in the West African religious practice of Obeah—and also used for killing the white masters. This underside of the garden makes it a potential site of resistance, rebellion, and revolt in the West Indies. It also allows us to see the ramifications of using the garden allegorically, especially since the motif of the garden was used in imperial rhetoric as a rationale for colonization. Owing to this double valence, we might say that the garden is a site of literal and figurative hybridity; indeed, Kincaid uses the garden as a metaphor for cultural hybridity.

Salman Rushdie, Homi Bhabha, and Stuart Hall all have appropriated hybridity as a metaphor in relation to the diasporic subject, with Hall's work the most directly engaged in theorizing Caribbean identity in terms of hybridity. For Hall, the new cultural identities emerging from the diaspora and from colonial experience should be understood as "cultures of hybridity" (310): he argues that by mingling the old and the new, these identities conflate different cultural traditions into a dynamically original mixed culture. Similarly, Robin Cohen has emphasized the cultural syncretism of a Caribbean diaspora's hybridity. Cohen even attempts to classify the different diasporas in terms of a "horticultural image": in what he calls "the good gardener's guide to diasporas," Cohen categorizes the Caribbean diaspora as "Cultural/hybrid/postmodern," using the horticultural term "cross-pollinating" (177–78). Although he admits to having let his "imagination roam freely" (179), Cohen's attempt confirms a tendency to understand Caribbean diasporas in terms of hybridity and garden metaphors.

The garden as a metaphor for hybridity allows the Caribbean diaspora writer to draw fruitfully on her past memories and thereby create a series of connections, or what Doris Sommer calls "allegorical relationships" (326). Drawing on Paul de Man's theory of allegory in a postcolonial context, Sommer argues that this trope allows personal narratives to stand for larger political conditions. In this way, Kincaid uses her gardening experience to create a series of historical, geographical, botanical, and familial connections that intermingle in the metaphor of the garden. The garden as a metaphor for (as well as a literal site of) hybridity derives from its potential for connecting cross-cultural memories. In *My Garden (Book)*, Kincaid makes of her garden a place where memories of the Caribbean intersect with her life in the diaspora: "I only marveled at the way the garden is for me an exercise in memory, a way of remembering my own immediate past, a way of getting to a past that is my own (the Caribbean Sea) and the past as it is indirectly related to me (the conquest of Mexico and its surroundings)" (8). She suggests that the garden itself fuses memory, geography, and culture in a dynamic and creative way: "it dawned on me that the garden I was making (and am still making and will always be making) resembled the map of the Caribbean and the sea that surrounds it" (7–8). In this view, the past, far from being static, acquires dynamism in the garden by mobilizing connections between history, geography, politics, literature, and culture. Kincaid considers memory an active, creative force because it connects cultures across time: "Memory is a gardener's real palette; memory as it summons up the past, memory as it shapes the present, memory as it dictates the future" (*My Favorite Plant* xvi). Through her garden, Kincaid sees how her personal past is tied to politics and, specifically, to the history of imperialism. Hence she sees memory itself as characterized by hybridity, in that her personal associations with gardening necessarily evoke a larger cultural legacy, one that is part of her history though it is not part of her own direct experience. For example, in *My Garden (Book)* the Caribbean becomes "a garden of words and images made of words," because memory entails remembering particularly historical, proper, and flower names: "flowers turned into words, and the words in turn making the flower, the plant, the bean" (*My Favorite Plant* xix). Thus the garden form intersects with the history of imperialism in that it recalls how flowers acquired their common and scientific names.

*   *   *

My Garden (Book) directly connects horticulture and imperialism. "What is the relationship between gardening and conquest?" Kincaid asks (116). Her answer lies in naming, because a name establishes meaning by categorizing the thing named. Key to naming is the belief that there is more than a merely contingent relationship between the word and the thing it names. Kincaid explains that naming is central to the allegory of the garden, because in the tales of conquest, flowers form part of the allegorical embellishment of the landscape:

> This is how my garden began; then again, it would not be at all false to say that just at that moment I was reading a book and that book (written by the historian William Prescott) happened to be about the conquest of Mexico, or New Spain, as it was then called, and I came upon the flower called marigold and the flower called dahlia and the flower called zinnia, and after that the garden was to me more than the garden as I used to think of it. After that the garden was also something else. (6)

This "something else" refers to the garden as a site where history and conquest meet in naming the exotic other. Kincaid characterizes Prescott's account of conquest as "the best history of conquest that I have ever read" (117), because it emphasizes the ideology of landscape, in which the scene of conquest is permeated by the Edenic vision of the land. Quoting Prescott, Kincaid writes:

> When the Spanish marauder Hernando Cortez and his army invaded Mexico, they met "floating gardens ... teeming with flowers and vegetables, and moving like rafts over the waters"; as they looked down on the valley of Mexico, seeing it for the first time, a "picturesque assemblage of water, woodland, and cultivated plains, its shining cities and shadowy hills, was spread out like some gay and gorgeous panorama before them," and "stretching far away at their feet were seen noble forests of oak, sycamore, and cedar, and beyond, yellow fields of maize and the towering maguey, intermingled with orchards and blooming gardens"; there were "flowers, which, with their variegated and gaudy colors, form the greatest attraction of our greenhouses." (117)

For Kincaid, the moment of starting her own garden and the moment of reading about conquest telescope into a meditation on the importance of possession via naming. It is perhaps not surprising that reading and gardening come together in her understanding of history's ideological implications, since, as Richard H. Grove argues in *Green Imperialism*, "the connections between colonial forest control and attempts to control indigenous colonised people became well established on the Caribbean islands" (266). The garden connects Kincaid to the culture of imperialism.[2]

At the moment of conquest, the Caribbean became an arbitrary zone of words and things. Naming is key to Kincaid's critique of conquest because imperial accounts of the West Indian landscape depicted it as abundant in flora but empty of civilization. In imperial chronicles, the myth of the land as garden was concurrent with the erasure of the indigenous population and the depletion of tropical vegetation by deforestation. Reminiscent of Adam in the Garden of Eden, conquerors portrayed the Caribbean islands as Edenic gardens to be mapped and claimed on behalf of imperial power. Unnaming, naming, and renaming are here processes of historical and geographical importance that range beyond the purely theoretical. For instance, the chronicles and histories of conquest document the confusions evoked by these arbitrary acts of naming in the Caribbean. We see the New World depicted as a paradise in the many references to the "virginity" of the flora, yet rival nomenclature caused so many disputes and so much confusion among the imperial powers that it affected the histories of conquest. In this way, the driving myth of Eden became somewhat dissociated from the ideology of peace and order that it originally represented, as a passage from Captain Thomas Southey's *Chronological History of the West Indies* (1827) indicates:

> Much confusion has arisen from the same name being given to different islands in the West Indies, and from the same island having different names.
>
> There is Barbadoes, Barbudo, and the Saints were at one time called Barbata.
>
> Columbus named Isla Larga St. Fernandina, which name was afterwards given to Cuba, although Columbus had named that island Juana.
>
> St. Christopher's is familiarly called St. Kitt's.
>
> St. Salvador's is also called Cat Island.
>
> Puerto Rico was often called San Juan. Its proximity to St. John's increases the confusion. There is Caricou, one of the Grenadines, and Curaçao. The Bahamas were the Lucayos.
>
> Espaniola, St. Domingo, and Hayti, are all names for one island; and St. Domingo is the name of the principal city in the Spanish part of the same island.
>
> There are two islands called Anguila, one to windward of St. Martin's, the other among the Bahamas in the Canal de Santaren. (1: i)

What especially interests me about this passage is less its factual accuracy than its symptomatic status, its revealing how the historical processes of naming and renaming—processes central to techniques of imperial domination and control—created a map of the Caribbean that was so confusing as to *confound* control.[3] Imperial power and imperial knowledge are here in conflict, rather than operating in concert. Indeed, in a moment of desperation, Columbus once named the West Indies "The Eleven Thousand Virgins," asserting the virginity of the land by analogy with the virginity of the saints in a sweeping generalization. According to Kincaid, this happened after Columbus became "exhausted" by having to name consecutively so many places (*My Garden* 158).

It was not only the West Indies but also their flora that were named. Of great significance for Kincaid is the story of the flower known by the indigenous population of Mexico as cocoxochitl. This flowering plant, whose bloom Cortez metaphorized in his accounts of conquest, was transported and hybridized by the Dutch botanist James Dahl, who subsequently renamed it *dahlia* in his own honor. For Kincaid, this story illustrates the global character and power of imperialism. She quotes William Robinson's *The Wild Garden* (1894): "the idea of the wild garden is placing plants of other countries, as hardy as our hardiest wild flowers, in places where they will flourish without further care or costs" (228–29). But, adds Kincaid, those wild flowers of 1894 have become "very commonplace now" in England (228). And it is the very commonplaceness of things, brought about by imperialism, that allows dahlias to appear as an attraction of the Mughal Gardens in India.[4]

Kincaid describes how this transfer of plants gained momentum with the emergence of scientific reason in Europe: "Accounts of botanical gardens begin with men who have sworn to forsake the company of women and have attached themselves to other things, the pursuit of only thinking, contemplating the world as it is or ought to be and, as a relief from this or complementary to this, the capture, isolation, and imprisoning of plants" (*My Garden* 151). An example of this type of figure is Carolus Linnaeus, the Swedish botanist who, in what Kincaid refers to as the Adamic role of giving "names to the things he saw growing before him," created the Latin-based system of nomenclature for cataloguing plants that is still in use. Linnaeus funded expeditions around the globe and stimulated great competition among the Western empires for acquiring specimens, to increase the imperial knowledge of plants. As colonization progressed, the garden became an institutionalized site connecting the metropolis with its colonies—a site that conjoined labor and resistance in the empire. From being considered the preferred metaphor for describing the landscape, the garden became a site of transculturation. The West Indies as gardens became what Mary Louise

Pratt calls "contact zones"—spaces of first encounter and of the transfer of knowledge between cultures characterized by an imbalance of power (4). Metropolitan gardens—for example, those in London—also acquired the status of contact zones, because they served as spaces of transculturation for the West Indian *floral* diasporas. In this way, on both shores of the Atlantic, gardens became diasporic spaces and energetic centers of hybridity.

In the 1830s, the term "gardenesque" was invented in England to describe the various effects that the transplanted "exotics" added to British gardens. In *The Garden Triumphant*, David Stuart describes this penchant for hybridity:

> There was . . . a quite astonishing burst of activity on the part of plant breeders. The old florists had been working away on their traditional genera for several centuries, and so the idea of breeding plants was widely disseminated, as were the techniques for doing it. Now, the wild enthusiasm for the new, especially for new species, poured over into a widespread passion for new varieties of plants. (149)

By 1897, Victorian England had gained the title "The Motherland of Orchids," having broken the European record of two-hundred hybrid species of orchid. The imperial powers competed for what they named floral wealth. Historians Joan Morgan and Alison Richards describe the nineteenth-century English hybrid "mania":

> The marriage of formal gardening and exotic plants introduced an intensity of colour and pattern that had never been seen before, and provided a powerful visual language in which to express the mood of the time. It was a style at once old and completely new, domestic and controlled, yet expansionist and outward-looking. It could only be made possible by new technology, yet lent itself to the nostalgic and heraldic associations required by old and new aristocrats alike. Whether measured in terms of architectural and engineering triumphs, the tens of thousands of bedding plants needed to fill the parterre, or the immense labour required to maintain the high level of finish on which the whole effect depended, it was an unsurpassed opportunity for the display of wealth and taste. (16)

Georgian and Victorian gardens became a common fixture for the English gentry as colonization intensified, and "exotic" plants accelerated the processes of taxonomy and hybridization. Hybridists, as botanists sometimes were known, also changed the country landscape. As the empire grew and London's population increased, the Victorian country house became the preferred place for house parties. This demand transformed country estates into a showcase for the creative design of Victorian pleasure gardens. Jane Austen's Mansfield Park, with its gardens and landscape that exemplify the garden form at the time of early settlement of the West Indies, is a case in point. Antigua, Kincaid's homeland, is the colony that sustains Mansfield Park in the novel (see Said 80–97).

The pleasure gardens of the Victorian country house represented the culmination of a long period of accumulated botanical knowledge that was collected and modified in the slowly emerging cultural institution of the botanical garden. As imperial conquest accelerated and empires consolidated their territories, the demand for the botanical garden grew. Previously attached to schools of medicine, botanical gardens became increasingly independent with the spread of European colonization. As new institutions, these gardens acquired the characteristics of a hybrid themselves, by becoming both places of pleasure, where people could admire the beauty of "exotic" plants, and engines of a new agricultural revolution that fueled the imperial powers in their economic expansion. For Kincaid, the botanical garden epitomizes the first stage of dispossession brought about by conquest and the first institution built on systems of floral transfer. If in the age of empire flora and fauna were globalized, then the botanical garden typifies the processes of transculturation that were established. The botanical garden became an icon of imperial power, and in it the empire and the diaspora merged into one: "The botanical garden reinforced for me how powerful were the people who had conquered me; they could bring to me the botany of the world they owned" (My Garden 120). As an institution, the botanical garden played a crucial role in shifting the West Indian economy from one based on independent farming of minor products to one based on plantations and African slavery, and subsequently to the production of multiple crops that came to replace the centrality of sugarcane in the post-Emancipation Caribbean. Eventually Kew Gardens would take the lead as the primary botanical institution mediating not only metropolitan interests but also those of the West Indian plantation owners as they moved from slavery to employing free and indentured labor.

Having influenced botanical trade at least since the late eighteenth century, by 1848 Kew in London was at the vanguard of British imperialism, according to garden historian Brent Elliott (66). Kew was consulted by the governors of the West Indies and by the metropolitan investors, also called "The London Merchants," on New World ventures (Penson 10; Burn 52–91). Always in need of more efficient plant-based industries, the investors in empire looked to Kew for the collection of plants worldwide and for their perfection; once hybridized, the plants moved from the category of wild to that of cultivated. The field of economic botany was developed as Kew established a new role for botanical gardens in general. As Lucile H. Brockway has noted in *Science and Colonial Expansion*, Kew was at the center of "a network of government botanical stations . . . stretching from Jamaica to Singapore to Fiji. This new technical knowledge, of improved species and improved methods of cultivation and harvesting, was then transmitted to the colonial planters and was a crucial factor in the success of the new plantation crops and plant-based industries" (6–7). Historian Robin Blackburn also has argued, in *The Making of New World Slavery*, that these "advanced forms of technical and economic organization" connected the emerging plantation society with slavery in the West Indies (3). Transculturation changed the role of gardens within both the metropolitan and the colonial arenas. In the West, the garden changed agricultural, social, scientific, economic, and political institutions, while in the West Indies, it altered not only economic institutions but also their racial makeup.

The taxonomy model of Kew, with its effective plant-breeding techniques, represents the culmination of a long process that was not restricted to botany; indeed, eighteenth-century Antigua witnessed experiments in slave-breeding, as part of an ongoing attempt to create more efficient workers.[5] For example, the Codrington plantation in Barbuda, a small island territory of Antigua, was considered a "stud farm" or "nursery" for the breeding of slaves (Augier et al. 161). The hyperathletic disposition of Barbudan slaves, however, may have been less a matter of breeding than of a condition sustained by the "abundance of provisions from their large garden plots" (Lowenthal and Clark 515), garden plots that served a number of purposes, including resistance. While in *The Overthrow of Colonial Slavery* Blackburn describes the period ranging from the end of the eighteenth century to the middle of the nineteenth as a time of "successive challenges to the regimes of colonial slavery, leading to the destruction either of the colonial relationship, or of the slave system, or of both, in one after another of all the major New World colonies" (3), slave resistance in Antigua started well before this period. During the "sugar revolution" (1670–1763), the West Indies had increasingly become "sugar colonies," or "sugar islands," and a fertile soil for slave rebellions (Parry and Sherlock 142), with the first attempt at collective resistance in Antigua occurring in 1736. Although the rebellion was crushed, historian David Barry Gaspar argues that as a "well-organized, islandwide affair, the slave conspiracy of 1736, had it succeeded, would have catapulted Antigua onto the stage of world history as the first territory in the slave heartland of the Caribbean in which slaves seized full control" (*Bondmen and Rebels* xiii). Instead, it was the successful French St. Domingue (Haiti) revolution of 1791–1803 that inspired revolts elsewhere in the Caribbean and has become a source of inspiration for West Indian writers such as

C. L. R. James.[6] Connecting with this long tradition of West Indian resistance, *My Garden (Book)* reverses the "emptiness" of the Caribbean landscape by emphasizing the loss that hovers over the postimperial gardens. Kincaid visits England—or, as she refers to it, the "old suitcase"—and evaluates the imperial gardens long after the demise of empire, when British gardens have become spaces of cultural and historical dislocation. She reminisces, "I was in a country whose inhabitants (they call themselves subjects, not citizens) do not know how to live in the present and cannot imagine living in the future, they can live only in the past, because it, the past, has a clear outcome, a winning outcome" (111–12). Kincaid and photographer Lynn Geesaman meditate on the postimperial gardens in Europe as "scenes of punishing order, scenes that glorify the exact, scenes of chaos playing with a notion of the understandable arrangement (Damme, Belgium), scenes of abandonment (Palatine Hill, Italy), scenes of emptiness (Ostia Antica, Italy), scenes of loneliness (Parc de Caradeuc, France)" (*Poetics of Place* 7). In Kincaid's view, Europe's postimperial gardens no longer show the glory of empire but rather exhibit the death and desolation of the macabre; they remain haunted by the ghosts of the slave trade and the lost colonies. The postimperial gardens remind the subaltern viewer of the historical context of empire from which they emerged.

For Kincaid, the postimperial gardens are haunted by the labor, possession, and forced migration of colonial times. She claims that postimperial gardens evoke the desolation of a dead gardener; the postimperial gardens have been transformed into graveyards of empire, because the gardeners have died. As Kincaid explains, "A garden will die with its owner, a garden will die with the death of the person who made it" (*My Garden* 129). Hence the imperial garden died with the loss of empire. The gardener's death becomes a marked memory in the garden: "Walking around the garden, then, I am full of thoughts of doom, I am full of thoughts of life beyond my own imagining" (*My Garden* 61).

In *My Garden (Book)*, the garden of mourning inscribed with words is the graveyard. There we find names, dates, endless words of good wishes, and sometimes even a short biographical inscription. It is a space of death where writing, order, and flowers coalesce with the alterity of a "beyond." With this in mind, Kincaid compares the rationalized New England graveyard to Antigua's graveyards: whereas the first is built according to reason, the Caribbean graveyard embodies a difference. Kincaid says that her garden in the diaspora is "like a graveyard, but not a graveyard in New England, with its orderliness and neatness and sense of that's-that, but more like a graveyard in a place where I am from, a warm place, where the grave is topped off with a huge mound of loose earth, because death is just another way of being, and the dead will not stay put, and sometimes their actions are more significant, more profound than when they were alive, and so no square structure made out of concrete can contain them" (69). The Caribbean graveyard connects with, rather than distances itself from, death. Gaspar characterizes the graveyard as a location of resistance in the West Indies: "The dirt used in the ritual concoctions [of Obeah] came from the graves of deceased relatives or other slaves, and indeed, many induction ceremonies were performed at grave sites, as the rebels sought assistance and approval from the ancestral spirits" ("Sense" 45). During Antigua's 1736 rebellion, the graveyard was the place where the slaves took their oath of war. The official document *A Genuine Narrative of the Intended Conspiracy of the Negroes at Antigua* (1737) describes this oath: "The manner of administering the Oath, was by drinking a Health in Liquor, either Rum, or some other kind, with Grave-Dirt, and sometimes Cock's Blood infused" (13). As graveyard, the postcolonial garden connects Kincaid not only to death but also to "another way of being"—that is, to a landscape beyond the immediate one of the garden-graveyard. This landscape beyond is dual: a warm place (the West Indies) and a place of death (the Obeah, *jablesse*, voodoo, the spiritual, fantastic, and otherworld of West African religion in the Caribbean).[7] Hence the Caribbean slave garden remains for Kincaid a memory and sign of resistance.

In *The Anti-Slavery Examiner: Emancipation in the West Indies* (1838), Jas A. Thome and J. Horace Kimball inform us that in Antigua each slave house "is to have a garden" (54); but these gardens are "dressed with Obeah," that is, full of poisonous traps to prevent "the theft of their contents" (86). This is important not only in that slaves were allowed to have a garden plot, but also because they were allowed to "grow whatever they like . . . even arsenic or bitter cassava" (115).[8] The gardens were central to slave resistance and to the practice of Obeah. As a syncretic transcultural religion, Obeah is a hybrid spiritual form that uses both magic and sorcery; in the West Indies it became even more hybridized by incorporating aspects of Christianity. For its spells, Obeah employs special herbs, objects, or potions made from livers and gall bladders. A key practice in this West African religion was the cultivation of poisonous seeds to kill the white masters, as West Indian proprietor Matthew Gregory Lewis elaborated in his 1834 memoir:

> There are many excellent qualities in the negro character; their worst faults appear to be, this prejudice respecting Obeah, and the facility with which they are frequently induced to poison to the right hand and to the left. . . .
>
> One of the deadliest poisons used by negroes (and a great variety is perfectly well known to most of them) is prepared from the root of the cassava. Its juice being expressed and allowed to ferment, a small worm is generated, the substance of which being

received into the stomach is of a nature the most pernicious. A small portion of this worm is concealed under one of the thumb-nails, which are suffered to grow long for this purpose; then when the negro has contrived to persuade his intended victim to eat or drink with him, he takes an opportunity, while handing to him a dish or cup, to let the worm fall, which never fails to destroy the person who swallows it. Another means of destruction is to be found (as I am assured) in almost every negro garden throughout the island: it is the arsenic bean, neither useful for food nor ornamental in its appearance; nor can the negroes, when questioned, give any reason for affording it a place in their gardens. (Mistron 75–76)

As this passage indicates, resistance was tied to the garden plot where slaves grew cassava and the highly poisonous "arsenic bean." Gardens in which were cultivated "wild plants" that yielded poison were perceived as key to slave rebellions (*Antigua* 2: 51). In the West Indies, resistance and Obeah practices were deeply connected to gardening; hence the garden's appropriation by the diaspora writer makes of it an allegory for both conquest *and* resistance. The garden as metaphor—established by the rhetoric of conquest to rationalize the decimation of the West Indian landscape—has its underside in the practices of West Indian slave resistance. In *My Garden* (*Book*) Kincaid writes, "On my night table now is a large stack of books and all of them concern the Atlantic slave trade and how the world in which I live sprang from it" (64). It is conquest, its institutions and possessions, that has marked the garden with mourning and resistance. Nevertheless, the garden also became the space to mourn the memory of those killed by history: "But what am I to do with this droopy, weepy sadness in the middle of summer, with its color and shape reminding me of mourning, as it does in spring remind me of mourning, but mourning the death of something that happened long ago[?]" (12).

*   *   *

Kincaid depicts imperial conquest in terms of an encounter with "the death of something that happened long ago" in her short story "Ovando" (1989), whose title refers to the historical figure Nicolas de Ovando, first governor of the West Indies (1502–1509). The governorship was settled in the island of St. Domingo (today the Dominican Republic), under Spanish control. Attempting to fulfill what he took to be the destiny of conquest and colonization, Ovando imposed a system of "sharing" in the West Indies. "Sharing" was his euphemism for the distribution of the indigenous population as a labor force in the service of European settlers. By enslaving the natives, Ovando's "sharing" system had the effect of initiating a process of exterminating the indigenous population.[9] This is particularly important for Kincaid because her grandmother was one of the few surviving Carib Indians in the West Indies. "Sharing" in the West Indies marks the initial death of the Carib subaltern.

As intensive field labor accelerated the Carib's extermination, it also had an impact on the native flora's deforestation. Hence Ovando represents in West Indian history both the enslavement of the indigenous population and the beginnings of a depletion of the islands' natural resources. This historical context illuminates Kincaid's story, which is narrated by an indigenous voice at the moment of conquest. It is a first-person narrative by an Antillean subject describing Ovando's moves and his maddening colonial enterprises. As the story develops, the voice of the narrator progressively fades, thereby mirroring the macabre metamorphosis of Ovando's body.

"Ovando" begins with Frey Nicolas de Ovando knocking on the door of a native Antillean's home. The single phrase "a knock at the door" creates a feeling of expectancy and suspense reminiscent of a horror story. The native Antillean voice describes the encounter with his or her unexpected yet seemingly unavoidable historical visitor:

> It is Frey Nicolas de Ovando. I was surprised. I was not expecting him. But then on reflecting, I could see that though I was not expecting him, he was bound to come. On reflecting, I could see that while I sat I thought, Someone will come to me; if no one comes to me, then I will go to someone. (75)

Ovando's abrupt appearance at the door is taken as inevitable in the sense that an encounter between worlds was sure to happen. Thus the narrative revolves around not when but rather how the encounter between worlds took place.

Ovando surprises not only by showing up uninvited, but also by his physical appearance. He is pictured as a corpse: "Not a shred of flesh was left on his bones" (75). The anonymous narrator describes Ovando as "a complete skeleton except for his brain which remained; and was growing smaller by the millennium," thereby indicating the extent to which Ovando is an allegorical rather than a realistically depicted historical figure. Although Ovando "stank," the narrator receives him with open arms:

> "Ovando," I said, "Ovando," and I smiled at him and threw my arms open to embrace this stinky relic of a person. Many people have said that this was my first big mistake, and I always say, How could it be a mistake to show sympathy, to show trust, to show affection to another human being, on first meeting?

In this parable, Kincaid allegorizes the moment of conquest as a house visit, picturing the house's threshold as a "contact zone." She represents the West Indies as a home that is already domesticated—far from an "empty" landscape. Thus Kincaid reverses the accounts found in historical chronicles. Nevertheless, the visitor acts as if there were no native host, but only a space waiting to be filled:

> With a wave of my hand I threw the door open and said, "Come in." I did this with great exaggeration, for it was unnecessary. You see, he was already inside. And so too when I said, "Sit down, make yourself at home, in fact think of this as your new home," not only was he already sitting down but he said, "Yes, this is the new home I have been looking for, and I already like it so much that I have sent for my relatives in Spain, Portugal, France, England, Germany, Italy, Belgium and The Netherlands." (75–76)

In this scene, Ovando imposes himself much as the colonizer imposed on the native. The European exodus to the Americas during the time of conquest is figured through the many national origins of Ovando's relatives, and the narrator, continuing in an absurdist allegorical mode, indicates that Ovando brought not only his relatives but also culture: "He carried with him the following things: bibles, cathedrals, museums (for he was already an established collector), libraries (banks, really, in which he stored the contents of his diminishing brain), the contents of a drawing room" (75).

In this story, the allegory of the garden-island becomes overlaid with the allegory of death and conquest. Even though Ovando pictures the West Indies as a "paradise" (78), he writes his accounts of empire by destroying the garden that he is making into myth. Ovando deforests the islands into leaves of paper "six inches long and six inches wide" (80), leaving behind only stumps, in order to write the narrative of his conquests:

> The document that he had prepared for me was only six inches long and six inches wide, but it was made from the pulp of one hundred and ten trees and these trees had taken ten millennia to reach the exquisite state of beauty in which Ovando found them.... These trees Ovando had ordered cut down so that only stumps remained, and boiled and pounded and dried, and the process repeated again and again until they were reduced to something that measured six inches by six inches. Holding it up to the light, he said, "Do you see?" (80)

This powerful question is posed not only by Ovando to the narrator, but also by Kincaid to her contemporary audience: Do you see the connection between deforestation and the writing of imperial history?

Ovando destroys not only nature but also the indigenous Carib voice narrating the story. As several critics have noted, the narrative style of "Ovando" shifts from one in which the native voice is quoted directly to one devoid of direct speech. Ovando's own rotting body allegorizes this decimation of native life and voice; hence the decomposing form of the conqueror signals the spreading sickness of the empire, in which the corroding body of death colonizes all gardens. Ovando's pestilent body is depicted as "covered with sores . . . he lay on a bed of broken glass bottles" (82). In this bed, Ovando lies touching and exposing his infested "child-sized penis"—an image that is repeated, with a difference, in *My Brother*. Ovando's decaying penis figures his dissemination of death and destruction—a dissemination that Kincaid understands her brother to reap centuries later. Just as they did with the dahlias, the imperial powers perfected and transported their deterioration. Hence Kincaid's representing colonial power through images of putrefaction.

"Ovando" ends with the narrator's acknowledging a fear of becoming possessed by her own allegory, as if being obsessed by the subject of imperial conquest were itself another form of colonization. For the Carib narrator, the European conqueror suffered from an excessive self-love, which translated into his desire to occupy all space with his own image:

> Such a love is a worm asleep in every heart, and must never be awakened; such a love lies like kindling in every heart, and must never be lit. A charge against Ovando, then, is that he loved himself so that all other selves and all other things became nothing to him. I became nothing to Ovando. My relatives became nothing to Ovando. Everything that could trace its lineage through me became nothing to Ovando. And so it came to be that Ovando loved nothing, lived in nothing and died in just that way. I cannot judge Ovando. I have exhausted myself laying out before him his transgressions. I am exhausted from shielding myself so that his sins do not obsess and so possess me. (82–83)

The Carib voice telling the story finally fades—"exhausted"—coincident with the spread of illness during conquest. "Ovando" narrates the spread of imperial disease and so functions as an allegory that explains the death of the indigenous and subaltern. It is a death that the West Indies continues to mourn at a historical level. In Kincaid, this mourning for the deaths of conquest is tied to the death of her queer brother from AIDS-related illness. Thus in "Ovando" and for Kincaid's brother, the death of the subaltern connects lost memories to the silences of history.

In 1997, Kincaid published *My Brother*, a memoir of her brother Devon Drew. Structured in the form of two long essays, *My Brother* relates the memory of her brother's sickness and his death from AIDS on January 19, 1996. Typical of her introspective autobiographical style, Kincaid weaves descriptions of her life in the Caribbean diaspora with an account of the disease and death of her brother in Antigua. *My Brother* is based on a different type of mourning, however, since it grieves the loss of a brother whom its author did not know very well, having left Antigua for New York when he was a child.[10] The book provides a powerful narrative of mourning and memory in the diaspora, a paradoxical mourning that requires getting acquainted with the person at the same time that one is grieving his loss. Although death and loss have been present as motifs in Kincaid's earlier work, such as *At the Bottom of the River* and *Annie John*, *My Brother* confronts a specifically familial death and the processes of loss and decay of a deteriorating body. Furthermore, this decaying body conceals the alterity of a sexual difference.

Devon, the youngest of all Kincaid's brothers, was thirty-three years old when he died. In what has been depicted as "unsparing honesty" (Graham) and an "unflinching account" (Rubin), Kincaid recounts her brother's involvement in Rastafarian music, Antigua's drug culture, and sexual promiscuity.[11] Despite the reviewers' impulse to sensationalize this narrative, Kincaid's book is not about only sex, drugs, and Caribbean rock 'n' roll; rather, *My Brother* attempts to contextualize her mourning in the Caribbean diaspora via the memory of a sexual alterity in the West Indies. The narrative begins with Kincaid tending to her brother in Antigua's main public hospital. She tells us of his degenerating body and the memories that emerge with decay and the proximity of loss. She goes on to describe his temporary recuperation with the help of AZT drugs that she sends him from the United States (necessary since Antigua does not have, or does not want to allocate, the resources needed to provide for the treatment of people with AIDS). Kincaid also describes the culture of stigmatization that people with AIDS in Antigua suffer. Most poignant of all is the memory of how she discovered that her dead brother was queer: Kincaid learned of her brother's sexuality a few days after he died, during a visit to Chicago, from a lesbian friend of his who used to lend her house in Antigua as a sort of safe haven for same-sex couples to manifest their culturally unsanctioned sexuality. Hence the moment when Kincaid claims not to have known her brother is identical to the moment when she starts mourning him in the Caribbean diaspora.

Besides a passion for music, her brother had an inclination for gardens, much like Kincaid herself. Her own life of gardening and reading about the garden is disrupted by news of her brother's illness in Antigua:

> At the time the phone call came telling me of my brother's illness, among the many comforts, luxuries, that I enjoyed was reading a book, *The Education of a Gardener*, written by a man named Russell Page. . . . The next time I opened this book I was sitting on the lawn in front of Gweneth O'Reilly ward and my brother was sitting in a chair next to me. It was many days later. He could barely walk, he could barely sit up, he was like an old man. The walk from his bed to the lawn had exhausted him. We looked out on an ordinary Antiguan landscape. There was a deliberate planting of willow trees, planted, I suspect, a long time ago, when Antigua was still a colony and the colonial government would have been responsible for the running of the hospital. . . . And when I picked up that book again, *The Education of a Gardener*, I looked at my brother, for he was a gardener also, and I wondered, if his life had taken a certain turn, if he had caused his life to take a different turn, might he have written a book with such a title? (10–11)

Kincaid connects the garden to writing and to the diaspora. Her brother lacked the experience of living in the diaspora and—remaining in Antigua— did not "take a different turn." Still, her brother had a passion for gardening and for reading history, especially Thomas Coke's *A History of the West Indies* (1808–11), where he read of Colonel Codrington's "cultivat[ing] the sugar cane with extraordinary success in Barbadoes; and having obtained certain intelligence that the soil of Antigua was well adapted to its propagation, he became one of its resident inhabitants . . . his name will be long remembered in the West Indies" (2: 411).

While her brother's disease was in remission with the help of AZT, Kincaid used to go for walks with him around the botanical gardens. She reminisces about these walks in *My Brother*:

> My brother and I walked up to the botanical gardens and found they were closed for repairs; they had been neglected for many years, many specimens had died, but now someone—most likely a Canadian, because they are so generous to the self-destructive of the world—a Canadian had given money to have the botanical gardens restored. We walked around the perimeter, and using a book on tropical botany that I carried and also relying on our own knowledge, we identified many plants. But then we came to

a tree that we could not identify, not on our own, not from the book. It was a tree, only a tree, and it was either just emerging from complete dormancy or it was half-dead, half-alive. My brother and I became obsessed with this tree, its bark, its leaves, its shape; we wondered where it was really from, what sort of tree it was. If it crossed his mind that this tree, coming out of a dormancy, a natural sleep, a temporary death, or just half-dead, bore any resemblance to him right then and there, he did not say, he did not let me know in any way. (79–80)

Conflating her brother's status with that of an enigmatic "half-dead" tree, Kincaid connects the postcolonial body to a neocolonial condition via the imagery of the decaying postcolonial botanical garden. This image also connects the botanical garden's need for a constant influx of foreign capital with the Antiguan AIDS-ridden body's need for a steady supply of foreign drugs. For Kincaid, the decaying institutional ruins of empire—such as the botanical garden—mirror the queer subaltern's condition.

The metaphors of spreading neocolonialism return us to the historical allegories of "Ovando," the garden, and imperial expansion. In a crucial scene in *My Brother*, it becomes clear that from Kincaid's perspective, her brother's illness repeats imperial degeneration:

I stood looking at him for a long time before he realized I was there. And then when he did, he suddenly threw the sheets away from himself, tore his pajama bottoms away from his waist, revealing his penis, and then he grabbed his penis in his hand and held it up, and *his penis looked like a bruised flower that had been cut short on the stem*; it was covered with sores and on the sores was a white substance, almost creamy, almost floury, a fungus. When he grabbed his penis in his hand, he suddenly pointed it at me, a sort of thrusting gesture, and he said in a voice that was full of deep panic and deep fear, "Jamaica, look at this, just look at this." Everything about this one gesture was disorienting; what to do, what to say; to see my brother's grown-up-man penis, and to see his penis looking like that, to see him no longer able to understand that perhaps he shouldn't just show me—his sister—his penis, without preparing me to see his penis. I did not want to see his penis; at that moment I did not want to see any penis at all. (91; emphasis added)

Her brother's corroded penis replicates the image of Ovando's penis. As a bruised flower or truncated stem, Devon's penis also is reminiscent of the stumps left behind in a deforested garden. For this Caribbean diaspora writer, the images of Ovando and her brother become conflated in the historical allegories of imperialism. Both are visualized via allegories of the garden. Whereas Ovando allegorizes colonialism, her brother allegorizes the subaltern neocolonial condition. Yet both meet in the garden, where, according to Kincaid, Ovando sows death and her brother harvests it.

Kincaid's brother represents the alterity at the heart of her writing's allegory—that is, he represents a certain wildness of unlawful desire. As she explains, her brother's death "raises another kind of interest, another kind of haunting," that of a nonheteronormative sexuality (178). Although her brother remains sexually enigmatic (in the sense that he is neither obviously gay nor yet unequivocally straight), Kincaid politicizes his sexuality by exposing through writing a subaltern sexuality for which no discourse yet exists in Antigua's history. His queerness thus represents a condition of internal exile that comes to stand for the subaltern's sexual alterity.[12] Her brother's alterity, his otherness, is yet more troubling because he is living with AIDS and having unprotected sexual encounters with local young women, in order to conceal his homosexual practices. His death reveals a neocolonial Antiguan condition of despair on the part of disenfranchised members of society. And for the Caribbean diaspora writer, this death evokes a different type of connection:

> I was haunted by everything that had happened since he died and everything that had happened before he died, and everything that was happening as I went from the city of Chicago and its view of the frozen lake of blue, a blue that was not permanent, a blue that would change with the season (a thing my brother would never know, a change of season, for he never left the place in which he was born). (168)

What haunts this Caribbean diaspora writer is the difference between her condition and that of her subaltern brother: his internal exile as queer contrasts sharply with her own exile in the diaspora. The difference lies also in the contrast between writing personal history and simply reading official history, since her brother could read only a history that had written him out of existence. Queer Antiguans represent a gap or silence within postcolonial history. Just as the West Indian slave gardens haunt the empire, the alterity of subaltern and sexual difference hovers over the myth of the West Indies as Eden. The legacy of the conquest's myths, with Eden as primordial symbol of gender difference, is challenged in a new way by articulating the death of the queer subaltern. Hence the Caribbean subaltern's death indexes the repressed spaces of national history.

*   *   *

Kincaid mourns the silences of Antiguan history in more than one way. From the diaspora, she mourns the subaltern's internal exile by connecting her brother's death from AIDS with a memory of his infancy. She does this by recounting a poignant episode when her brother was a baby and she was instructed to take care of him. It is a memory that hovers over the entire text, building upon a sentiment of inadequacy, because she considers his life as a truncated version of her own. She sees the failings of the neocolonial subject in its postcolonial national condition from the vantage point of the diaspora writer. Her writing establishes a connection between the memory of her brother's childhood and the despairing life in Caribbean society:

> My brother, the one who is dying, who has died, who while dying could not take himself to the bathroom and freely control his bowel movements, then as a little boy, two years old, wore diapers and needed to have someone change them from time to time when they grew soiled. That day (and I cannot remember if it was a Monday, a Tuesday, or a Wednesday, but I do know with certainty that it was not a Saturday or a Sunday) when I had been reading instead of taking care of him, I did not notice that in his diaper was a deposit of my brother's stool, and by the time my mother returned from her errands—and she did notice it—the deposit of stool had hardened and taken the shape of a measure of weight, something used in a grocery store or in the fish market or the meat market or the market where only ground provisions are sold; it was the size of that measure signifying a pound. And in it, this picture of my brother's hardened stool, a memory, a moment of my own life is frozen; for his diaper sagged with a weight that was not gold but its opposite, a weight whose value would not bring us good fortune, a weight that only emphasized our family's despair: our fortunes, our prospects were not more than the contents of my brothers diaper, and the contents were only shit. (*My Brother* 130–31)

What she calls elsewhere the "repressed memory" of a "hardened stool" is tied not only to an economic value but also to the weight of writing, to the mourning for books, and hence to the tools of the diaspora writer. As a teenager, Kincaid's passion was increasingly invested in literature and distant from the family's despair. If memory is allegorized as a "hardened stool," it is because it carries a history of loss—a loss that for Kincaid leads to the reading of literature:

It was because I had neglected my brother when he was two years old and instead read a book that my mother gathered up all the books I owned and put them on a pile on her stone heap, sprinkling them with kerosene and then setting them alight; I cannot remember the titles of these books, I cannot remember what they were about (they would have been novels, at fifteen I read only novels), but it would not be so strange if I spent the rest of my life trying to bring those books back to my life by writing them again and again until they were perfect, unscathed by fire of any kind. (197–98)

The burning of books triggers in Kincaid the need to write. We have to go to her early novel *Annie John* to discover specifically which book needs to be rewritten by this Caribbean diaspora writer. In this semi-autobiographical novel, the protagonist-narrator explains her melancholy in terms of literature:

In the year I turned fifteen, I felt more unhappy than I ever imagined anyone could be. . . . I tried to imagine that I was like a girl in one of the books I had read—a girl who had suffered much at the hands of a cruel step-parent, or a girl who suddenly found herself without any parents at all. When reading about such a girl, I would heap even more suffering on her if I felt the author hadn't gone far enough. In the end, of course, everything was resolved happily for the girl. . . . But I was not in a book. I was always just sitting there with the thimble that weighed worlds fastened deep inside me, the sun beating down on me. Everything I used to care about had turned sour. (85–86)

Though *Jane Eyre* is never mentioned, the girl pictured here is clearly Charlotte Brontë's eponymous heroine. This passage appears in a chapter titled "Somewhere, Belgium," which refers to Brontë's experiences—fictionalized in *Villette* (1853) and *The Professor* (1857)—during the period she lived in Brussels. *Jane Eyre* was the young Kincaid's favorite novel; its narrative of torment is one that the adult writer tries to compose and perfect "again and again." She wants to perfect it because the suffering depicted in *Jane Eyre* is light by comparison with the cruelty of West Indian history. Brontë's novel is part of Kincaid's history because, I surmise, it was in the pile of books burned by her mother. If this is the case, then mourning her brother and his "hardened stool" would be connected to mourning the loss of *Jane Eyre*. Furthermore, the chapter title "Somewhere, Belgium" pictures Brontë herself as a writer living abroad. The burning of *Jane Eyre* also evokes

Brontë's character Bertha, the diasporic West Indian "madwoman" who burns Thornfield Hall, with its haunted parks and parterres.

Juxtaposing the passage from *Annie John* with the book-burning scene in *My Brother* allows us to grasp what I call the hybridity of memory and of mourning. Mourning is hybrid because its elements are intertextual and transcultural. This makes mourning a space of cross-cultural connection for the diaspora writer: "my brother dying, the memory of my books being burned because I had neglected my brother who was dying when he was a small child. . . . And then again, and then again" (137). The hybridity of mourning enables Kincaid to relive these connections because by mourning her brother she mourns also a larger cultural condition. She mourns a memory that is both personal *and* historical, one that is of social urgency *and* literary significance. In this way, her hybrid memory connects this diaspora writer intertextually and socially to the West Indian context and its social needs. The hybridity of mourning is key to the diaspora writer, because memories in the diaspora are hybrid. In *My Brother*, mourning connects the diaspora writer to the queer subaltern's death, but also to the hybrid memory of a "hardened stool" and of a *Jane Eyre* in flames.

The hybridity of memory in this Caribbean diaspora writer consequently entails an understanding of mourning as a hybrid process. By elaborating the history of hybridity as a concept in the Caribbean context, my account extends and revises Robert Young's critique of this term in postcolonial theory; but whereas Young focuses on the term's deployment in British imperialism, I have emphasized hybridity's potential for resistance to imperialism by showing how a Caribbean diaspora writer makes hybridization central to her political critique. I would like to suggest how understanding the hybridity of mourning—its simultaneously personal and political aspects—helps to revise current theories of mourning in postcolonial studies. Mourning is a central focus of Kincaid's writing and therefore of critical discussion of her work. But Kincaid's critics tend to assume that mourning leads to regeneration and health: mourning is a stage that must be superseded via "working through" (Freud's *Dürcharbeiten*). For Kincaid's critics, mourning serves the purpose of building a bridge to a new self or an improved identity. Rather than being considered a process of making connections that are fruitful in and of themselves, mourning is treated as an investment that leads to profit, as trees lead to paper. For these critics, mourning has to be overcome; its value lies only in what follows. In this model, mourning is tacitly pathologized, its value being only exchange value.[13]

By depathologizing mourning, my argument about Kincaid suggests that mourning is a cultural and historical, not only an individual or psychological, process, and that it occurs through writing. For this diaspora writer, mourning is not a pathological stage that must be overcome; rather, mourning is the culturally normative yet highly political strategy through which a diaspora writer makes transcultural connections. In making this argument about mourning as a mode of connectivity, I draw on and extend Edward Said's comments, in *Culture and Imperialism*, about "new types of connections." Said concludes:

> Once we accept the actual configuration of literary experiences overlapping with one another and interdependent, despite national boundaries and coercively legislated national autonomies, history and geography are transfigured in new maps, in new far less stable entities, in new types of connections. Exile, far from being the fate of nearly forgotten unfortunates who are dispossessed and expatriated, becomes something closer to a norm, an experience of crossing boundaries and charting new territories in defiance of the classic canonic enclosures, however much its loss and sadness should be acknowledged and registered. Newly changed models and types jostle against the older ones. (317)

When we factor into this account a "newly changed model" of mourning, Kincaid's case dramatizes Said's general claims about the diaspora condition. The hybridity of mourning is a way of describing these connections, because by mourning personal losses, the diaspora writer creates an allegory of imperialism and so makes an implicitly political critique. It is through the allusiveness of her prose that Kincaid evokes this allegory and hybridization. Allusiveness is more than a purely literary style or technique for Kincaid, because allusions can be a way of making connections that are also cultural and political. Hence the importance for her of writing, since writing crystallizes her life in the Caribbean diaspora and connects her mourning with the death of her brother and with the Caribbean subaltern's condition.

Speaking of the death of her brother, who could not write his own garden book, Kincaid meditates on the relation between death and writing:

> I became a writer out of desperation, so when I first heard my brother was dying I was familiar with the act of saving myself: I would write about him. I would write about his dying.... When I heard about my brother's illness and his dying, I knew, instinctively, that to understand it, or to make an attempt at understanding his dying, and not to die with him, I would write about it. (195–96)

Unlike the case of the gardener whose death cuts short the life of the garden, the death of her brother allows the coming to life of the diaspora writer.

If at the end of this narrative of mourning in *My Brother* Kincaid tries to remember for whom and why she writes, it is because what remains is the connectivity—"again and again"—of mourning "different forms" of death in the diaspora. "And so I wrote about the dead for the dead," she says (197). The Caribbean diaspora writer, as postcolonial, is not haunted by death, for death is simply "another form of being," a zone of hybrid connectedness. The garden and mourning become allegories of political reflection that reconnect her to memories of a decaying past. For Kincaid, the hybridity of mourning points to diasporic memories as hybrid forms of otherness. Beyond *Hamlet*, as the sign par excellence of a pathological mourning, and beyond the pathologies of empire, the work of mourning connects the diaspora writer to hybrid forms of loss and hence to a diasporic understanding of death and rootedness.

Notes

1. With respect to the criticism on Kincaid, my essay offers a very different account of mourning, one that goes against the grain of established readings. A principal motif in the criticism has been Kincaid's relationship with her mother, and the complex connection between mother and motherland. Moira Ferguson, for example, examines the "ambiguously represented mother" as a figure that conflates the biological and colonial (2). For similar approaches, see Susheila Nasta on histories of exile literature; Wendy Dutton on Kincaid's "mother obsessed" discourse; and Patricia Ismond on the question of the "damaged psyche."

2. Although taking center stage in *My Garden* (*Book*), this connection was established in Kincaid's and Eric Fischl's *Annie, Gwen, Lilly, Pam and Tulip* (1986), a children's book in which personified flowers narrate an allegory of imperial conquest. The flowers fear the disruption of their Edenic paradise: "In this, our perfect place: here patches of flowers in bloom, forged, as we have seen, from one whole and complete thing and enveloped in tremendous truth and moving beauty; in this way we live and die and live again forever . . . I hear the voice say, Hullo! Hullo! Hullo! How new and strange and cold is the voice; the words strike at me like pellets released from a slingshot; the voice moves swiftly in many different directions and I feel that it aims to disturb and conquer" (5). For useful historical accounts of the relation between empire and horticulture, see Crosby and Cook.

3. Although my critique of this passage focuses on the symptomatic inconsistencies of imperial power/knowledge relations, mention also might be made of some of its factual inaccuracies. For instance, Puerto Rico was not simply "often called" San Juan but actually was named San Juan Bautista (St. John the Baptist) by Columbus himself, and it was only later that the name of its capital, Puerto Rico, became the name of the island. We might also register that the native-Antillean name for the island was originally "Borikén," a name that was erased in the colonization process. Further inaccuracies consist in the fact that Espaniola, St. Domingo, and Hayti are not names for the same island; in fact, Espaniola is this island's name. Since Espaniola is the territory of two independent nations, St. Domingo refers only to the Spanish-speaking eastern side of the island, and Hayti refers solely to the French-colonized western side of the island.

4. Helen Tiffin discusses Kincaid's novel *Lucy* in terms of what she calls the "daffodil complex." The protagonist "Lucy"—a young Antiguan woman living in New York—becomes angry after seeing daffodils for the first time. In Antigua there are no daffodil plants, yet at

school she had been forced to memorize Wordsworth's "I Wandered Lonely as a Cloud," a poem in which daffodils figure the compensatory value of memory. While in the poem the memory of daffodils brings joy—"And then my heart with pleasure fills, / And dances with the daffodils"—in the novel, the memory of daffodils unleashes Lucy's murderous fury. See also Donnell for a reading of daffodils in Kincaid as metaphors of cultural resistance. For a discussion of the relation between literature and schooling in the Caribbean bildungsroman, see Tapping.

5. As a consequence of importing plant-breeding techniques into the Caribbean labor context, the success of the botanical gardens also influenced the historical narratives of colonial Antigua by encouraging genealogies of blood and family tree lineage. The preoccupation with breeding was not reserved for plants and slaves but became an obsession in the writing of history, too, as epitomized in Vere Langford Oliver's *History of the Island of Antigua* (1894), one of the few historical accounts of Antigua written in the nineteenth century. Its two volumes consist solely of pedigrees of the families of Antigua's elite class.

6. For a historical account of the Haitian revolution that underscores its importance in the long history of Caribbean resistance, see James's *The Black Jacobins*.

7. Obeah is "a system of beliefs grounded in spirituality and an acknowledgement of the supernatural and involving aspects of witchcraft, sorcery, magic, spells, and healing" (Frye 198). In a different register, *jablesse* refers to a vampiric figure in Caribbean folklore, "a person who can turn into anything. . . . Their eyes shine like lamps, so bright that you can't look," as Kincaid defines it in *At the Bottom of the River* (9). For a discussion of such phenomena in Kincaid's literary imagination, see Paravisini-Gebert (esp. 54–57).

8. Thome and Kimball emphasize here just one aspect of the provision garden, a long-established tradition in Caribbean slave societies that was to be augmented in post-Emancipation Antigua. The existence of slave gardens, generally referred to as "provision grounds" or "provision gardens," is well documented for periods long before emancipation in the British Caribbean. In comparison to the other British islands, however, Antigua had fewer provision gardens due to its high population density and limited agricultural land. This situation accentuated the importance of the existing garden plots and added to their cultural value. These gardens provided the dietary subsistence not only of the slaves but also of the plantation owners, as well as yielding produce that was traded by the slaves in their own markets. Some slaves were even able to purchase their own freedom from the revenue made at these markets. For more on the economic and social role of the provision gardens in Caribbean plantocracies, see Green (esp. 25–27). For the importance of provision gardens in the politics of rebellion in post-Emancipation Jamaica, see Bakan (esp. 22–26) and Heuman (esp. 183–84). Kincaid's allegory of the postcolonial garden as a space of resistance is not constrained by Antiguan history but includes the greater Caribbean cultural experience, in the same way that her garden in the diaspora attempts to represent not just Antigua but the overall map of the Caribbean Sea, including its many islands.

9. Ovando's "sharing" system led not only to the enslavement of the indigenous population, but also subsequently created a demand for further slaves, because enslavement and harsh working conditions killed off the natives in large numbers. The continuing demand for slaves prompted the king of Spain to grant a permit, in the sixteenth century, for the importation of Africans to the New World. This chain of events initiated the African diaspora and led to the creation of a hybrid population in the West Indies. For a detailed history of this encounter, see Burns (esp. 35–58); Garcia (esp. 24–32); and Newton (esp. 17–33).

10. The impact of Devon's birth on Kincaid's fiction is an established topic in Kincaid criticism. See Simmons (esp. 100–15); Paravisini-Gebert (esp. 106–107); Natov; Murdoch, and Caton.

11. These quotations are taken from the cover of the paperback edition of *My Brother*.

12. For a different reading, which stresses the role of the subaltern as a marked absence in diaspora texts, see Aparajita Sagar's very suggestive essay "'Dr. Freud for Visitor.'"

13. This understanding of mourning dominates not only Kincaid criticism, but also postcolonial theory and recent psychoanalytic theories of subjectivity. See, for example, E. San Juan's *Beyond Postcolonial Theory* and Judith Butler's *The Psychic Life of Power*.

WORKS CITED

Antigua and the Antiguans: A Full Account of the Colony and Its Inhabitants from the Time of the Caribs to the Present Day, Interspersed with Anecdotes and Legends. 2 vols. London: Saunders and Otley, 1844.

Augier, F. R., S. C. Gordon, D. G. Hall, and M. Reckford. *The Making of the West Indies*. London: Longmans, Grees, 1960.

Austen, Jane. *Mansfield Park*. 1814. New York: Modern Library, 1995.

Bakan, Abigail B. *Ideology and Class Conflict in Jamaica: The Politics of Rebellion*. Montreal: McGill-Queen's UP, 1990.

Bhabha, Homi K. *The Location of Culture*. London: Routledge, 1994.

Blackburn, Robin. *The Making of New World Slavery: From the Baroque to the Modern, 1492–1800*. London: Verso, 1997.

———. *The Overthrow of Colonial Slavery, 1776–1848*. London: Verso, 1988.

Brockway, Lucile H. *Science and Colonial Expansion: The Role of the British Botanic Gardens*. New York: Academic P, 1979.

Brontë, Charlotte. *Jane Eyre*. 1847. New York: Modern Library, 1997.

———. *The Professor*. 1857. New York: Modern Library, 1997.

———. *Villette*. 1853. New York: Modern Library, 1997.

Burn, W[illiam] L[aurence]. *The British West Indies*. London: Mayflower, 1951.

Burns, Sir Alan Cuthbert. *History of the British West Indies*. 1954. London: Allen and Unwin, 1965.

Butler, Judith. *The Psychic Life of Power: Theories in Subjection*. Stanford: Stanford UP, 1997.

Caton, Louis F. "Romantic Struggles: The *Bildungsroman* and Mother–Daughter Bonding in Jamaica Kincaid's *Annie John*." *Melus* 21.3 (Fall 1996): 125–42.

Cohen, Robin. *Global Diasporas: An Introduction*. Seattle: U of Washington P, 1997.

Coke, Thomas. *A History of the West Indies*. 1808–11. 3 vols. Miami, FL: Mnemosyne P, 1969.

Cook, Noble David. *Born to Die: Disease and New World Conquest, 1492–1650*. Cambridge: Cambridge UP, 1998.

Crosby, Alfred W. *Ecological Imperialism: The Biological Expansion of Europe, 900–1900*. Cambridge: Cambridge UP, 1993.

Donnell, Alison. "Dreaming of Daffodils: Cultural Resistance in the Narratives of Theory." *Kunapipi* 14.2 (1992): 45–52.

Dutton, Wendy. "Merge and Separate: Jamaica Kincaid's Fiction." *World Literature Today* 63.3 (Summer 1989): 406–10.

Elliott, Brent. *Victorian Gardens*. London: B. T. Batsford, 1986.

Ferguson, Moira. *Jamaica Kincaid: Where the Land Meets the Body*. Charlottesville: UP of Virginia, 1994.

Fernández Olmos, Margarite, and Lizabeth Paravisini-Gebert, eds. *Sacred Possessions: Vodou, Santería, Obeah, and the Caribbean*. New Brunswick, NJ: Rutgers UP, 1997.

Frye, Karla Y. E. "'An Article of Faith': Obeah and Hybrid Identities in Elizabeth Nunez-Harrell's *When Rocks Dance.*" Fernández Olmos and Paravisini-Gebert 195–215.

Garcia, A. *History of the West Indies.* London: George G. Harrap, 1965.

Gaspar, David Barry. *Bondmen and Rebels: A Study of Master–Slave Relations in Antigua with Implications for Colonial British America.* Baltimore, MD: Johns Hopkins UP, 1985.

———. "From 'The Sense of their Slavery'; Slave Women and Resistance in Antigua, 1632–1763." Mistron 43–47. [Also in *More Than Chattel: Black Women and Slavery in the Americas.* Ed. David Barry Gaspar and Darlene Clark Hine. Bloomington: Indiana UP, 1996. 218–38.]

A Genuine Narrative of the Intended Conspiracy of the Negroes at Antigua. 1737. New York: Arno, 1972.

Green, William A. *British Slave Emancipation: The Sugar Colonies and the Great Experiment, 1830–1865.* 1976. Oxford: Clarendon, 1991.

Grove, Richard H. *Green Imperialism: Colonial Expansion, Tropical Island Edens and the Origins of Environmentalism, 1600–1860.* New York: Cambridge UP, 1995.

Hall, Stuart. "The Question of Cultural Identity." *Modernity and Its Futures.* Ed. Stuart Hall, David Held, and Tony McGrew. Cambridge: Polity P, 1992. 273–316.

Heuman, Gad J. *"The Killing Time": The Morant Bay Rebellion in Jamaica.* Knoxville: U of Tennessee P, 1994.

Ismond, Patricia. "Jamaica Kincaid: 'First they must be children.'" *World Literature Written in English* 28.2 (Autumn 1988): 336–41.

James, C. L. R. *The Black Jacobins: Toussaint L'Overture and the San Domingo Revolution.* 1963. New York: Vintage, 1989.

Kincaid, Jamaica. *Annie John.* 1983. New York: Plume, 1986.

———. *At the Bottom of the River.* 1978. New York: Farrar, 1984.

———. *The Autobiography of My Mother.* 1996. New York: Plume, 1997.

———. *Lucy.* New York: Farrar, 1990.

———. *My Brother.* 1997. New York: Noonday, 1998.

———, ed. *My Favorite Plant: Writers and Gardeners on the Plants They Love.* New York: Farrar, 1998.

———. *My Garden (Book).* New York: Farrar, 1999.

———. "Ovando." *Conjunctions* 14 (1989): 75–83. Rpt. in *Mistresses of the Dark: 25 Macabre Tales by Master Storytellers.* Ed. Stefan Dziemianowicz, Denise Little, and Robert Weinberg. New York: Barnes and Noble, 1998. 216–24.

Kincaid, Jamaica, and Eric Fischl. *Annie, Gwen, Lilly, Pam and Tulip.* 1986. New York: Knopf, 1989.

Kincaid, Jamaica, and Lynn Geesaman. *Poetics of Place.* New York: Umbrage Editions, 1998.

Lewis, Matthew Gregory. *Journal of a West India Proprietor, Kept During a Residence in the Island of Jamaica.* 1834. Mistron 75–79.

Lowenthal, David, and Colin G. Clarke. "Slave-Breeding in Barbuda: The Past of a Negro Myth." *The New York Academy of Sciences* 292 (1977): 510–33.

Mistron, Deborah, ed. *Understanding Jamaica Kincaid's Annie John.* Westport, CT: Greenwood, 1999.

Morgan, Joan, and Alison Richards. *A Paradise out of a Common Field: The Pleasures and Plenty of the Victorian Garden.* New York: Harper, 1990.

Murdoch, Adlai H. "Severing the (M)Other Connection: The Representation of Cultural Identity in Jamaica Kincaid's *Annie John.*" *Callaloo* 13.2 (Spring 1990): 325–40.

Nasta, Susheila. "Motherlands, Mothercultures, Mothertongues: Women's Writing in the Caribbean." *Shades of Empire in Colonial and Post-Colonial Literatures*. Ed. C. C. Barfoot and Theo D'haen. Amsterdam: Rodopi, 1993. 211–20.

Natov, Roni. "Mothers and Daughters: Jamaica Kincaid's Pre-Oedipal Narrative." *Children's Literature* 18 (1990): 1–16.

Newton, Arthur Percival. *The European Nations in the West Indies, 1493–1688*. London: A. and C. Black, 1933.

Oliver, Vere Langford. *The History of the Island of Antigua: One of the Leeward Caribbees in the West Indies, From the First Settlement in 1635 to the Present Time*. 2 vols. London: Mitchell and Hughes, 1894–99.

Paravisini-Gebert, Lizabeth. *Jamaica Kincaid: A Critical Companion*. Westport, CT: Greenwood, 1999.

Parry, J. H. and P. M. Sherlock. *A Short History of the West Indies*. London: Macmillan, 1963.

Penson, Lillian M. *The Colonial Agents of the British West Indies*. London: Frank Cass, 1971.

Pratt, Mary Louise. *Imperial Eyes: Travel Writing and Transculturation*. London: Routledge, 1992.

Rushdie, Salman. *Imaginary Homelands: Essays and Criticism, 1981–1991*. New York: Penguin, 1991.

Sagar, Aparajita. "'Dr. Freud for Visitor': Afro-Caribbean Writers and the Question of Diaspora." *Semiotics 1994*. Ed. C. W. Spinks and John Deely. New York: Peter Lang, 1995. 471–80.

Said, Edward W. *Culture and Imperialism*. New York: Vintage, 1993.

San Juan, E., Jr. *Beyond Postcolonial Theory*. 1998. New York: St. Martin's, 1999.

Simmons, Diane. *Jamaica Kincaid*. New York: Twayne, 1994.

Sommer, Doris. "Allegory and Dialectics: A Match Made in Romance." *Gendered Agents: Women and Institutional Knowledge*. Ed. Silvestra Mariniello and Paul A. Bové. Durham, NC: Duke UP, 1998. 325–48.

Southey, Captain Thomas. *Chronological History of the West Indies*. 3 vols. 1827. London: Frank Cass, 1968.

Stuart, David. *The Garden Triumphant: A Victorian Legacy*. New York: Harper, 1988.

Tapping, Craig. "Children and History in the Caribbean Novel: George Lamming's *In the Castle of My Skin* and Jamaica Kincaid's *Annie John*." *Kunapipi* 11.2 (1989): 51–59.

Thome, Jas A., and J. Horace Kimball. *The Anti-Slavery Examiner: Emancipation in the West Indies: A Six Months' Tour of Antigua, Barbadoes, and Jamaica, in the Year 1837*. 1838. Mistron 52–55.

Tiffin, Helen. "Cold Hearts and (Foreign) Tongues: Recitation and the Reclamation of the Female Body in the Works of Erna Brodber and Jamaica Kincaid." *Callaloo* 16.4 (Fall 1993): 909–21.

Young, Robert J. C. *Colonial Desire: Hybridity in Theory, Culture and Race*. London: Routledge, 1995.

MARIA HELENA LIMA

Imaginary Homelands in Jamaica Kincaid's Narratives of Development

They should never have left their home, their precious England, a place they loved so much, a place they had to leave but could never forget. And so everywhere they went they turned it into England; and everybody they met they turned English. But no place could ever really be England, and nobody who did not look exactly like them would ever be English, so you can imagine the destruction of people and land that came from that. (*A Small Place* 24)

It was because I had neglected my brother when he was two years old and instead read a book that my mother gathered up all the books I owned and put them on a pile on her stone heap, sprinkling them with kerosene and then setting them alight; I cannot remember the titles of these books, I cannot remember what they were about (they would have been novels, at fifteen I read only novels), but it would not be so strange if I spent the rest of my life trying to bring those books back to my life by writing them again and again until they were perfect, unscathed by fire of any kind. For a very long time I had the perfect reader for what I would write and place in the unscathed books; the source of the books has not died, it only comes alive again and

From *Callaloo* 25, no. 3 (Summer 2002). © 2002 by Charles H. Rowell.

again in different forms and other segments. The perfect reader
has died, but I cannot see any reason not to write for him anyway,
for I can sooner get used to never hearing from him—the perfect
reader—than to not being able to write for him at all. (*My
Brother* 196–97)

Towards the end of *My Brother*, Jamaica Kincaid confesses that she became
"a writer out of desperation"; that the act of writing about her own life (in
fictional accounts of the artist's youth) has actually saved that life. Kincaid's
ongoing narrative, then, is cumulative rather than linear: when seen together
her characters constitute a single bildung—that of the writer. In *My Brother*,
readers will find the same overbearing mother, whose "love for her children
when they are children is spectacular, unequaled [. . .] in the history of a
mother's love," but whose "mechanism for loving them falls apart" when
her children are trying to become adults and pursue a career as a writer (17).
Antigua is the "same" underdeveloped place Kincaid has spent most of her
writing life up to now trying to recreate. Her last book is only different from
the others on the surface, in that it does not disguise itself as fiction. Kincaid
attempts to understand both her brother's life in Antigua and her (non-)
place in it until the moment he begins to die of AIDS.[1] In order "not to die
with him," Kincaid tells her readers, "[she] would write about it" (195–96).
Writing this book, obviously, is not meant to save her brother's life: she notes
that her book is "about the dead for the dead" (197).

It is on the "for the dead" part of the statement that I want to focus,
since, in a way, *My Brother* is also meant as an eulogy/epitaph for William
Shawn, her editor/father-in-law, whom she claims is her "perfect reader,"
and who died just before her brother. With the intricacy that characterizes
her style, Kincaid weaves layers of complexity as she links the loss of her
brother to that of her "perfect reader" when telling the story of why she
becomes a writer: in an effort to bring back to life the books her mother has
burned to punish her for reading books rather than fulfilling what should
have been natural to her as a woman—taking care of her baby brother.

Although Kincaid does not hide the guilt she feels for that first neglect
(when her brother was a baby), it is hard to tell what the dominant feeling is
in her description of the last time she sees her brother alive:

I did not kiss him goodbye when I was returning home to my
family, I did not give him a goodbye hug. I said to him at the end
of my visit (four days), Goodbye, and he said, So this is it, no hug
no nothing? (and he said it in that way, in conventional English,
*not in the English that instantly reveals the humiliation of history, the
humiliation of the past not remade into art*). (108, my emphasis)

It is, I believe, significant that Kincaid brings more of the Antiguan creole into *My Brother* than she has done in her other works. This move from Standard English to Creole speech is meant not only to underscore the class differences between Kincaid and her family of origin, but it also makes manifest, as François Lionnet writes of Michelle Cliff, "the double consciousness of the post-colonial, bilingual, and bicultural writer who lives and writes across the margins of different traditions and cultural universes" (324). What is different in Kincaid's use is the way she seems to devalue the Creole form by calling it "the English that instantly reveals the humiliation of history, the humiliation of the past not remade into art." Can readers therefore consider Kincaid's autobiographical fiction to this date—her continuing bildungsroman—an effort to remake the humiliation of the past into art? I am, of course, assuming here that Kincaid means not only the individual humiliation of growing up undervalued and with little hope, but the collective humiliation of history that she describes in *A Small Place*. If her ongoing bildungsroman is indeed her effort to remake the humiliation of the past into art, who is she really writing for?[2]

Caribbean writers "at home" and in the diaspora have used the bildungsroman form to represent their quest for personal and national identity, to explore precisely the complexities and contradictions of growing up in a region where (neo-)colonial relationships exacerbate an already oppressive patriarchal situation. In "Decolonizing Genre: Jamaica Kincaid and the *Bildungsroman*," I've tried to understand how Kincaid has modified the conventions of the European novel of development, to offer her own counternarrative to "progressive development" and "coherent identity." Now I want to focus primarily on *Lucy* to continue to explore Jamaica Kincaid's use of the bildungsroman form and also attempt to answer the question of intended audience I have just raised. The genre's traditional goal of accommodation to the existing society, of ending the novel with a character's "precise stand and assessment of himself and his place in society" (Hirsch 298) seems even less possible in the Caribbean context, where a history of foreign domination, slavery, imperialism, and neocolonialism parallels a not always evident heritage of revolt, resistance and struggle to assert cultural and intellectual freedom.[3]

I cannot help but continue to wonder what dangers lie in the form itself, given its central historical role in determining our notions of human identity. Since humanism's unstated goal, in both social and cultural realms, was to constitute a "center of humanity" that would function as an ideal norm and model of emulation for all peoples, what is the bildungsroman genre, recognizably one of the main carriers of humanist ideology, indeed helping to reproduce? If Marc Redfield is correct in his assessment of the reason for the indestructibility of the bildungsroman—that the content of the genre is never simply a "content," but is always also Bildung, the formation of the human as the producer of itself (380)—can the form be anything but normative? Since the bildungsroman narrates the acculturation of a self—the integration of a particular "I" into the general subjectivity of a community, and thus, finally, into the universal subjectivity of mankind—the genre can be said to repeat, as its identity or content, its own synthesis of particular instance and general form (Redfield 378). While the "choice" of the bildungsroman in a way helps to reproduce the cultural imperialism that inevitably separates the Third World intellectual from the community and culture of her birth, Kincaid's rewriting of many of the conventions that have shaped the genre also allows us to see its use in the Caribbean and in the diaspora as a form of resistance. As I have argued before, the set of available narrative conventions that allows a Western novelist to constitute her character's subjectivity does not serve as a model for the life-history of a girl growing up in a primarily female-centered world in Antigua before independence. Kincaid reconstructs the bildungsroman by transforming its narrative values. Like *Annie John*, *Lucy* does not conform to the structural model for the genre that Susan Suleiman identifies: she does not seem to evolve from *ignorance* (of self) into *knowledge* (of self). She does not move from *passivity* to *action* (Suleiman 65). *Lucy* continues to explore the intersections of colonialism, racism, sexism, and heterosexism in contexts that almost prevent access to the "selfhood" that traditional renderings of the genre have claimed possible. We can almost say Lucy and Annie John are the same character—both versions of the developing artist herself.

Leaving home at age 19 to become an au-pair for a wealthy New York City family is central to the character's development as a writer. Although she is fulfilling Annie's dream of "living apart from [her] family in a place where no one knew much about [her]; almost no one knew [her] name, and [she] was free more or less to come and go as [she] pleased," the feeling of "bliss, the feeling of happiness, the feeling of longing fulfilled that [she] had thought would come with this situation was nowhere to be found inside [her]" (158). Exile for Annie John/Lucy, however, is more than the "act of planned separation from her mother" (Mahlis 170). In New York, Lucy finds herself in an "expanding world" (55) that seems to require representation. Using photography to reshape her reality, she "would try to make a print that made more beautiful the thing [she] had seen, that would reveal to [her] some of the things [she] had not seen" (160). While Lucy does not feel she succeeds, Kincaid's readers are able to notice the artist-in-formation in the way she defamiliarizes the ordinary experiences of life, making the strange familiar, and the familiar, strange. Visiting the Metropolitan Museum of Art, she feels connected to other artists, a sign that although she does not realize at that point that she is indeed an artist, she "will be with the people who stand apart" (98). While Lucy "identifies with the yearnings of [Gauguin]" (95), the situation surrounding their exile differs greatly: she first has to wear the mantle of a servant.

Exile has been the first significant feature of anglophone Caribbean writing, according to Kamau Brathwaite, as he identifies the need—or the imagined need—to emigrate to metropolitan centers in order to exist as writers.[4] At the same time, migration creates the desire for home, which in turn, as Carole Boyce Davies explains, produces the rewriting of home: "home as a contradictory, contested space," and home as a longing for that single origin (113). For in Kincaid's narrative the post-colonial protagonist is trapped within a futile but continuous process of gesturing towards the "source" of identity, towards the grounds of cultural origins, towards conflicting images of home. While the traditional bildungsroman requires a constructed harmony between external and internal factors to provide, according to Franco Moretti, "a homeland to the individual" (116), Kincaid's novel of development exposes the impossibility of such a fictional harmony. While in most 19th-century novels the youthful protagonist leaves home in quest of selfhood only to discover that the "truth" lies in what he has left behind and so returns home (Peterson 23), for Kincaid's protagonist there is no possibility of return. Lucy is immediately disappointed with the "reality" of places in the developed north that exist primarily in her imagination.

In *Lucy*, the Americas are also to be understood as places of many continuous displacements: of the original pre-Columbian inhabitants, the Arawaks, Caribs and Amerindians, permanently displaced from their homelands and decimated; of the displacements of slavery, colonization and conquest. Lucy characterizes the maid's room she occupies in the New York apartment as "a box in which cargo traveling a long way should be shipped. But I was not cargo. I was only an unhappy young woman living in a maid's room" (7). The New World also stands for the endless ways in which Caribbean peoples have been destined to "migrate," of the Antillean as the prototype of the modern or postmodern New World nomad, as Stuart Hall writes, continually moving between center and periphery ("Cultural" 234).[5] The nomadism that is enforced through hostile labor conditions in the Caribbean, as Supriya Nair argues, makes "migration, unfinished identities, and lack of regular employment far less causes for celebration than they seem from [Paul] Gilroy's [*Black Atlantic*] vantage point" (71).

Kincaid continues her subtle critique of center–periphery relations in the character of Mariah, a typical North American liberal, who spends her time with organizations trying to save the earth, failing to make any "connection between their comforts and the decline of the world that lay before them" (72). Lucy feels sure that Mariah's kindness is the result of her "comfortable circumstances." And her kindness is also the reason why Lucy cannot point out to her that

> if all the things she wanted to save in the world were saved, she might find herself in reduced circumstances; I couldn't bring myself to ask her to examine Lewis's daily conversations with his stockbroker, to see if they bore any relation to the things she saw passing away forever before her eyes. (73)

One of Lucy's many unanswered questions is how a person gets to be that way, the way of Mariah, "the sort of victor who can claim to be the vanquished also" (41). In an interview with Moira Ferguson, however, Kincaid seems to recognize in herself a person who "contributes to pretty horrendous things" (183). For, like her character Mariah, Kincaid lives "in a nice house in a country that does pretty horrendous things" (183). The longer Kincaid feels like an American, the harder it will become for her to continue to "express the voice of the decolonised subject [. . .] journeying back and forth between empires and colonies of the past and the present," as Giovanna Covi posits, "always refusing to adopt the language of either the vanquished or the victors" (60). It will be more difficult for her protagonist (and for Kincaid) not to acknowledge *both* in herself and do away with the binary altogether—at least in her writing.[6]

While Kincaid claims that if she had "not become a writer, [she] would have been insane" (Ferguson 169), she places her writing directly in the British tradition, naming Charlotte Brontë, Virginia Woolf, Wordsworth, and Shakespeare as sole influences: she had "never read a West Indian writer when [she] started to write" (Ferguson 169). Such youthful reading experiences take on crucial importance in the lives of the protagonists of the novels of development Kincaid writes, since their reactions and desires are to a large extent guided by the literature they read.[7] Mariah is unable to understand Lucy's rage at daffodils: where Mariah sees beautiful flowers, Lucy can only see sorrow and bitterness because she has had to memorize "a long poem about some flowers [she] would not see in real life until [she] was nineteen" (30). As early as age fourteen, Lucy has refused to sing "Rule, Britannia! Britannia, rule the waves; Britons never, never shall be slaves" in choir practice; that she was "not a Briton and that until not too long ago [she] would have been a slave" (134–35). While in the traditional bildungsroman the process of growth for the individual occurs largely through the medium of literature, as both Peterson and Kontje emphasize, since the heroes of the period are all avid readers, in post-colonial novels of development reading almost prevents development. Lucy does not realize how changing her name would have meant compliance rather than rebellion. After contemplating

Emily, Charlotte, or Jane, among "the names of the authoresses whose books [she] loved" (149) for her new name, Lucy almost settles on Enid, after Enid Blyton, an extremely popular British writer of children's literature, whom Bob Dixon exposes as extremely racist in the characters she creates. Lucy keeps her given name, fortunately, once she knows its origin:

> The stories of the fallen were well known to me, but I had not known that my own situation could even distantly be related to them. Lucy, a girl's name for Lucifer. That my mother would have found me devil-like did not surprise me, for I often thought of her as god-like, and are not the children of gods devils? (153)

To compensate for the homesickness she initially feels, Lucy writes home using "flourishing words and phrases" to "say how lovely everything was," "as if [she] were *living life in a greeting card*" (10, my emphasis). Whereas before, when reading about homesickness in books, Lucy would feel impatient with the character who would "leave a not very nice situation and go somewhere else, *somewhere a lot better*, and then long to go back *where it was not very nice*," now she understands the feeling and "[longs] to be back in the place that [she comes] from" (6, my emphases). Kincaid makes clear the confusing doubleness of the colonized self who oscillates between what she sees and the images she has been fed:

> In a day-dream I used to have, all these places were points of happiness to me; all these places were lifeboats to my small drowning soul, for I would imagine myself entering and leaving them, and just that—entering and leaving over and over again—would see me through a bad feeling I did not have a name for. I only knew it felt a little like sadness but heavier than that. Now that I saw these places, they looked ordinary, dirty, worn down by so many people entering and leaving them in real life, and it occurred to me that I could not be the only person in the world for whom they were a fixture of fantasy. It was not my first bout with the disappointment of reality and it would not be my last. (4–5)

Despite being homesick, Lucy refuses to respond to her mother's letters, but she cannot stop recalling and recreating her throughout the novel: a "face that was godlike, *for it seemed to know its own origins, to know all the things of which it was made*" (94, my emphasis). Lucy and Annie John share the overwhelming longing for the absent mother/island, and the futile attempts at escaping that influence:

for I had spent so much time saying I did not want to be like my
mother that I missed the whole story: I was not like my mother—I
was my mother. [. . .] I knew that if I read only one [of the nineteen
unopened letters], I would die from longing for her. (90–91)

While the patterns of the female European novel of development have
been largely circular—women in fiction remain at home—(Ferguson, M. A.
228), Annie John/Lucy chooses not to replicate the life of her mother and
instead leaves Antigua. In doing so, ironically, they recreate the mother's own
journey away from Pa Chess and the island of Dominica, thus reinforcing a
familial pattern of rupture. The contradictions in mastering the educational
system, in apparently rejecting the mother and in leaving for the mother
country (or neocolonial equivalent) make them both seem completely
indoctrinated in western values and beliefs. But by the end of the novel, we
know what Lucy has rejected, but not what she will adhere to. While the
entire process of the bildungsroman aims towards that moment when the
individual applies the knowledge acquired, Lucy seems not to have learned
anything. When we leave Lucy at age 20, she knows as little about herself as
she starts out with; the only certainty she has is of *not* belonging:

> Everything I could see looked unreal to me; everything I could
> see made me feel I would never be part of it, never penetrate to
> the inside, never be taken in. (154)

Growing up in a society of extreme diversity and grave fragmentation of
both European and African cultures does not allow for any coherent sense of
self. In none of these worlds can Lucy/Annie John posit herself as a subject:
she will not be British in the way that the educational system has tried to
make her, and she refuses to be the docile woman her mother expects her to
become:

> Whatever my future held, nursing would not be a part of it. I had
> to wonder what made anyone think a nurse could be made of me.
> I was not good at taking orders from anyone, not good at waiting
> on other people. Why did someone not think that I would make
> a good doctor or a good magistrate or a good someone who runs
> things? (92)

Lucy wants to believe that the girl her parents expected her to be had gone
out of existence in the one year away from home; that since, as she writes
home, "life as a slut was quite enjoyable[, she] would not come home ever"
(30). Her mother's reply is similar to the one Annie John hears before leaving

Antigua: "that she would always love me, she would always be my mother, my home would never be anywhere but with her" (128). Lucy seems permanently displaced, both here [New York] and there [Antigua], and neither here *nor* there at one and the same time.

The solution for Lucy's longing for home [mother and island] is, as in *Annie John* and other Caribbean novels of development, to become a writer. In both novels, the female writing subject comes into existence to try to recover that something—the lost mother/stolen land—as a reaction to the homelessness imposed both by patriarchy and colonization.[8] When Lucy/Kincaid invents herself as an artist, her art becomes her homeland. While the search for identity always involves a search for origins, according to Stuart Hall, it is impossible to locate in the Caribbean a single origin for its peoples:

> Questions of Caribbean culture and identity are not separate from the problem of political mobilization, economic and cultural development. [...] Questions of identity are always questions about representation. They are questions about the invention, not simply the discovery of tradition. They are always exercises in selective memory. ("Negotiating" 5)

At issue, then, is the relationship between the experience of cultural displacement and the construction of cultural identity. Reading Elizabeth Bishop's "In the Waiting Room," the poem Kincaid claims showed her how to write (Krelkamp 168), offers yet another clue to the gradual process of education of the artist.[9] The occasion of Bishop's poem seems simple enough: a child in a waiting room who, reading the *National Geographic* of February 1918, realizes she does not have to be "one of them." The speaker's questioning follows:

> Why should I be my aunt,
> or me, or anyone?
> What similarities—
> boots, hands, the family voice
> I felt in my throat, or even
> the *National Geographic*
> And those awful hanging breasts—
> held us all together
> Or made us all just one?
> How—I didn't know any
> word for it—how 'unlikely' ...
> How had I come to be here,
> like them, [...]

Works Cited

Bammer, Angelika, ed. *Displacements: Cultural Identities in Question*. Bloomington and Indianapolis: Indiana University Press, 1994.

Brathwaite, Edward Kamau. *The History of the Voice: The Development of Nation Language in Anglophone Caribbean Poetry*. London: New Beacon, 1984.

Castle, Gregory. "The Book of Youth: Reading Joyce's Bildungsroman." *Genre* 22.1 (Spring 1989): 21–40.

Covi, Giovanna. "Jamaica Kincaid's Prismatic Self and the Decolonisation of Language and Thought." *Framing the Word: Gender and Genre in Caribbean Women's Writing*. Ed. Joan Anim-Addo. London: Whiting & Birch Ltd., 1996. 37–67.

Davies, Carole Boyce. *Black Women, Writing and Identity*. London and New York: Routledge, 1994.

Dixon, Bob. *Catching Them Young: Sex, Race, and Class in Children's Fiction*. London: Pluto, 1977.

Ferguson, Mary Anne. "The Female Novel of Development and the Myth of Psyche." *The Voyage In: Fictions of Female Development*. Ed. Elizabeth Abel et al. Hanover, NH: University Press of New England, 1983. 228–43.

Ferguson, Moira. "A Lot of Memory: An Interview with Jamaica Kincaid." *The Kenyon Review* 161 (1994): 163–88.

Gmelch, George. *Double Passage: The Lives of Caribbean Migrants Abroad and Back Home*. Ann Arbor: University of Michigan Press, 1992.

Hall, Stuart. "Cultural Identity and Diaspora." *Identity: Community, Culture, Difference*. Ed. Jonathan Rutherford. London: Lawrence & Wishart, 1990. 222–37.

———. "Negotiating Caribbean Identities." *New Left Review* 209 (January/February 1995): 3–14.

Hirsch, Marianne. "The Novel of Formation as Genre: Between Great Expectations and Lost Illusions." *Genre* 12 (1979): 293–311.

Krelkamp, Ivan. "Jamaica Kincaid." *Writing for Your Life #3*. Pushcart, NY: W.W. Norton, 1997. 166–70.

Kincaid, Jamaica. *Annie John*. New York: Farrar, Straus & Giroux, 1985.

———. "In History" (orig. in *Callaloo*). *The Best American Essays, 1999*. Ed. Cynthia Ozick. Boston & New York: Houghton Mifflin Co., 1998. 163–72.

———. "The Little Revenge from the Periphery." *Transition: An International Review* 73 (Spring 1997): 68–73.

———. *Lucy*. New York: Plume, 1990.

———. *My Brother*. New York: Farrar, Straus and Giroux, 1997.

———. *A Small Place*. New York: Farrar, Straus and Giroux, 1988.

Kontje, Todd. "The German *Bildungsroman* as Metafiction." *Michigan Germanic Studies* 13.2 (1987): 140–55.

Lima, Maria Helena. "Decolonizing Genre: Jamaica Kincaid and the *Bildungsroman*." *Genre* 26.4 (Winter 1993): 431–59.

Lionnet, Françoise. "Of Mangoes and Maroons: Language, History, and the Multicultural Subject of Michelle Cliff's *Abeng*." *De/Colonizing the Subject: The Politics of Gender in Women's Autobiography*. Ed. Sidonie Smith & Julia Watson. Minneapolis: University of Minnesota Press, 1992. 321–45.

Mahlis, Kristen. "Gender and Exile: Jamaica Kincaid's *Lucy*." *Modern Fiction Studies* 44 (Spring 1998): 164–82.

Nair, Supriya. "Expressive Countercultures and Postmodern Utopia: A Caribbean Context." *Research in African Literatures* 27.4 (Winter 1996): 71–87.

Moretti, Franco. "The Comfort of Civilization." *Representations* 12 (Fall 1985): 115–39.

Olwig, Karen Fog. "Global Relations, Local Identities: Family Land as a Cultural Site in the West Indies." General Seminar Paper, Institute for Global Studies in Culture, Power & History, Johns Hopkins University (December 6, 1994).

Peterson, Carla L. *The Determined Reader: Gender and Culture in the Novel from Napoleon to Victoria*. New Brunswick, NJ: Rutgers University Press, 1986.

Redfield, Marc. "Ghostly Bildung: Gender, Genre, Aesthetic Ideology, and Wilhelm Meisters Lehrjahre." *Genre* 26.4 (Winter 1993): 377–407.

Smith, John H. "Sexual Difference, *Bildung*, and the *Bildungsroman*." *Michigan Germanic Studies* 13.2 (Fall 1987): 206–25.

Suleiman, Susan Rubin. *Authoritarian Fictions: The Ideological Novel as a Literary Genre*. New York: Columbia University Press, 1983.

ELIZABETH J. WEST

In the Beginning There Was Death:
Spiritual Desolation and the Search for Self in
Jamaica Kincaid's Autobiography of My Mother

Jamaica Kincaid's novels have invited considerable commentary on the mother-daughter relationships of her fictional heroines. While the undercurrent critique of white domination in *Annie John* (1978) and the inimical vision of British imperialism in *Lucy* (1990) have gone unacknowledged by many scholars, the unrelenting harshness of *The Autobiography of My Mother* (1996) does not allow for such critical neglect.[1] For Kincaid's fictional female trilogy—Annie, Lucy and Xuela—"alienation from the mother becomes a metaphor for . . . alienation from an island culture that has been completely dominated by the imperialist power of England."[2] With its focus on Christianity's place in the lives of those dispossessed by western exploitation, *The Autobiography of My Mother* is more explicit in its indictment of imperialism. Through the enigmatic existential protagonist, Xuela, Kincaid traces the resultant spiritual wasteland that is the legacy for this post-Colonial victim who rejects the master's God, but whose disconnectedness with her ancestral past leaves her unable to reclaim the gods of her past. *The Autobiography of My Mother* is not Kincaid's first fictional contemplation of identity and colonialism.[3] In *Annie John*, the protagonist suffers a mental breakdown that "can also be read as a breakdown with the past, with tradition."[4] Like Xuela, Annie finds herself reconciling her African-based inheritance with a contrasting but dominant western

From *South Central Review* 20, no. 2/4 (Summer–Winter 2003). © *South Central Review*.

presence. When Annie suffers a mental breakdown, she is restored to health through the community of women and their ties to African spiritual practices.[5] In contrast to Annie's narrative of identity, Xuela's narrative will neither confirm her identity nor free her from a despairing past. Xuela will find no community to provide her a meaningful sense of place and self—the self she ultimately constructs is defined by loss and isolation.

Social paradigms of race and gender complicate Xuela's search for self, but it is her concurrent spiritual struggle that ultimately shapes the empty self that emerges. She finds that Christianity offers no personal solace, and that for Blacks collectively Christianity offers little more than unfulfilled promises of solace and deliverance. The vacuity of the Christian message cannot be answered by looking back to the spiritual legacy of the ancestors, for the African-based spirituality that had once connected African-descent people has been lost. For Xuela, this loss translates to personal loss; in particular, it precipitates her inability to construct a meaningful identity. The paradox of Xuela's identity is articulated by Xuela herself. She understands and accepts that she was born into a legacy of defeat, and her answer to this fate is to construct a self that is insulated and self-serving:

> I am of the vanquished, I am of the defeated . . . for me the future must remain capable of casting a light on the past such that in my defeat lies the beginning of my great revenge. My impulse is to the good, my good is to serve myself. I am not a people, I am not a nation. I only wish from time to time to make my actions of a people, to make my actions be the actions of a nation.[6]

She presumes to see life in its veritable emptiness—a vision that escapes the racial victor (Whites) as well as the racially vanquished (Blacks). The power of her vision, however, only offers a life filled with a lingering emptiness, for she sees death as the ultimate power over life. From infancy, death will signal pivotal moments in her life: "My mother died at the moment I was born . . . at my beginning was this woman whose face I had never seen, but at my end was nothing, no one between me and the black room of the world" (AOMM 3). This bleakness, recounted in the first lines of the novel, will resonate throughout. While the novel exemplifies Kincaid's masterful manipulation of language, it offers a despairing and gloomy message. From beginning to end, the narrator maintains this desolate vision, and she will conclude her narrative with the despair of the beginning, confirming once again that "death is the only reality, for it is the only certainty, inevitable to all things" (AOMM, 228).

What then does a novel like Kincaid's *Autobiography of My Mother* offer its readers? What can we make of it as a black novel when we consider that it is not controlled by "master discourses of race?"[7] The despair of Kincaid's protagonist is not entirely connected to an explicit or sustained racial theme, which perhaps leaves readers frustrated. While Kincaid calls attention to the protagonist's recognition of her racialized self, the novel does not position race as the controlling discourse. Xuela's search for self is thwarted in greater part by the spiritual void in her life than by a prevailing struggle with racial issues. Her moments of racial reflectiveness do not prompt her to action that alters the course of the narrative. Instead, issues of personal/subjective desire emerge and influence her choices.

Claudia Tate argues that novels with themes that are "external to [the] racial/social argument" of the text result in an "enigmatic surplus [that] disrupts the novel's conscious plot around racial/social protest or affirmation."[8] Enlisting W. E. B. DuBois's not-so-highly praised novel, *Dark Princess*, Tate suggests that "the novel's finale engenders our wonder and amazement but fails to evoke our empathy, compassion, or identification . . . offer[ing] us no site for entry."[9] *The Autobiography of My Mother* exemplifies Tate's analogy of black authored texts with surplus desire that "generate meaning in the novel that is external to its racial/social argument."[10] Xuela is less a victim of the ills of racism than a victim of a sustained longing resulting from a trauma experienced at birth. This character, who for the most part remains unnamed in a narrative that she controls, longs for what she will never have—a mother. That longing will translate into a spiritual longing that will also go unanswered. Her elusive father, who is her only living connection to her mother, will deny Xuela both a tie to himself and to her mother. Having no mother and no functional father, Kincaid's enigmatic heroine has no link to the past and no road to the future. Her mythical mother, had she lived, may have proven a link to the ancestral spirits. Acknowledging only the gods of the victors, however, Xuela's father does not give merit to an African ancestral connection.

The Autobiography of My Mother maintains a critique on racism; in particular, the narrator addresses issues of white privilege and black despair. Early in the novel Xuela positions herself as the racial other. She recalls speaking first in the language of the oppressor: "That the first words I said were in the language of a people I would never like or love is now a mystery to me: everything in my life, good or bad, to which I am inextricably bound is a source of pain" (AOMM 7). Although Xuela speaks the language of the conqueror before uttering her native tongue, her instinctive rejection of things British surfaces early. As a toddler she accidentally breaks a plate belonging to her surrogate mother, Ma Eunice. The plate, painted with "a picture of the English countryside idealized," and labeled "HEAVEN," was a treasured icon (AOMM 9). Xuela realizes the importance of the plate to Ma Eunice; however, she is unable to apologize. She instinctively rejects the message of reverence for the oppressor suggested in the image painted on the plate.

While Xuela repeatedly identifies the British as those who have gained privilege by their abuse and exploitation of racial others, she fails to mediate her personal narrative into this theme. She is black, but hers is a complicated identity. Her mother was "of the Carib people" who had been exterminated by the British and were disliked by those of African descent. Her father was the product of a union between a Scots-man and a woman of African descent. Given popular constructions of race, Xuela is identified as black. However, Xuela sees herself as both a physical and spiritual hybrid. She will identify herself as having come from many but belonging to none. She discloses the complexity of racial realities and racial constructions but does not demonstrate that her own story is significantly influenced by this social paradox. The novel ends with a racial discourse and a discourse of personal desire that have not been merged into a unified narrative.

Xuela's personal longing begins at the moment of her birth with the traumatic loss of her mother. From early childhood she seeks her mother, though she knows that it is a futile search: "I missed the face I had never seen; I looked over my shoulder to see if someone was coming, as if I were expecting someone to come ... I was just looking for that face, the face I would never see, even if I lived forever" (AOMM 5). She experiences apparitions in which her mother appears, but she is always denied the vision of her mother's face: "She came down the ladder again and again, over and over, just her heels and the hem of her white dress visible; down, down, over and over" (AOMM 31). By the age of seven Xuela has become quite familiar with this vision, and she accepts that she will never look upon her mother's face. But this acceptance represents a resignation—not a resolution. Hence, the narrative continues as a contemplation of loss and a desire for a mother. The memory of the loss will remain, and in the closing moments of the text the protagonist will again remind readers that hers is a narrative of maternal disconnectedness: "That attachment, physical and spiritual, that confusion of who is who, flesh and flesh, which was absent between my mother and her mother was also absent between my mother and myself, for she died at the moment I was born, and though I can sensibly say to myself such a thing cannot be helped—for who can help dying—again how can any child understand such a thing, so profound as abandonment? I have refused to bear any children" (AOMM 199).

As the narrative unfolds the reader learns that this loss represents a legacy of loss: in infancy her mother was abandoned and left at the gates of a convent, and her father was abandoned in his youth by his father. Her father will not physically abandon her; however, he becomes himself a symbol of unfulfilled desire. She longs for a connectedness to her father who will never allow her entry into his inner world or share with her his memory of her mother. This father, who shortly after her mother's death delivers Xuela to the door of his laundry woman, will prove the living conscious source of her self-consumed existence:

> When my mother died, leaving me a small child vulnerable to all the world, my father took me and placed me in the care of the same woman he paid to wash his clothes. It is possible that he emphasized to her the difference between the two bundles: one was his child, not his only child in the world but the only child he had with the only woman he had married so far; the other was his soiled clothes. He would have handled one more gently than the other, he would have given more careful instructions for the care of one over the other, he would have expected better care for one than the other, but which one I do not know, because he was a very vain man, his appearance was very important to him. That I was a burden to him, I know; that his soiled clothes were a burden to him, I know; that he did not know how to take care of me by himself, or how to clean his own clothes himself, I know. (AOMM 4)

Throughout the narrative, the vision of her father triggers feelings of overwhelming despair and disillusionment. She will, however, occasionally contemplate the possibility of goodness in her father, but the distance between father and daughter will remain. Xuela's only admirable memory of her father is his handwriting which she remembers as "such a beautiful thing to behold. It covered the page with strong curves and strong dashes and strong slashes" (AOMM 95). Ironically, she is in awe of his handwriting, but she cannot read it. Her inability to read her father's writing exemplifies her inability to read her father—even though he, like his handwriting, seems bigger than life. His world is off limits to her; she cannot read his handwriting just as she cannot read his face or his actions.

Having no mother and no functional father, Xuela faces an unconquerable void. She understands that she will never possess the self knowledge, connectedness, or inheritance that parents impart to their children: "Observing any human being from infancy, seeing someone come into existence, like a new flower in a bud . . . all this is something so wonderful to behold; the pleasure for the observer, the beholder, is an invisible current between the two, observed and observer, beheld and beholder, and I believe that no life is complete, no life is really whole, without this invisible current, which is in many ways a definition of love. No one observed and beheld me, I observed and beheld myself" (AOMM 56). Xuela, then, learns of self through a self-reflexive process—she cannot gaze into the eyes of a parent and find her image. She will, like her father, create herself, and she will, ironically, create a self that mirrors the father she so despises. She has inherited his soul even though he has disinherited her materially. He denies her the spiritual inheritance that she desires, and she does not require his material means, for she has learned from him the ruthless road to possessing wealth. Like her father, she will come to weigh the interest of self as primary. She acknowledges and is empowered by her self-interest: "My own face was a comfort to me, my own body was a comfort to me, and no matter how swept away I would become by anyone or anything, in the end I allowed nothing to replace my own being in my own mind" (AOMM 100). And just as her father had chosen a spouse he did not love, she too would forgo love and choose instead a spouse who would answer her desire for material gain.

At its core, the complex estrangement between Xuela and her father may be an outgrowth of the effects of racism. Certainly, her father has been influenced by a society in which a white father can so easily abandon his family of color. Certainly, Xuela has been influenced by the question of identity that is imposed on one who is a hybrid of races, but in her self-absorbed narrative, race is de-centered as the master discourse. Xuela struggles with issues of personal loss and personal desire that cannot be answered by an emerging racial consciousness. She marries a white man, but she finds no community or kinship with Whites. While she is looked upon as black, she forms no substantive connections with Blacks. There is no opportunity for kinship with the Carib people of whom her mother was a descendant, for they have long been killed off by conquering Whites. Xuela represents the existential protagonist who seats herself at the center of her world, constructing codes of ethics and morality that originate in her own self-conceived and self-validated paradigms. She does not appropriate the discourse of spiritual enlightenment often found in the bildungsroman. While the novel recounts Xuela's coming of age, it disrupts this literary convention by not only negating Christianity as the source of the protagonist's transformation, but by further dismissing spirituality as a source of self-empowerment. In the post-Colonial world of this displaced heroine, no spiritual solace is found: Christianity is innately corrupt and the connection between Africans and their pre-Colonial spirituality has been severed. In the absence of spiritual bonds, race is not sufficient to tie Xuela to Blacks in her community. The result is a spiritual wasteland that confirms her alienation and loss.

Through her inversions of Christian myths and ideals, Xuela unveils Christianity's failure. Her own beginning overturns the biblical creation story that marks the beginning of life as a generative moment. For Xuela the beginning is a paradox marked not by life, but rather by death and loss: the beginning for Xuela marks death for her mother. In contrast to the creation story that promises life and hope, Xuela's narrative suggests that the beginning is only a cruel paradox in which life emerges out of death, and life itself is only a journey to death. Instead of the gift of Eden that God awards the first humans, Xuela finds life a "false paradise . . . full of life, full of death, able to sustain the one, inevitably to claim the other" (AOMM 32). Born out of this paradox, Xuela repeatedly subverts the anticipated spiritual revelation commonly appropriated in coming-of-age narratives. She experiences no moment of spiritual revelation that ties her to community, leads her to identity, or answers her personal yearnings.

The paradoxical gaining of life through the death of another will prove a recurrent trope in *The Autobiography of My Mother*. The narrator reminds the reader repeatedly that her birth occurred with the concurrent death of her mother. In a choral-like chant near the novel's end she reflects on her mother's life, confirming and reconfirming one fact about her mother: "she died at the moment I was born" (AOMM 198). Her own emergence into life through the death of her mother compels Xuela to deny the emergence of life through her own body. With god-like authority, she denies life to those who might threaten her own. Her first abortion awakened her to the power she possessed to will out unwanted life. She remembers the subsequent revelation of self that was born out of this destructive act: "I was a new person then, I knew things I had not known before, I knew things that you can know only if you have been through what I had just been through. I had carried my own life in my own hands" (AOMM 83). Through the near death experience brought on by the physical trauma of her abortion, Xuela is born again. In an unconscious state she sets off on a mystical journey in which the imagery of her resurrection is juxtaposed with that of the risen Christ. On a journey that begins out of a sacrilegious act, Xuela beholds images revered by Christians: "At Massacre the entire Church of St. Paul and St. Anne was wrapped in purple and black cloth as if it were Good Friday" (AOMM 87). Good Friday is the holiday celebrated by Christians in remembrance of God's promise of eternal life. Christians remember it as the day of Christ's resurrection, and the color purple signifies the eminence of God's chosen son. In contrast to the risen Christ, the chosen son, who, resurrected from the dead, promises eternal life to humankind, Xuela, the dispossessed daughter, is resurrected from the dead through her denial of life to another. Following her first abortion Xuela returns to the home of Lise, the woman who has befriended her. Here, with Lise and her husband, who fathered the life that Xuela has expelled, the novel's inversion of Christian iconography is once again highlighted. Xuela recalls that they stood in a "little triangle, a trinity, not made in heaven, not made in hell, a wordless trinity" (AOMM 93). Just as the image of the holy trinity—God the father, Jesus the son, and the holy spirit—remains a paradox in Christian theology, the image of Xuela, Lise LaBatte, and Jacques LaBatte standing in a kind of trinity is also a paradox. Unlike the holy trinity that originates out of God's gift of life to humankind, theirs is a union conceived in the unholy act of adultery and confirmed with the taking of life.

The loss of life will mark two other paradoxical moments of human connectedness for Xuela. While she insists that her father's children are not her sister and brother, she comes to feel a familial bond with them through death experiences. With the death of her brother, Xuela is able to regard him as a sibling: "My brother died. In death he became my brother" (AOMM 110), she explains. Similarly, her momentary connectedness to her sister occurs when they share a death experience. Xuela and her sister have maintained a mutual disregard that goes uninterrupted with the exception of one episode:

> She became my sister when shortly after she was expelled from school she found herself with child and I helped her rid herself of this condition . . . I hid her in my small room behind the kitchen . . . I made her strong potions of teas. When the child inside her still refused to come out, I put my hand up inside her womb and forcibly removed it. (AOMM 114)

When this crisis is over Xuela's sister offers her no gratitude for her services. In fact, while Xuela's deed offers her a moment of connectedness to her sister, it cements her sister's dislike for her: "I never became her sister; she never took me into her confidence, she never thanked me; in fact, the powerful clasp in which she could see I held my own life only led to more suspicion and misunderstanding" (AOMM 115). With her father, Xuela will likewise know no familial connectedness, but his death precipitates a moment of renewed life for her. She remembers her father's death as a kind of redemption:

> I had been living at the end of the world for my whole life; it had been so when I was born, for my mother had died when I was born. But now, with my father dead, I was living at the brink of eternity, it was as if this quality of my life was suddenly raised from its usual self, embossed with its old meaning. (AOMM 213)

Death is regenerative for Xuela; it marks the beginning of her life, it affords her the few moments of familial bonding that she experiences, and it endows her with renewed enlightenment and empowerment. As the source of Xuela's empowerment and regeneration, death, the omnipresent power, signifies the novel's subversion of Christianity's greatest promise. Whereas in Christian myth God is the power that rules over death and grants humankind eternal life, Xuela's ideology holds death as the ultimate authority. The novel's allusion to the biblical figure Lazarus exemplifies this inversion. The appropriation of this well-known figure negates the Christian belief in God's power over death and the redemption of the poor in the hereafter. In John 11:1–44 the story is told of Jesus raising Lazarus from the grave. Dead for four days, Lazarus is brought back to life to demonstrate God's power of resurrection. A biblical account of another Lazarus contrasts the life of a symbolic rich man with that of the beggar, Lazarus. Lazarus, though poor and dejected in the carnal world, triumphs in the afterlife while the rich man is condemned to hell (Luke 16:19–31). In her narrative Xuela will recall two encounters with a poor man named Lazarus; however, this Lazarus is not resurrected from the dead, and he does not come to know the promise of heavenly recompense. On the contrary, Xuela's Lazarus is the embodiment of death, of the hopelessness of life, and his life suggests that there is no just reward for the poor—in this life or another.

In addition to being a poor man, Xuela's Lazarus is a gravedigger—that image of the doorkeeper to the gates of death. Though he may have been given the name Lazarus as an act of faith, this Lazarus cannot escape that eminent and omnipotent power—death. Xuela detects the contradiction between what his name signifies and what his fate will be:

> his name would have been given to him in a moment of innocent hope; his mother would have thought that such a name, rich and powerful as it was with divine second chance, would somehow protect him from the living death that was his actual life; but it had been of no use, he was born the Dead and he would die the Dead. (AOMM 140)

This Lazarus will be exploited by Xuela's father, a rich man who, unlike the rich man in the biblical tale, suffers no consequences for his acts. And this Lazarus will not realize redemption in the afterlife. While Xuela attempts to intercede on Lazarus's behalf when he comes to her father in need, she does not find the success of the biblical Mary and Margaret who are able to employ Jesus to come to the aid of Lazarus. In fact, Xuela will herself become the object of her father's scorn because of her plea for Lazarus. He angrily shows Xuela the nails that he has told Lazarus he does not have. Refusing Lazarus the nails he needs to build a roof, Xuela's father denies him fundamental protection. Lazarus has no physical home and he knows no spiritual refuge; his name symbolizes the Christian promise of redemption and salvation, but he is the embodiment of human despair and hopelessness.

The novel's negation of Christianity's power and sacredness is also revealed with Xuela's allusion to the biblical book, Romans. As a young child

Xuela writes secret letters venting her feelings of victimization suffered at the hand of her teacher. A boy named Roman uncovers her letters and turns them in:

> My letters did not remain a secret. A boy named Roman had seen me putting them in their secret place, and behind my back, he removed them. He had no empathy, no pity; any instinct to protect the weak had been destroyed in him. He took my letters to our teacher. (AOMM 20)

The boy Roman, evil and cunning, clearly contrasts the image of sacredness associated with the biblical book, Romans. The inversion of Christian iconography is further evident in the contrasting nature of Xuela's secular letters and Paul's spiritual letters. Paul's letters have not been authored in the interest of self but for the greater cause of spreading the Christian message. Though Xuela addresses these letters to her father, she has no intention of sending them. She has authored these letters to provide herself solace and vindication. As author, Xuela stands in contrast to Paul, but her ethnic hybridity is reminiscent of Paul's cross cultural identity. Though a Christian apostle, Paul is a Jew by birth; while a Jew, he is a Roman citizen.[11] Xuela embodies a similar hybrid of cultures: though she is assumed to be black, her mother is a descendant of the Carib people, and her father is of mixed African and Scottish blood. With his acceptance of Christ's message that all are one under God, Paul successfully negotiates his Jewishness and his belief in Christianity. Xuela, however, is a splintered self who finds no spiritual message that enables her to merge her multiple selves into a unity of self.

Undermining a tradition of Christian myths and claims, *The Autobiography of My Mother* suggests the failure of Christianity in the lives of the conquered Africans. Kincaid's protagonist recognizes that adaptation to Christianity has not brought Africans the prosperity that it brought the conquering Whites. In her teacher, the young Xuela witnesses the discord that Christianity cultivates. A woman of African ancestry educated by Methodist missionaries, Xuela's teacher had learned to view her ancestry with shame, and it was a sentiment widespread among this community of African descendants:

> My teacher ... was of the African people, that I could see, and she found in this a source of humiliation and self-loathing, and she wore despair like an article of clothing, like a mantle, or a staff on which she leaned constantly, a birthright which she would pass on to us. She did not love us; we did not love her; we did not love one another, not then, not ever. (AOMM 15)

For her teacher and for Africans at large, colonialism and Christianity had displaced self love and ancestral ties. Christianity had been the tool of exploitation employed by the conquerors and later by the conquered themselves. In Xuela's own father we see the parasitic nature of Christianity personified. A self-made man, her father came into his wealth by exploiting those in his community. The more respected he became, the more corrupt and the more religious he became: "My father had become a Methodist, he attended church every Sunday; he taught Sunday school. The more he robbed, the more money he had, the more he went to church; it is not an unheard-of linking" (AOMM 40).

Church, then, is the institution that confirms the defeat of the conquered. Xuela observes Blacks as they submit themselves each Sunday to this self-defeating ritual:

> This activity—going to church, coming from church—had about it an atmosphere of a decree. It also signified defeat yet again, for what would the outcome have been of all the lives of the conquered if they had not come to believe in the gods of the people who had conquered them? (AOMM 133)

Xuela contends that the conquered African people, dispossessed of their own spiritual heritage and denied the Christian promise of redemption, are left to despair. She recalls the history of the church in the small town of Roseau, a history that symbolizes the spiritual dispossession of colonized Africans:

> But this church, typical of its time and place in every way, was built, inch by inch, by enslaved people, and many of the people who were slaves died while building this church, and their masters then had them buried in such a way that when the Day of Judgment came and all the dead were risen, the enslaved faces would not be turned toward the eternal light of heaven but toward the eternal darkness of hell. (AOMM 133)

Stripped of their own legacy and denied a place in Anglo religious tradition, these Africans lack cultural identity and strength, and as in the case of Xuela's teacher, they are filled with self-loathing.

The conquered do not entirely submit. Some hold on to ancestral ways. Ultimately, however, they find that ancestral myths collapse under the overreaching influence of Christianity. This subjugation of African myth to western spiritual hegemony is illustrated early in the novel with Xuela's account of her young classmate who disappeared after being called into the river by an apparition of a woman. Xuela recalls observing this naked woman who in their eyes was beautiful. Hers was a beauty that they understood and were drawn to because she resembled them: ". . . she was dark brown in skin, her hair was black and shiny and twisted into small coils all around her head. Her face was like a moon, a soft, brown, glistening moon" (AOMM 35). Mesmerized and unable to move away, they watched her. Though she embodied a beauty and a familiarity that attracted them, they were nevertheless uneasy. One boy in the group, swayed to come nearer, swam farther and farther in his attempt to reach her. He finally drowned from exhaustion, and he and the apparition disappeared. The children who witnessed this mystical event are made to doubt what they have seen. The story will live on as a folkloric tale bearing little resemblance to the truth of their experience. But as an adult looking back, Xuela understands why those in her community, even the children who had witnessed it firsthand, could not accept this event as real:

> Everything about us is held in doubt and we the defeated define all that is unreal, all that is not human, all that is without love, all that is without mercy. Our experience cannot be interpreted by us; we do not know the truth of it. Our God was not the correct one, our understanding of heaven and hell was not a respectable one. Belief in that apparition of a naked woman with outstretched arms beckoning a small boy to his death was the belief of the illegitimate, the poor, the low. I believed in that apparition then and I believe in it now. (AOMM 37–38)

Those Blacks who attempt to maintain ancestral practices meet with failure in this community that finds little or no value in African-based practices and ideals. Such is the case with Madame LaBatte's spell gone wrong. While a young woman, she is unable to secure a marriage proposal from Jacques LaBatte who has refused other women wanting to marry him. She calls on mystical practices to lure him, but the spell quickly wears off and Monsieur LaBatte is no longer under her command. In fact, she becomes the victim as this relationship drains her of life and will. Similarly, when Xuela's stepmother calls on the god of her ancestors to save her dying son, she witnesses the powerlessness of this resource. Xuela recalls the paradoxical image of the boy's mother praying to the ancestral god while his father calls on the Christian god:

> Inside that yellow house with the brown windows, my father's son was lying on a bed of clean rags that was on the floor. They were special rags; they had been perfumed with oils rendered from things vegetable and animal. It was to protect him from

evil spirits. He was on the floor so that the spirits could not get to him from underneath. His mother believed in obeah. His father held the beliefs of the people who had subjugated him. (AOMM 108)

In the end both gods fail the young boy. His death symbolizes the spiritual death of this community of displaced Africans who share no vital ties of ancestry. Like this mother and father whose beliefs are at odds, the community too is at odds. They are a house divided between the ways of the conqueror and the ways of the ancestors. These traditions cannot coexist, and the result for this community is much like that for the frail boy who could not survive at the fringes of two disparate worlds.

Refusing to become one of the powerless, Xuela serves no god, but rather raises herself to godhood. She arrives at this state of self-proclaimed divinity through experiences that cultivate in her a desire for power. This is evident early in her childhood when shortly after Ma Rainey has reprimanded her for breaking her treasured plate, Xuela takes three young turtles and keeps them captive. Feeling helpless and victimized, Xuela wishes to emulate the power that Ma Rainey has exercised with her. She chooses three turtles as her victims, capturing them so that they completely depend on her. Punishing the turtles for withdrawing into their shells, she seals the holes from which they refuse to emerge. When she remembers them some days later, she returns to find them dead. She does not recall this event with sorrow or remorse, but with a godlike indifference. She had wished something of the turtles, they had denied her, and she had killed them in an attempt to gain their obedience. This incident, in part, symbolizes her struggle with Ma Rainey, who responds to Xuela's insolence by exercising her power to punish her, to make her suffer. Xuela, in turn, discovers her own power through her experiment with the turtles. But she has surpassed Ma Rainey, for she has exercised the power to take life.

Xuela's association of power with death evolves into a more conscious philosophy as she matures. The incident between Xuela and her teacher reveals this emerging consciousness. In a moment that echoes the powerlessness Xuela felt at the hands of Ma Rainey, Xuela again finds solace in knowing her power to take life. When her teacher reads her letter and verbally reprimands her before her classmates, Xuela becomes fixated with a spider on the wall. She remembers her overwhelming desire to destroy this spider: ". . . I wanted to reach out and crush it with the bare palm of my hand, because I wondered if it was the same kind of spider or a relative of the spider that had sucked saliva from the corner of my mouth the night before as I lay sleeping, leaving three small, painful bites" (AOMM 21). Xuela does not kill the spider, but her desire to kill demonstrates her connection of death and power. When the confrontation with her teacher leads to Xuela's removal from the school, she realizes that this incident has ultimately resulted in the fulfillment of her desire to leave. If, as Xuela suspects, she had saved her own life by her actions, it had been inadvertently; however, shortly after arriving at the house of her father and his new wife she will be required to deliberately orchestrate a plan to save herself from death. Instinctively knowing that the necklace her stepmother has given her as a gift is in fact a death object, Xuela presents this necklace as a gift to her stepmother's favorite dog, who soon afterward dies. At this point Xuela has transformed her power to the deliberate act of taking life. She killed the turtles accidentally, and she only imagined killing the female spider; however, when she places the necklace on the dog, knowing that it is an instrument of death, she has, for the first time, deliberately taken life. Xuela's indifference at the taking of life will be brought to fruition with her refusal to allow life to come from her body, and her subsequent self-inflicted abortions exemplify her determination to control life and death.

Recognizing and exercising her power to determine the course of her life, Xuela relishes in her "self." This celebration of the self leads her to an ongoing practice of self-sensual/sexual gratification. Though she seeks intimacy with men, she regularly pleases herself, and she holds nothing in life before herself. Xuela becomes for Xuela the greatest presence in life—no greater source of knowledge, of pleasure, or power can she find. She is the god in her world, and her own face becomes the graven image that reifies her authority:

> When I could not see my face, I could feel that I had become hard; I could feel that to love was beyond me, that I had gained such authority over my own ability to be that I could cause my own demise with complete calm. I knew, too, that I could cause the demise of others with the same complete calm. It was seeing my own face that comforted me. I began to worship myself . . . in the end I allowed nothing to replace my own being in my own mind. (AOMM 99–100)

Xuela revels in her power of self-rule, but ultimately she must recognize and concede to powers greater than herself. Her god-like reach is limited: what she seeks most she will never possess. Reminiscent of the biblical Eve who seeks knowledge that is beyond human capacity, Xuela admits that what she desires most she can never have. She confesses, "to know all is an impossibility, but only such a thing would satisfy me," and at the close of the novel Xuela signals her submission to that authority to whom all must submit—death (AOMM 226–28).

Although Xuela must ultimately submit to death, this does not diminish her compelling role as the seer. She sees Christianity draining the lifeline of Africans, she sees Africans unable to maintain the ways of their ancestors, she sees Africans as a disempowered people, she sees Whites as usurpers, and she asserts her rejection of all these legacies. Xuela will create herself, and this construction of self begins in the aftermath of her first abortion. She recounts the dream that revealed the legacy that would define her:

> I walked through my inheritance, an island of villages and rivers and mountains and people who began and ended with murder and theft and not very much love. I claimed it in a dream. Exhausted from the agony of expelling from my body a child I could not love and so did not want, I dreamed of all the things that were mine. (AOMM 89)

She is awakened out of this dream by her father whose presence reminds her of the uncertainty and the void in her life. She has claimed the inheritance of the unloved, of the dejected, of the abused. It is fitting, then, that after she comes to know her mother, she will choose the inheritance of her mother. Xuela reconstructs her mother's image and life through what she has been told, and the image that emerges confirms the picture offered at the novel's beginning—her mother will stand again as an icon of death and loss. She imagines that from a young age her orphaned mother had been shaped by the nuns into a "quiet, shy, long-suffering, unquestioning, modest, wishing-to-die-soon person," and that upon first meeting her mother, her father noticed "her sadness, her weakness, her long-lost-ness, the crumbling of ancestral lines, her dejectedness, the false humility that was really defeat" (AOMM 199–200).

Although she has claimed powers of life and death and vision, Xuela becomes one of the dispossessed, the vanquished. And while she has claimed herself godlike, she has no greater knowledge of self than the defeated masses who have become victims of western domination. She finally concedes that life is a paradox, a mystery that remains unknowable. Her choice to retreat to the homeland of her mother signals this defeat, for she has identified her mother as one among the defeated. Her retrospection near the close of the novel suggests that giving the account of her life as an autobiography of her mother reveals her inextricable tie to the world of the defeated:

> This account of my life has been an account of my mother's life as much as it has been an account of mine, and even so, again it is an account of the life of the children I did not have, as it is their account of me. In me is the voice I never heard, the face I never

saw, the being I came from. In me are the voices that should have come out of me, the faces I never allowed to form, the eyes I never allowed to see me. This account is an account of the person I did not allow myself to become. (AOMM 227–28)

Xuela's self-reflection at the end of the narrative is not altogether convincing, and this marks the novel's thematic shortcoming. That this heroine who consciously chooses and relishes in her self-interestedness and isolationism should abruptly shift to a sentimental discourse of unfound love and unfulfilled desire suggests an attempt to endear the protagonist to the reader. Xuela's extreme individualism and her dispassionate tie to others represent the self that she has deliberately constructed. She has privileged the material and corporeal world and claimed herself superior to others because she sees the fruitlessness of all else. Her arrogance and distance may leave readers unmoved by her story, but her spirit of resistance offers readers a site of connection. With her final sentimental lament, however, Xuela has compromised the defiance that has defined her heroic nature. Xuela's inconsistent narrative exemplifies a body of fiction by contemporary black women writers that critic bell hooks suggests is both powerful and problematic. This fiction is significant "in that it clearly names the ways structures of domination, racism, sexism, and class exploitation oppress and make it practically impossible for black women to survive if they do not engage in meaningful resistance on some level," but a prevailing shortcoming in many of these works is that often they "fail to depict any location for the construction of new identities."[12] This failing is evidenced in Kincaid's heroine, Xuela. Throughout the narrative, Xuela reiterates the charge that Christianity is a tool of western exploitation; however, it is her belief that the African-descent victims of western domination are unable to meaningfully connect with their pre-Colonial spiritual inheritance that informs her overwhelming desolate vision. Her determination to avoid the paralyzing reach of Christianity distinguishes her from the community of victims among whom she lives, but her insight does not lead her to the construction of a healthy self. While readers may applaud Xuela's defiance, they may be less inclined to embrace the empty self that evolves from her superior insight. Xuela is defined by loss, and she is finally consumed by that legacy. She is daring enough to explore the nature of her existence, but she lacks the courage to seek life.

Xuela represents the evolution of a fictional self that Kincaid arrives at through a series of works. Xuela's ontological introspection is foreshadowed in Kincaid's earlier work, *At the Bottom of the River* (1978), a collection of sketches that explores questions of identity and being. In particular, the speaker's search for knowledge of self in the final vignette is a precursor to

Xuela's desire to know the unknowable. Here, however, the speaker accepts the unknowable nature of human existence and accepts that if life is "a violent burst of light, like flint stuck sharply in the dark," then one "must continually strive to exist between the day and the day."[13] Out of the understanding that one cannot know, this speaker, unlike Xuela, is able to construct meaning out of her existence.

In the two novels that followed *At the Bottom of the River—Annie John* (1983) and *Lucy* (1990)—Kincaid's fictionalized contemplations occur through less abstract characterizations and with clearer musings on the African self in the face of western domination. The protagonists' piercing denunciations of Christianity in these novels symbolize their break with western ideologies. However, for both Annie and Lucy, African spirituality contributes to their construction of an African-rooted self, and their disengagement from Christianity is ironically exemplified by their self-subscribed allegiance with the Christian personification of evil—Lucifer.[14] Although Lucy's frequent proclamations of detachment foreshadow Xuela's self-imposed isolation, she, like Annie, maintains a reverence for African-based spirituality. Annie and Lucy are still connected to the world outside themselves—they are connected to others. While they recognize the hypocrisy and untruth veiled in western claims of civility, Annie and Lucy are not driven to the spiritual abyss that claims Xuela. Xuela is the nexus as well as the denouement to Kincaid's narrative trilogy. Going beyond Annie and Lucy's rejection of western spirituality, Xuela pronounces African-based spirituality inept and effectively dead. She accepts the resultant void, living at the margin of two worlds, claiming to be part of neither. Disengaged from humanity and any meaningful ideology, Xuela resides in a cosmos of her own. Having left no point of entry for human connection, Xuela's final lament can only echo within the confines of her self-imposed and once celebrated isolationism.

NOTES

1. In her essay, "Jamaica Kincaid's Writing and the Maternal Colonial Matrix," Laura Niesen de Abruna comments on the inclination of reviewers to emphasize Kincaid's exploration of mother–daughter relationships while ignoring her commentary on colonialism (*Caribbean Women Writers: Fiction in English*, eds. Mary Condé and Thorunn Lonsdale [New York: St. Martin's Press, 1999], 172–183).

2. Laura Niesen de Abruna, "Jamaica Kincaid's Writing and the Maternal Colonial Matrix," in Condé and Thorunn, 173.

3. For recent critical discussions on identity and colonialism in Kincaid's works, see Moira Ferguson's *Jamaica Kincaid: Where the Land Meets the Body* (Charlottesville: University Press of Virginia, 1994); and Diane Simmons's *Jamaica Kincaid* (New York: Twayne, 1994). See Belinda Edmondson's *Making Men: Gender, Literary Authority, and Women's Writing in*

Caribbean Narrative (Durham: Duke University Press, 1999) for discussion on constructing identity in works by Kincaid and other Caribbean women writers.

4. Wendy Dutton, "Merge and Separate: Jamaica Kincaid's Fiction," *World Literature Today* 63 (1989): 409.

5. H. Adlai Murdoch's "Serving the Mother Connection: The Representation of Cultural Identity in Jamaica Kincaid's *Annie John*" (*Callaloo* 13 [1990]: 325–340) and Craig Tapping's "Children and History in the Caribbean Novel: George Lamming's *In the Castle of My Skin* and Jamaica Kincaid's *Annie John*" (*Kunapipi* 11 [1989]: 51–59) explore the journey to selfhood in *Annie John*.

6. Jamaica Kincaid, *The Autobiography of My Mother* (New York: Farrar Straus Giroux, 1992), 215–16. This text will also be referred to as AOMM.

7. Claudia Tate, *Psychoanalysis and Black Novels* (New York: Oxford University Press, 1998), 10. Though *Autobiography of My Mother* is not among the texts considered in Claudia Tate's critical work, Tate's call to consider the implications of black authored novels that lack a race-centered narrative can be applied to a reading of *Autobiography of My Mother*.

8. Claudia Tate, *Psychoanalysis*, 13.

9. Claudia Tate, *Psychoanalysis*, 82.

10. Claudia Tate, *Psychoanalysis*, 9.

11. For details of Paul's ancestry see Romans 11:1; Philippians 3:5; Acts 16:37; Acts 22:25–28. Also, Werner Keller's *The Bible as History* provides an account of Paul's identity (pp. 357–63).

12. bell hooks, *Black Looks: Race and Representation* (Boston: South End Press, 1992), 50–51.

13. Jamaica Kincaid, *At the Bottom of the River* (New York: Farrar Straus Giroux, 1983), 73.

14. Jamaica Kincaid, *Annie John* (New York: Farrar Straus Giroux, 1983), 94–95. Kincaid, *Lucy* (New York: Farrar Straus Giroux, 1990), 139, 152–53. In both novels the protagonists are described by their mothers as Lucifer. Neither Annie or Lucy find this offensive, perhaps because despite his evil nature, Lucifer stands as the antithesis to Christianity.

J. BROOKS BOUSON

"Like Him and His Own Father before Him, I Have a Line Drawn through Me": Imagining the Life of the Absent Father in Mr. Potter

"*How do I write?* Why do I write? What do I write? This is what I am writing: I am writing 'Mr. Potter.' It begins in this way; this is its first sentence: 'Mr. Potter was my father, my father's name was Mr. Potter.' So much went into that one sentence; much happened before I settled on those 11 words" ("Those Words"). So Kincaid writes in a June 1999 *New York Times* "Writers on Writing" essay as she remarks on the difficult beginnings—the "many days of this and that and back and forth"—of what would eventually become *Mr. Potter*, her fictional memoir of her biological father, Roderick Nathaniel Potter. She describes her attempt to conjure up Mr. Potter's life—"He is a young man, and I am not yet born. Oh, I believe I am seeing him as a little boy"—only to find that his life remains "frozen in the vault that was his name and the vault of being only my father." As Kincaid goes about her domestic and daily routines, she continues to think about Mr. Potter, who, finally, one day is "driving a motorcar and dressing in a way imitative of men who had enormous amounts of money," but that day of writing comes with a cost, leaving Kincaid "bereft and exhausted and feeling empty" ("Those Words"). If in her description of the writing process, Kincaid seems to will Mr. Potter into a kind of imaginative and literary existence—"I look at Mr. Potter, in my own way, a way I am imagining, a way that is most certainly true and real" ("Those Words")—her essay also points to the reluctant and halting

From *Jamaica Kincaid: Writing Memory, Writing Back to the Mother.* © 2005 by the State University of New York.

159

beginnings of her 2002 novel, which deals with the absent yet everpresent father and the missing yet everpresent part of her identity: "Elaine Cynthia Potter," the daughter-narrator of *Mr. Potter*, who can readily be identified with Kincaid as she continues her ongoing process of autobiographical-fictional self-representation.

"[H]e is dead and beyond reading and writing and beyond contesting my authority to render him in my own image," Kincaid remarks in *Mr. Potter* (193), which refers not only to the death of her biological father in 1992 at the age of seventy but also to the death of her mother, Annie Drew, who died in 1999 at the age of eighty. Commenting that although the book is about her "real father," it is "not a biography," she recalls, "I didn't know him at all.[1] I only had his birth certificate, death certificate, and his parents' death certificates" (*Essence*). But she also acknowledges her use of her family history in *Mr. Potter*, explaining, "I have always used the facts of autobiography and manipulated them with language so they are transformed into something else" (Heer). "Always I'm writing about these actual people in my past. I don't write about them to know them in any biographical way. I like to think of them in some sort of existential way" (Walker).

Even though Mr. Potter and the daughter-narrator have an "intimate connection," as Kincaid remarks, Mr. Potter is nevertheless "only a spectre"[2] in the narrator's life. Because Mr. Potter is "oral, not literate," Kincaid deliberately draws on the language of oral culture to create his world. "His world had to be made of the very thing he couldn't do, read or write. I make a world by repeating things, using bricks of language. A great deal of my imagination came about by reading things that were originally meant to be oral, such as the Bible, Homer and myths. When I was writing, I was tapping into more of the sources that formed me than any other writing I had done" (Heer). Kincaid also associates the style of *Mr. Potter*, which is heavily repetitive both in its verbal patterns and in its telling and retelling of Mr. Potter's story, with her mother's storytelling when she was growing up in Antigua. "My mother would tell me stories about herself, about me being born, about her family. That's the voice I heard, primarily. The stories she told me she told me again and again" (Heer). In her fictional memoir of her biological father, Kincaid repeats over and over something her mother said of him—that "A line runs through him," which as a girl Kincaid understood "as a curse, that he was a bad man and on top of that he was doomed" (101).

Unlike her mother, who is overpresent in her life—and memories—her father is an absence. Yet, as Kincaid's daughter-narrator remarks, "My father's absence will forever hang over my present and my present, at any given moment, will echo his absence" (192). By imagining and writing the life of her absent father, she can make him "whole and complete" and break the "silence" of the illiterate chauffeur who never "had a voice to begin with" (193, 189). Giving an oral quality to her account through her progressive and constantly repeated but also interrupted telling of Mr. Potter's story, Kincaid exposes the shameful story of her illegitimacy,[3] a heritage passed down through the paternal line. Even as Kincaid writes about her biological father in *Mr. Potter*, she also writes back to her mother. Asked how the "idea" of the novel came to her, Kincaid explained, "It came to me in thinking about my mother. The more I thought of her life, and how it was that I grew up without knowing this person that she loathed and who was my father, the more I wanted to write this book. Here was a person she absolutely detested. She never introduced me to him and he never had any interest in me" (McLarin). If in part Kincaid attempts to talk back to her mother and reverse Mr. Potter's curse—the curse of illegitimacy that he, in turn, passed down to Kincaid—she nevertheless speaks in her mother's voice as she expresses her resentment toward and contempt for her absentee father. Kincaid also re-creates the haunted world of obsessive memory in *Mr. Potter* through the refrain-like and often-repeated words of shame that come to echo in the daughter-narrator's memory and in her narrative—"I have a line drawn through me."

Recalling her characterization of Antiguans in *A Small Place* as small-minded people living small lives in a small place, Kincaid highlights the wholly unimaginative and circumscribed life of her biological father. A descendent of African slaves and a mixed-race man on whose face is written "'Africa' and 'Europe,'" Mr. Potter is "not unfamiliar with upheavals and displacements and murder and terror," for his existence in Antigua "had been made possible by such things, but he did not dwell on them and he could not dwell on them any more than he could dwell on breathing" (11, 7). In *Mr. Potter*, as she does in *My Brother*, Kincaid associates the Creole speech of Mr. Potter with a history of humiliation. When Mr. Potter says, "'Me name Potter, Potter me name,'" his voice is "so full of all that had gone wrong in the world for almost five hundred years that it could break the heart of an ordinary stone" (23). To Mr. Shoul, the Middle Eastern owner of the taxi business where Mr. Potter works, Mr. Potter is without importance, and to Dr. Weizenger, a Czechoslovakian doctor[4] who is one of Mr. Potter's passengers, Mr. Potter is a physically repulsive and worthless human being. Kincaid's daughter-narrator is sympathetic to the historical and social plight of Mr. Potter as a representative black Antiguan, but she also harshly criticizes him for his small-mindedness and narcissism: "[E]vents great or small did not enter his mind, nothing entered his mind, his mind was already filled up with Mr. Potter" (27).

Because Mr. Potter cannot read or write, he cannot "understand himself" or "make himself known to others" or "know himself" (21). "I think

to be able to read is to make a crucial separation between your self and the
world," Kincaid states. The ability to read and write "is not just about some
UN standard of literacy. It's really symbolic of the ability to know yourself,
to separate the different parts of yourself so that you can speak to the world
and yourself" (Heer). Literacy fosters the ability to separate from the world
and also to appreciate its beauty, Kincaid suggests in *Mr. Potter* as she, using
romanticized, literary speech, describes the quality of light in Antigua, where
the sunlight is "so bright that it eventually made everything that came in
contact with it transparent and then translucent" (19). If to the prosaic Mr.
Potter the sun merely shines down in its "usual way," to the daughter-narrator
the Antiguan sunlight is "the very definition of light . . . light that was itself
and also a metaphor for all other aspiring forms of brightness" (16). When
Mr. Potter is suddenly thrilled by the light—"('E ah make me trimble up
inside, 'e ah make me feel funny)"—the daughter-narrator voices thoughts
and feelings that her illiterate father is incapable of feeling or expressing:
"[T]he light was substance itself and the light gave substance to everything
else: the trees became the trees but only more so, and the ground in which
they anchored themselves remained the ground but only more so, and the
sky above revealed more and more of the sky and into the heavens, into
eternity, and then returned to the earth" (19, 20). Mr. Potter sees the world
"in that special light," but he does not think "This is Happiness itself," for he
is not "separated from himself," and as he clearly sees the world and all that
is in it, words fail the illiterate taxi driver (21).

    Rendered by Kincaid as inarticulate—indeed, his most common
expression is a series of "Eh, eh!" sounds—Mr. Potter lacks the capacity
for deep thought or an emotional or aesthetic response to his Antiguan
surroundings. Instead, as he drives his taxi, he is "almost in a stupor": "Mr.
Potter drove along and nothing crossed his mind and the world was blank
and the world remained blank" (34). An uninviting, if not unlikely, subject
for a fictional memoir, Mr. Potter is presented as someone living a vacuous
life-in-the-present. He lacks not only a historical and autobiographical
awareness—a sense of family history and of the causal links between his
childhood and adult selves—but also an interior life. Presenting her father's
unstoried life as a story, Kincaid connects his past to his present and adds
narrative, indeed novelistic, dimension to his empty, barren life. The absent
father, thus, is given a kind of narrative presence as he is authored—and
authorized by—the daughter-writer who preserves family history and
transforms it into literature.

    Yet even as Kincaid uses her writing to aestheticize and give a kind
of verbal substance to her biological father—and to her life in his—she also
vents her anger as she exposes the shameful secret of her illegitimacy. As
she, in effect, elevates the life of Mr. Potter by writing his life story, she

also asserts her verbal authority over him, using her writing to settle old scores against her absentee father, a shallow, unloving man who abandoned Kincaid's mother when she was seven months pregnant and rejected his daughter. Once treated in a contemptuous way by Mr. Potter, who refused to acknowledge his daughter's existence and turned his back on his four-year-old daughter the one time she approached him, ironically enough, to ask for money so she could buy writing paper, Kincaid returns paternal contempt with her own daughterly countercontempt in *Mr. Potter*.

The daughter-writer, Kincaid talks and writes back to her biological father as she continues her autobiographical project of writing stories about her family—the story of Annie Drew in *The Autobiography of My Mother*, of Devon Drew in *My Brother*, and of Roderick Nathaniel Potter in *Mr. Potter*—as a way to come to terms with her own painful Antiguan past. In *Mr. Potter*, as Kincaid ruminates over the past in her inner dialogue with her parents, she also brings into a kind of self-dialogue the two parts of her identity; that of "Elaine Cynthia Potter," the illegitimate, and thereby shamed and powerless, daughter, and "Jamaica Kincaid," the successful and powerful author. The split between "Elaine Cynthia Potter" and "Jamaica Kincaid" also looks back to Kincaid's beginnings as a writer in New York City. As Kincaid recalls her early days in New York, she comments that reading and writing gave her a "sense of self" and "self-possession," allowing her to reflect on her situation and "put into words" who she was and making her realize that she did not want to be Elaine, the powerless girl sent by her parents to the United States to work as an au pair "at their will" (Deziel). Attempting to artistically repair the rift in her identity and write over the line drawn through her, Kincaid works to give a kind of artistic and bookish legitimacy to her shameful, discarded identity as "Elaine Cynthia Potter," the illegitimate daughter of Mr. Potter who grew up with a "line drawn through" her.

Mr. Potter's Family Legacy

Explaining that she refers to her biological father as "Mr. Potter" because that is the name she "came to know him by," Kincaid's narrator slowly tells the story of Roderick Potter, a simple, unquestioning man who "did not long to know of all the Potters that he came from and how it came to be so that he came from them," and who "did not seek to interrogate the past to give meaning to the present and the future" (87, 25). The son of Nathaniel Potter, a fisherman, and Elfrida Robinson, who committed suicide by walking into the sea when her son was five years old, Mr. Potter is afraid of and hates the sea, which to him is "so much water . . . so much nothing" (12). While Mr. Potter is unaware of the cause of his hatred of the sea, readers are able to make sense of this feeling as they piece together his family history, which Kincaid places against the larger backdrop of the African diaspora.

Elaborating on a story she tells in *Annie John*,[5] Kincaid recounts the history of the narrator's grandfather, Nathaniel Potter, who, like his son, Roderick, is illiterate and unreflective: "Who am I? never entered into his thoughts . . . and Nathaniel could not read and he could not write" (57). While Nathaniel was taught by his fisherman father how to construct a fishing boat and make and mend fishing nets, he does not understand that his father was a shaping force in his life, and he cannot "give an account of himself, not even one that began with 'I was born'" (42). Unable to read or write, he is an unreflective, storyless, historyless man. "He was so much a part of the glory of the world and he could not see himself. Naked at all times, no matter what covered his body, that was Nathaniel Potter. The sun fell into the black before him; the moon rose up from the black behind him: and in between was history, all that had happened, and at its end was a man named Nathaniel Potter and who was only that, Nathaniel Potter. And he asked himself . . . What? He asked himself, not a thing" (42–43). Unloved and therefore unloving, Nathaniel does not "miss love, for it had never been part of his very being" (43).

Nathaniel's fisherman's life, which depends on the sea's bounty, becomes uncertain and indecipherable when, suddenly and inexplicably, his fish pots and fishnets come up empty day after day. Expressing his anger at what he perceives as a God-decreed fate, Nathaniel curses God and, in an irreverent act of defiance, removes his trousers, faces his bare buttocks to the sky, and angrily asks God to kiss his ass. Intoning biblical cadences and speech to describe the biblical-obeah curse that befalls the fisherman, the narrator tells of his gruesome death at the age of forty-seven in passages that recall Kincaid's earlier account in *My Brother* of the transformation of Devon's AIDS-ravaged body into a disgusting and dissmelling object. "[A] curse fell on Nathaniel Potter and this curse took the form of small boils appearing on his arms and then on his legs and then on the rest of his body and then at last covering his face. And the small boils festered and leaked a pus that had a smell like nothing that had ever lived before and all his bodily fluids were turned into the pus that leaked out of him. . . . And when he died, his body had blackened, as if he had been trapped in the harshest of fires" (47).

Nathaniel leaves behind twenty-one children—although he knows of only eleven children that he has fathered with eight different women—and not one of his children, including Roderick, can read or write. In a self-referential aside that directs attention to the daughter-narrator's—and by extension, Kincaid's—presence in the text, the narrator remarks of her grandfather, "I can read and I am also writing all of this at this very moment; at this very moment I am thinking of Nathaniel Potter and I can place my thoughts about him and all that he was, and all that he could have been into words. These are all words, all of them, these words are my own" (48). The ability to "place" her thoughts in words gives Kincaid's narrator the power and authority to have the last word about the substance and meaning—or lack of meaning—of Nathaniel's life expressed in his imagined final words. "A very long 'Oooooohhhhh!!!' sighed Nathaniel Potter just before he died and many times before that and it was his only legacy to all his children and all who would come from them: this sound of helplessness combined with despair: 'Oooooohhhhh,' they all cried and cry, all who came from Nathaniel Potter" (57).

The only child of Elfrida Robinson, Roderick Nathaniel Potter is born in a one-room house in the village of English Harbour in 1922. "And Mr. Potter was not an original man, he was not made from words, his father was Nathaniel and his mother was Elfrida and neither of them could read or write; his beginning was just the way of everyone, as would be his end" (55–56). No one cares about his birth; his appearance does not make "the world pause," and he is "held with contempt" by the midwife (61, 63). One of "the despised," Mr. Potter is brought safely into the world, wrapped in a blanket, and placed next to his sixteen-year-old mother on a bed of clean rags. "[B]ut to what end? To no end at all" (67).

Yet another example of the unloving, rejecting mother that haunts Kincaid's narratives, Elfrida, after caring for Roderick for the first week of his life, tires of him and longs to rid herself of him. Leaving him alone on a bed of rags, she can hear him crying when he is hungry or lonely "and sometimes her heart broke in two when she heard his cries and sometimes her heart hardened. . . . And her breasts became parched, barren of her milky fluids (she had willed them so)" (69). An unloving mother, Elfrida is a motherless girl, as was her mother and her mother's mother, a condition reaching back to 1492—Elfrida's motherless condition, like Xuela's in *The Autobiography of My Mother*, standing as a metaphor for the African diaspora and loss of the African motherland. Passing on this legacy to her son, Elfrida, in 1927, gives away the five-year-old Roderick and then, on an ordinary day, walks into the sea, which takes her in "not with love, not with indifference, not with meaning of any kind" (76). To Roderick, who cannot recall his mother's face or name, his dead mother becomes associated with a blank space of darkness and light. Although Elfrida was a woman of no account, Kincaid's narrator cannot forget that she was the mother of her biological father, and although Elfrida was soon forgotten by Nathaniel and her son and others who knew her or knew of her, Kincaid's narrator now thinks of her.

A motherless and fatherless child handed over to people who do not care for him—the Shepherds—Roderick is a familiar Kincaidian figure: the humiliated and vulnerable child. If in rare moments of childhood playfulness he is "in harmony with his joy and is himself," he also is one of the "ordinarily degraded" (80). Calling attention to her imaginative attempt to conjure up the childhood of Roderick and give his empty life narrative dimension, the narrator directs readers to envision the hardships he endures: "See the small boy, Roderick Nathaniel Potter, asleep on a bed of old and dirty rags. . . . See the small boy, so, tired, so hungry, before he falls asleep" (78). Left with Mr. Shepherd, the headmaster of the Shepherd school for wayward boys who finds the poor, hungry, and dirty boys in his school hateful—"their misfortune was a curse and to be cursed was deserving of hatred"—Roderick grows "dull and ugly, in the way of the forgotten" (96, 88).

Roderick Potter takes in Mr. Shepherd's "cruelty and ugliness with silence or indifference," and "all of it—cruelty, ugliness, silence, indifference"—becomes "a skin"; similarly, his mother's abandonment of him and his father's lack of fatherly feelings for him become "a skin," a "protective covering" without which he cannot live (93). Growing up in Mr. Shepherd's household, he is "despised for his vulnerability (his mother had abandoned him and had chosen the cold, vast vault that was the sea), held in contempt (for he could not protect himself, he could not protest when he was too tired to do one more thing that was required of him)" (94–95). Left "all alone in the world with nothing but a line drawn through him," Mr. Potter stands "before nothing, only Mr. Shepherd, the man who had been consigned to oversee his degradation in the world confirmed" (102). Despite his mistreatment at the hands of Mr. Shepherd, Roderick comes to identify with the vain and insensitive headmaster, who passes on to his charge not only "the love of contempt for all that was vulnerable and weak and in need and lost and in pain" but also a "love of self" coupled with "the love of appearing before people well dressed" (103–04).

Roderick Potter and Annie Victoria Richardson

"I was weak and vulnerable, not yet even a person, only seven months living in my mother's stomach when Mr. Potter first abandoned me; I was born in nineteen hundred and forty-nine and I never knew his face," Kincaid's narrator remarks of the abandoning Mr. Potter (104). A womanizer like his father, Mr. Potter visits many women in their one-room houses, fathering many girls who are all unloved by him—"and all of them a burden, all of them, these daughters, needing support of one kind or another: food, clothing, and then schoolbooks and above all, his love." Just when he is feeling good about himself, his daughters appear, one after another, "their forms wrapped in malice and general ill will" (119). "Who was he?" Kincaid's narrator asks. "And those daughters of his . . . those daughters of his with their cries of hunger and illness and ignorance, and their mothers who had words that were like weapons specially forged to make fatal wounds, and their sullying of his good name, for his name was good, his name was Mr. Potter, and accusing him of unfairness and betrayal of his fatherly duties and not being a good person" (119–20).

Retelling and elaborating on the story of her mother's early years in Antigua, Kincaid describes how Annie Victoria Richardson, at the age of sixteen, leaves Mahaut, Dominica, and comes to Antigua after quarreling with her father, who subsequently disinherits her.[6] A beautiful and still-young woman of twenty-five with long, black hair when she meets Mr. Potter, Annie lives in St. John's in a one-room house. "And my mother then was flames in her own fire, not waves in her own sea, she would be that later, after I was born and had become a grown woman, she would become that to me, an ocean with its unpredictable waves and undertow; she was then flames in her own fire and she was very beautiful and her beauty was mentioned sometimes with admiration and affection by others, sometimes with disapproval and scorn by some others, and it was as if her beauty was a blessing in the world sometimes, and as if her beauty was a sign of evil in the world sometimes" (135). Recalling earlier representations of the mother in Kincaid's works, Annie is described as a good/bad woman and a powerful presence, for in her passionate, unpredictable behavior, she is like a force of nature in her daughter's life.

Like Xuela in *The Autobiography of My Mother*, a character also drawn after Kincaid's mother, Annie Drew, Annie Richardson is a fierce and willful woman who repudiates motherhood. Before the age of thirty, she has four abortions, but when she tries to self-abort for the fifth time, she fails "and that failure was because of me, I could not be expelled from my mother's womb at her own will. All this my mother told me when I was forty-one years of age and had by then become the mother of two children" (136). The daughter-narrator, in an act of self-authoring, seeks the roots of her own life in the lives of her parents. Extending the bounds of the remembering self, she recounts her "memory" of her parents from the time before she was born: "I can see them breathing at the time they were being born and struggling into living and being, and I can see them passing through their lives as children and then into being the two people who came together and made me, and through all of this I see them in substantial particularity and I see them as specters, possibilities of the real, possibilities of the real as it pertains to me. And my name when I was born then was Elaine Cynthia, and Annie Richardson was my mother, and that is my substantial particularity and Mr. Potter is my specter" (137–38). In a passage that illustrates Kincaid's desire to know her characters in "some sort of existential way" (Walker), the daughter-narrator places her small life against the backdrop of the benign and violent forces of nature: "and the wind blows, and the sun shines, and the surface of the earth rises up and falls down in violent activity . . . and my mother Annie Victoria Richardson and my father Roderick Potter were, just then, at the time before I would be born, and even at the time I was born, were without interest in the world . . . and the forces that cause it to spin from one end to the other." Behind the "existential" and nihilistic awareness of the narrator lies a very personal story of Kincaid's lifelong obsession with, and inability to fully resolve, the hurts of the past: "and the sorrow I knew then, and the absence of permanent joy or spontaneous joy or frequent joy—all of this has remained unchanged from then to now, as I write this" (138).

Annie interrupts the smooth progress and certainties of Mr. Potter's life, for when she meets him, she is "already a series of beautifully poisonous eruptions . . . a whirlwind of sex and passion and female beauty and deception and pain and female humiliation and narcissism and vulnerability" (141). The narrator imagines that there is "a romance of some sort" between her parents but not any love "because my mother would not submit to anything, certainly not to love, with all its chaos, its demands, its unpredictability; and because Mr. Potter could not love anyone, not anyone who was his own" (163). The two live together, but when Annie is seven months pregnant, she quarrels with and then leaves Mr. Potter, taking all the money he has saved to buy a car so that he can become a self-employed chauffeur and thus "make of himself some semblance of a man" (142). When the daughter-narrator is born, her embattled parents hate each other with a hatred that causes Mr. Potter "to deny . . . the protection of his patrimony" (129). "[T]his hatred that existed between them became a part of my own life as I live it even today and I do not understand how this could be so, but it is true all the same" (130).

ELAINE CYNTHIA POTTER

"And my life began, absent Mr. Potter, in the dimly lit ward of the Holberton Hospital, with my mother's resentment silently beaming at him, with my mother's love for me and my mother's resentment silently beaming at me, and then I was swathed in yards of white cotton and laid to rest in the pose of the newborn which is also the pose of the dead" (146–47). Associating birth with death, Kincaid suggests, as she does elsewhere in her writings, the lethality of maternal resentment. An unwanted child born to parents who hate each other, the narrator is named "Elaine" not after a family member but after a daughter of the man Mr. Potter works for as a chauffeur, and thus the name *Elaine* becomes associated with people the mother ends up not liking or wishing well. Like Annie John, the daughter-narrator Elaine comes to know herself through her mother's stories. Elaine learns that she caused her mother, Annie, pain even before she was born—that her mother endured discomfort during her pregnancy and suffered a painful delivery—and Elaine also is told that she was such a greedy infant that her mother breastfed her until she was sucked dry, drained of her milk. Elaine learns of her essential "badness" through her mother's stories, and she comes to "remember" her one childhood encounter with Mr. Potter through a story her mother tells her.

In this story, which comes to define Elaine's girlhood and adult relation with her biological father, Mr. Potter rejects the four-year-old Elaine when she is sent by her mother to ask him for sixpence, so she can buy writing paper. Standing across the street from the garage where his taxi is kept, she waves at him and wishes him a good morning. Refusing to acknowledge her, Mr. Potter rolls his shoulders and then, turning his back on her, enters the garage. "Not only did he ignore me, he made sure that until the day he died, I did not exist at all" (126). In a subsequent retelling of this story, she remarks that Mr. Potter waved her away "as if I were an abandoned dog blocking his path, as if I were nothing to him at all and had suddenly and insanely decided to pursue an intimate relationship with him. 'Eh, eh,' said Mr. Potter" (146). If Elaine "remembers" the incident of waving to Mr. Potter because her mother has told her about it—"all of this my mother has told me, my entire life as I live it is all my mother has told me" (127)—she also comes to acknowledge the unreliability of her account. "I saw him from across the street and from across the street I asked him for money to buy books that I needed for school, but I do not remember any of this, it is only that my mother has told me so and my mother's tongue and the words that flow from it cannot be relied upon, she is now dead" (154). Retelling this story yet again, she remarks, "I have only a vague memory of him ignoring me as I passed him by in the street, of him slamming a door in my face when I was sent to ask him for money I needed to purchase my writing paper, and the full knowledge of the line drawn through me which I inherited from him" (160–61).

A "vague memory" and something she does "not remember" but was told, the story, which "cannot be relied on," nevertheless has a shaping influence on the daughter-narrator's identity, reinforcing the message of her illegitimacy and of her mother's power over her: fatherless, she comes "from the female line" and belongs "only" to her mother (161). In the "vacant" look on her face captured in a photograph of her taken when she was seven, the narrator sees evidence of "the absence of Mr. Potter" in her childhood, an absence that continues to reverberate in her adult life: "I have a line drawn through me, and that overwhelms everything that I know about myself at this moment" (145). Even though the narrator grows up entangled in her mother's life, she remains aware of the shadowy presence of Mr. Potter. "And who was I then, Potter or Richardson, for though my mother wove herself around me, wound me up in a cocoon of love and bitterness and anger and pain, and from this cocoon I shall never emerge, . . . through those unbreakable fibers I could feel Mr. Potter, the shadow of him, . . . a shadow more important than any person I might know" (154).

Kincaid's narrator expresses her sense of loss and regret at not knowing Mr. Potter: "Mr. Potter was a man and he was my father and I never knew him at all, had never touched him, or known how he smelled . . . or the look of him after he had an ordinary experience that related to touching or smelling or seeing or hearing" (160). Yet she also expresses hostility toward the unloving Mr. Potter who fathered many girl children with different women—women who all "longed for his presence," as she imagines it. "But Mr. Potter's caresses and embraces were like a razor and each woman and girl child of his who had received one of his embraces was left with skin shredded and hanging toward the floor and blood falling down to meet the floor and bones exposed and sinew, too, and nerves" (151). An irresponsible father who spurned his illegitimate daughters, Mr. Potter eventually achieved financial success as a chauffeur, owning three cars and living in a house with many rooms. Marrying a woman who bore him a daughter and then gave birth to a boy fathered by another man, Mr. Potter loved only the boy, whom he raised as his son, of all his children.

Making and Unmaking Mr. Potter

"What am I to call you?" the thirty-three-year-old Elaine asks Mr. Potter when she finally meets him[7] during a visit he makes to the United States (168). In her enraged response to Mr. Potter, the daughter-narrator resembles her mother, Annie, whose fierce anger is likened to a destructive, natural force. "And at that moment, should anger have surged through me like a force unpredictable in nature, should I have wished my father dead, should I have gone beyond mere wishing and walked over to him and grabbed him by the throat and squeezed his neck until his body lay limp at my feet, should I have thrown him out the window . . . ? And I did wish him dead and I did want him dead and I wanted my moments past, present, and future to be absent of him" (169–70). Yet despite her murderous rage, after he leaves she feels a sense of loss and despair, which she describes as an "empty space inside" her that is small when she is not aware of it and large when she is (170).

"'Potter dead, 'e dead you know, me ah tell you, eh, eh, me ah tell you,'" Annie tells her daughter, reporting the death of the seventy-year-old Mr. Potter, who dies in 1992 (185). When Elaine later looks for Mr. Potter's unmarked burial spot in the St. John's cemetery in Antigua, the grave master tells her about the family commotion that accompanied the burial of Mr. Potter as family members quarreled, ironically enough, over who was best loved by the unloving Mr. Potter and insulted each other because Mr. Potter, despite his considerable wealth, left them nothing. Those gathered at his gravesite recounted "stories of love and hatred," including one of his daughters, who said that Mr. Potter had raped her (50). "So much suffering was attached to Mr. Potter, so much suffering consumed him, so much suffering he left behind" (52). Mr. Potter was unmourned by those who knew him: "No one cried to show sorrow over his death and no one was sorry that he had died, they were only sorry they had known him, or sorry they had loved him, for he left them nothing at all" (185).

Unlike the illiterate Mr. Potter, Elaine can read and write, so she can "make" and "unmake" Mr. Potter (158). She is the "only one" able to write "the narrative that is his life" (87). "[B]ecause I learned how to read and how to write, only so is Mr. Potter's life known, his smallness becomes large, his anonymity is stripped away, his silence broken. Mr. Potter himself says nothing, nothing at all" (189). The man who lacked "private thoughts" or "thoughts of wonder" or "thoughts about his past, his future, and his present" (130) is given narrative and textual dimension by the daughter-writer who infuses her own rich literary sensibility into his diminished, empty existence—his lack—in her introspective and imaginative reconstruction of his life. In her existential musings on mutability and mortality, she enlarges his small life-in-the-present, giving it a kind of literary and textual depth and breadth by presenting it as an illustration of the ephemerality of human life. As she shows the connection between past and present—between Nathaniel and Elfrida's abandonment of Roderick and Roderick's abandonment of Elaine—she renders the story of Mr. Potter's life with a coherency beyond his grasp. And the narrator expresses sorrow at the death of Mr. Potter, who is unmourned by his family: "how sad never to again see the sun turn red sometimes and disappear sometimes; how sad never again to touch another person spontaneously, without thought, without reason, without justification, and to expect a similar response . . .; how sad never again to stand in the middle of nowhere and see the world in all its brightness and brimming over with possibilities innumerable heading toward you; how sad to know that you will be alive once and never so again, no matter how you rearrange your life and your very own self" (183).

As the narrator mourns the unmourned life of Mr. Potter, she attempts to grasp the whole of his life as she "start[s] again at the beginning: Mr. Potter's appearance in the world was a combination of sadness, joy, and a chasm of silent horror for his mother (Elfrida Robinson) and indifference to his father (Nathaniel Potter), who had so many children that none of them could matter at all" (188). Even though Mr. Potter's life and death were inconsequential, his small life is given meaning and enlarged by the daughter-narrator. And through her powers as a storyteller, she gives a kind of narrative presence to the father who was an absence in her life: "Hear Mr. Potter, who was my father; hear his children and hear the women who bore those children; hear the end of life itself rushing like a predictable wave in a known ocean to engulf Mr. Potter. . . . Hear Mr. Potter! See Mr. Potter! Touch Mr. Potter!" (194–95).

THE DAUGHTER-WRITER

No longer the disempowered daughter, Elaine, as the daughter-writer, can gain some mastery and control over the hurts of the past not only as she reconstructs and interprets the lives of her parents but also as she represents—and experiences—them as novelistic characters. The rejected daughter with the line drawn through her, she artistically revises the past as she becomes "the central figure" in the life of the man who turned his back on her and refused to acknowledge her as his daughter (153). By giving Mr. Potter a storied, novelistic identity, she makes him whole and complete. Yet she continues to observe and judge him and, like her mother, uses storytelling as a weapon, taking her daughter's revenge as a retrospective storyteller. She also talks and writes back to her mother, Annie, who told Elaine her life. "She is now dead, she is dead now," the daughter-narrator remarks of her hated mother (127). As Elaine stands near Mr. Potter's grave, she can see her mother's grave. "Her name was Annie Victoria Richardson and she did not have a line drawn through her, and for my whole life up to then, to see my mother dead was an event I was afraid I would never witness, I had waged a battle to see my own mother dead, and from time to time I was certain I would lose." Even as she stands above the graves of her parents—in the posture of the triumphant Xuela in *The Autobiography of My Mother*, who sees death as a humiliating defeat—Elaine recognizes their continuing influence on her life: "[T]hese three things, my father, me, my mother, remain the same into eternity, remain the same now, which is a definition of eternity" (192). She remains haunted by memories of her parents and of herself as the shamed, illegitimate daughter: "My name, Elaine Cynthia Potter, crossed out by the line that was drawn through it, I first abandoned and then changed to something else altogether, so that the line drawn through me, now, cannot find me, and if it did, would not recognize me, and that line cannot see me, but I can see it, following me each day as I do some ordinary thing" (143).

    In telling the story of her absentee father in *Mr. Potter*, Kincaid also tells the story of Elaine Cynthia Potter, the everpresent yet missing part of her identity. Kincaid retains her fierce anger about her past as she repeatedly and obsessively refers to the line of shame drawn through her, which she experiences as the attempted erasure of her identity. Yet even as Kincaid exposes the shame of Elaine Cynthia Potter in *Mr. Potter*, she also gives an artistic legitimacy to her cast-off identity. Like her parents, "Elaine Cynthia Potter" becomes a story authored and authorized by "Jamaica Kincaid" in her ongoing self-narration. Just as the real Elaine Cynthia Potter once sought refuge in the bookish world of novels, so Kincaid creates a bookish refuge for "Elaine Cynthia Potter" in *Mr. Potter*.

Kincaid does not claim that she can ever forget the past or heal the shame of the remembered girl with the line drawn through her. By ending her fictional memoir with the first eleven words she wrote when she began the novel—"Mr. Potter was my father, my father's name was Mr. Potter" (195)—she points to the persistence of her shame as she states the simple fact of her paternal origins. But in her self-fashioned identity as Jamaica Kincaid, she refuses to claim her inheritance or to pass her shame on to her children: "The line that is drawn through me, this line I have inherited, but I have not accepted my inheritance and so have not deeded it to anyone who shall follow me" (143). Because Kincaid cannot help but remember her Antiguan past, she remains haunted by Elaine Cynthia Potter, the shamed girl with the line drawn through her. Yet as the self-authored and thus self-possessed Jamaica Kincaid, she does find a kind of writer's solace as she gives a bookish presence and artistic legitimacy not only to her missing father but also to the missing part of her repudiated identity.

Notes

1. Kincaid recalls how a man once approached her and her mother and identified himself to Annie Drew as "'Walker, Potter's brother,'" leading Kincaid to wonder who "Potter" was. "They wouldn't explain," Kincaid recalls. "What's untypical is I didn't accept [their silence]. I should have said, 'Oh, yes' and just joined the parade. I said 'No.' I'm really not interested in a constant attempt to . . . make you think there wasn't a yesterday" (V. Jones). Commenting that *Mr. Potter* was "not meant" to be about her and her relationship with her "real father," Kincaid explains, "When I was writing it, I wasn't writing it to explore the fact that my father abandoned me, I was writing to explore what it means to be abandoned or what it means to live with someone who you would never know. The narrator may be 50-per-cent Mr. Potter, but she will never know him, and the only way he recognizes her is through the shape of her nose" (Macgowan).

2. Kincaid has described her biological father as "sort of typical of West Indian men: I mean, they have children, but they never seem to connect themselves with these children" (Cudjoe 219). When an interviewer asked Kincaid about her biological father in 1996, she remarked, tellingly, "He was as real to me as you. Yes, you'll go and I'll think, was there someone here?" (Jacobs).

3. Deborah Mistron's *Understanding Jamaica Kincaid's Annie John* includes information on social attitudes toward illegitimacy in Antigua during Kincaid's formative years. "Despite the fact that illegitimacy and mother-centered homes are accepted by the people, until quite recently (1986), and during the time that Annie John was growing up, illegitimate children were often discriminated against. Legitimate children often had more advantages, a higher social status, and more educational opportunities. Legitimate children were baptized on Sundays, at a church service; illegitimate ones were baptized separately during the week. Illegitimate children were often denied entrance to the better schools on the island and

thus had fewer educational and vocational opportunities.... In 1986, a law was passed in Antigua that prohibited discrimination against illegitimate children; it also gave them equal rights to inherit property from their fathers, even if the father had died without a will" (159). Mistron's analysis of Annie John's family situation is telling, pointing as it does to Kincaid's avoidance of the issue of her own illegitimacy in her early works. Mistron comments that Annie John's "father, typically, is older, with several previous relationships and children, but married to her mother, which gives Annie and her mother increased social status" (159).

Insight into the causes of illegitimacy in Antigua is found in an article Mistron includes by Mindie Lazarus-Black entitled "Bastardy, Gender Hierarchy, and the State: The Politics of Family Law Reform in Antigua and Barbuda" (originally published in *Law and Society Review* [Winter 1992]: 863–99). Remarking on Antigua's low marriage rate and high rate of illegitimacy, Lazarus-Black states: "In the early 1980s ... the marriage rate per one thousand persons was less than three, while the illegitimacy rate at birth averaged 80%. A variety of reasons account for these continued rates, including the legacy of laws that discouraged marriage and prohibited divorce, individuals' reluctance to marry until they have established a home and some financial security, an unwillingness on the part of men to wed until they feel they have 'sown their wild oats,' the critical relationship between marriage and individual religious salvation which becomes especially important in one's later years, and individuals' outright resistance to this form of state intervention in their personal lives. Visiting 'friends' and long-term, nonlegal relationships are common and prevail alongside formalized unions. Although both men and women say marriage is an ideal to which they aspire 'some day,' parenting outside of marriage is also highly valued. Within marriage, husbands and wives have segregated roles.... Both sexes believe firmly that a wife should defer to her husband when the couple faces important decisions.... A cultural prescriptive, common throughout the region, holds that men 'by nature' love to love more than one woman and ensures that many men will father 'outside' children even after they are wed" (180).

4. See *A Small Place* 28–29, 34.

5. See *Annie John* 121–22.

6. Kincaid recalls that when her mother's father died a wealthy man, he left his money to his other daughter who, in turn, left the family fortune to the illegitimate daughter of her husband. When Kincaid asked her mother, who had been disinherited after quarreling with her father, if she was "sorry" about what had happened, her mother replied, "'No, I was born with nothing, and I will die with nothing.' Something happened between her father and her, and she wouldn't compromise" (Ferguson, "Interview" 166). In another interview, Kincaid commented that her mother was disinherited because she married against her father's wishes (see Steavenson 37). See also *Annie John* 19–20.

7. In an interview, Kincaid describes this encounter with her biological father when he visited her in New York City in 1982. "He said he was my father, and I thought, 'How interesting,'" she recalls. "Then he actually began to make a claim of being my father, an emotional claim." When she asked him what she should call him and he answered "'Oh, why, Dad,'" the conversation ended, and they "never spoke again." "What I would have wanted him to say—how sorry he had been, how wrong he had been—he didn't say it. Then I didn't want to participate anymore," Kincaid explains. She also voices her anger at her father. "'You weren't my father when I was a year old, and you're my father now?' ... What do we do with the years in between? Do we just forget them? My tradition says 'Yes.' I say 'No'" (V. Jones). In another interview, Kincaid describes the aftermath of this encounter. "When he found me not interested in the idea of his being my dad, he actually disinherited me. It's in his will" (McLarin).

COLENA GARDNER-CORBETT

Escaping the Colonizer's Whip: The Binary Discipline

Readers who appreciate literature from a feminist perspective often rave about the insightful and misunderstood works of Jamaica Kincaid. Throughout Kincaid's collection of novels audiences are reminded of the author's past in Antigua. Her female characters give new meaning to "art imitating life," for not only does she portray herself in her works, but she evokes the belligerent protest toward colonist conformity developed through British colonization. In the midst of her biographical discovery, she conveys binary oppositions to compare norms of colonized society to those of postcolonial society. Attempting to dispel these binaries in her childhood, she leads a secret life because of her shame. Later, in her adolescence she exposes her true identity by claiming forbidden desires and sharing her experiences with those who are still living under the colonizer's whip. In adulthood, she tightly grasped the convictions that were never exposed in her youth, thus serving as a witness to other Antiguans who continued to remain as "doormats" in colonized British society.

The majority of Kincaid's works—*Annie John*, *Lucy*, *At the Bottom of the River*'s "Girl," *Autobiography of My Mother* and *My Brother*—convey coming-of-age stories about young girls breaking away from their disparaging maternal bonds. The author uses much of her childhood conflicts with maternal figures to symbolize her struggle between colonization and independence. Using

From *CLA Journal* 49, no. 1 (September 2005). © 2005 by the College Language Association.

maternal figures, Kincaid also explains oppressed people's escape from common canons arisen from colonial exploitation from within their mother country. This Antiguan daughter "[rejects] her mother . . . [as] . . . her attempt to escape the colonial yoke [which binds] her mother" (Alexander 47). In all of her works, she reiterates this constant theme of rejection from a mother figure because of the daughter's desire to protest the standards that are placed upon her. These standards are not Kincaid's culture, but they belong to the Eurocentric canon she is forced to abide under. Although Kincaid speaks with such infuriation, she candidly states that "her coming from Antigua is and has been a positive influence. She confesses that the happenstance of being Antiguan, like the happenstance of being black, has molded her in becoming who she is, a black Caribbean writer" (Alexander 29).

In her novels, Kincaid decodes *binary oppositions*.[1] Readers may witness various examples which display a constant contradiction throughout Kincaid's words, such as *chastisement* and *oppression*; *feminine* and *masculine*; *dirty* and *clean*; *child* and *adult*; *educated* and *ignorant*; *escape* and *free*; and *lady* and *the slut*. In using binary oppositions throughout Kincaid's works, the mother (colonizer) character attempts to brainwash these binary ideas into the young and innocent character in an effort to suffocate any effort of free thought. This common situation is reflective of the colonizer's plan for exploitation to begin at an early age. When the oppressed young develop into adults, these oppressed adults will not question the heterodox; the oppressed will perform trained exercises because they are conditioned; this is where Kincaid directs her anger. The mother country teaches her young that their natural ideals are wrong and will not be tolerated in the Eurocentric society. Therefore, it is acceptable for the colonized, the used, and the oppressed to feel inferior and not desire anything better than what they are given. The outcome is bleak for the colonized not to claim responsibility for their actions.

Literature: Propaganda

"Girl" was included in the collection of stories in *At the Bottom of the River* (1983). In "Girl" the narrator, a mother figure, is giving her daughter a list of instructions to meet feminine standards of their forced culture. Giovanna Covi elucidates the narrator's voice in Harold Bloom's *Modern Critical Views: Jamaica Kincaid*: "Kincaid's voice is that of a woman and an Afro-Caribbean/American and a post-modern at the same time. This combination is therefore not only disruptive of the institutional order, but also revolutionary in its continuous self-criticism and its rejection of all labels" (Covi 3). It is those same labels and institutions that push *Annie John* (1983) to leave her home of Antigua for England, to reclaim her life that once dangled at the strings of her mother, the master puppeteer. Annie

John is relative to Kincaid's actual life; she also left her home, Antigua, not for England but to attend college in the United States. It was during her studies in the United States that Kincaid worked as an au pair, similar to the caretaker in *Lucy* (1990). *Lucy* is based on Kincaid's experience in her employer's household and her observations on American culture through false eyes. Antigua is again revisited in *Autobiography of My Mother* (1996), in which Xuela is in search of answers about her existence. In her inability to piece the history of her birth mother, Xuela feels as if she has been shuffled and sold to anyone at the convenient price of her father. Although Xuela enjoys her exploitation, Kincaid portrays this boldly painted character as a woman who chooses to take control of negative situations by demonstrating her independence, embracing her sexuality, and exercising her right not to bear children. Xuela fosters sexuality and dispels the ingrained definition of a slut. In her most recent work, Kincaid's character later develops into a grown woman who plays herself in *My Brother* (1997). In her memoir on death and dying, Kincaid offers hope to the living, gives an awakening to the dead as her brother walks before and during his battle with AIDS. The author's premise of accepting responsibility and claiming one's own life reflects the binary opposition of life and death.

FEMININE: MASCULINE

Kincaid's main characters embrace not only life and death but also the difference within their sexuality. These women partake in measures that question their sexuality and oppose the standards set by canon society. In *Annie John*, Annie is balancing two sides of her inner consciousness. On one side, Annie (Kincaid) embraces the dainty femininity in her friend Gwen and on the other, masculinity in her friend the Red Girl. Each of these characters represents the two sides of Kincaid. Her mother favors Gwen but does not care for the Red Girl. Gwen was the picture of a model woman whom her mother desired Annie to become: "Gwen and everything about her were perfect, as if she were in a picture. Her panama hat, with the navy blue and gold satin ribbon—our school colors—around the brim. . . . The pleats in the tunic of her uniform were in place, as was to be expected. Her cotton socks fit neatly around her ankles, and her shoes shone from just being polished" (*Annie John* 47). Then Annie speaks of Gwen's mannerisms, observing that she was prim and proper, taking pride in her appearance. On the other hand, there is the Red Girl, who has "big, broad, flat feet, and they were naked to the bare ground; her dress was dirty, the skirt and blouse tearing away from each other at one side . . . her fingernails held at least ten anthills of dirt under them" (*Annie John* 57). The Red Girl delights herself in playing marbles, a mannish game that Annie's mother disapproves. She says it is a boy's game.

When Annie disobeys her mother by playing marbles, her mother attempts to find each one of them to throw them out, for she wishes to rid her daughter of the mannish qualities that are contrary to the colonized, conformed roles of a woman. Although Kincaid appreciates Annie's duality, she senses that her mother loathes her masculinity and would like her daughter to act like a little girl. She therefore gives her strict instruction on how women should act, what they should play with, and how they should appear when around the opposite sex.

Those same instructions in the novel *Annie John* may parallel the lessons in "Girl." Kincaid's combination of instruction, as well as oppression, compares with the roles or duties colonized society has placed on the women of Antigua:

> [O]n Sunday try to walk like a lady and not like the slut you are so bent on becoming; don't sing benna in Sunday school; you mustn't speak to wharf-rat boys, not even to give directions; don't eat fruits on the street—flies will follow you; but I don't sing benna on Sundays at all and never in Sunday school; this is how to sew on a button . . . this how to hem a dress when you see the hem coming down and so to prevent yourself from looking like a slut I know you so bent on becoming; this is how you iron your father's khaki shirt so that it doesn't have a crease . . . this is how to behave in the presence of men who don't know you very well, and this way they won't recognize immediately the slut I have warned you against becoming . . . don't squat down to play marbles—you are not a boy. ("Girl" 412)

All these instructions lead the female character to believe that she will only become what her mother asks of her and that is to clean, cook meals, and be a good wife for her husband. Although she gives the girl instructions on what honors mainstream Caribbean society desires, she does not consider what will please the girl. Thus, the matriarch fails to support the girl in establishing herself. In reading this short tale, some have found it to be an endearing reflection of a mother's protective intentions over her daughter, while other readers have viewed it as a reflection of women's potential under the colonized canon. Seodial Deena, for example, analyzes multiple works by post-colonial authors to decipher the historical and symbolic meanings behind exploitation on the basis of gender, race, and class canons set from colonialism. She asserts that women have not been valued in history and in colonial literature because they are seen as lowly figures in man's eye, and with these detrimental opinions of themselves handed down at early stages, many girls accept the inevitable destiny of becoming handmaids and whores for the dominant sex (Deena 17). Kincaid's matriarchal figures have learned to accept the positions given to them because their mothers were in those same roles given to them by their mothers. In "Girl," Kincaid presents this constant list of rules, this constant cycle placed upon them to live, but her other main female characters often reject the roles of the caretaker, mother, housewife, and sex-slave to their husbands, fathers, and male family members. Instead, they commit *female subordination*.[2]

Not only does Kincaid demonstrate the double standards set in the canon between male and female roles and how colonized society shuns those who do not claim their given roles; she also presents the self-hatred characteristic which reflects women's rejection of what they are destined to become. Instead, they look towards their male children, who are the apples of their husband's eye, whereas the girls are viewed as a curse in society. Kincaid, during her childhood, experienced this same type of treatment from her mother. In her memoir, *My Brother*, she conveys how double standards view girls as curses, according to which it is their fault if they become pregnant: "I was a girl she had been very strict with me and if she had not been I would have ended up with ten children by ten different men" (*My Brother* 28).

On the other hand, Kincaid felt that she was being treated unfairly when her mother subjected her to verbal abuse and took away her opportunities in an effort to save the family that her mother and father had failed in constructing (*My Brother* 135). Her baby brother, Devon, and her other brothers had an easier life, not only because Kincaid was the oldest sibling but also because as sons they were catered to. Thus, Kincaid saw her mother favor the boys over her, and despite Kincaid's accomplishments as a scholar and independent woman, she never thought she could please her mother. It was her brothers who were constantly in trouble or creating havoc, yet Kincaid's mother favored them:

> I felt I hated my mother, and even worse, I felt she hated me, too; my brother Devon, the one dying just then at that moment, was one year old and I did not wish him dead; I only wished that he had never been born, because it was his birth that plunged our family into financial despair. (*My Brother* 141)

Kincaid appreciated her education, enjoyed recreational activities with boys, but this was unacceptable for her family. Her mother did not understand her appreciation for learning. In fact, Kincaid's mother pulled her out of school in order to help take care of the sons while her mother cared for the sick father. Also, Kincaid was angered when her mother acted against education by forcing her into becoming a grooming caretaker. This was not the role that Kincaid wished to take on; she desired education, for this was the only freedom in her life. Kincaid was at a standstill with only what her mother wished for her, and that was upsetting because she felt sorry for her mother. She wondered why her mother did not enjoy life and why she wished to ruin that of her daughter:

> But there was a moment when in a fury at me for not taking care of her mistakes (my brother with the lump of shit in his diapers, his father who was sick and could not properly support his family, who even when well had made a family that he could not properly support, her mistake in marrying a man so lacking, so lacking) she looked in every crevice of our yard, under our house, under my bed ... and in all those places she found my books, the things that had come between me and the smooth flow of her life, her many children that she could not support, that she and her husband ... could not support, and in this fury ... she gathered all the books of mine she could find, and placing them on her stone head ... she doused them with kerosene ... and then set fire to them. (*My Brother* 134)

Kincaid's desires of becoming her own woman, having her own privacy by reading books, and educating herself were roles that her mother could not adopt at a point where things were never good for their family, but Kincaid saw it as a form of escape. She saw education as a freedom from the roles her mother wish to leave her with. Her mother would have never asked the sons to take the same responsibilities if they were of the same age because of their male gender. Like Kincaid's father (which she later discovers is not her biological father), her mother lets her husband disregard responsibility (by not helping them financially) and accepts the fact that he has affairs with other women who inflict curses upon the family. Kincaid leaves and takes responsibility, not waiting on a man to support her.

These notions of gender favoritism developed from a literary-theorist definition of self-hatred. In *Autobiography of My Mother*, Xuela became acquainted with her new stepmother, the woman who felt threatened by her because she was a child from a previous marriage. Xuela's stepmother did not like anything about her. Later Xuela reveals that her stepmother does not love her own female child either (*Autobiography* 53). Xuela's stepmother despised anything like her because she did not love herself; she did not love her life. Her stepmother's decision to bear children was only a trap to keep the man she loved. In fact, her stepmother valued her son more than she did the daughter:

> She bore a boy first, then she had a girl. This had two predictable outcomes: she left me alone and she valued her son more than her daughter. That she did not think very much of the person who was most like her, a daughter, a female, was so normal that it would have been noticed only if it had been otherwise: to people like us, despising anything that was most like ourselves was almost a law of nature. (*Autobiography* 51)

As a result of this non-existent love by any mother figure, Xuela never knew what real love felt like. She never loved herself and believed she would not bear children. She came to realize that if she could not love herself, she could not love anyone. This is her cry to women in Antigua: "Why bear children in your depressed state?" Not surprisingly, Xuela's half-sister would soon die an early death, attempting to chase love somewhere else. Kincaid learns to accept that her being a woman is a curse and that she will never be valued in a society where woman are only encouraged to become good housewives, handmaids, and submissive whores.

DIRTY: CLEAN

Another example of opposing canon of femininity through lack of cleanliness is observed in *Autobiography of My Mother*. Xuela discovers all the beauty within her by enjoying all that is natural on the human body, including dirt and odor. She learns to love her natural self, objecting to the colonized standards of a woman's appearance. She learns how she views cleanliness after becoming acquainted with her father's new wife:

> My father's wife showed me how to wash myself. It was not done with kindness. My human form and odor were an opportunity to heap scorn on me. I responded in a fashion by now characteristic of me: whatever I was told to hate I loved and loved the most. I loved the thin dirt behind my ears, the smell of my unwashed mouth, the smell that came from my legs, the smell in the pit of my arm, the smell of my unwashed feet. What ever about me caused offense, whatever was native to me, whatever I could not help and was not moral failing—those things about me I loved with the fervor of the devoted. (*Autobiography* 32)

Xuela celebrated all the things viewed as nasty and masculine, all opposite to feminine ideals of perfection, cleanliness, and purity.

Child: Adult

Kincaid's female characters' rebellion is an example of realizing independence. Kincaid selected to live as an adult and accept her responsibilities at an early age in her life. It was difficult for her to live her life, because her mother constantly desired control. Kincaid's problem is very symbolic, because it explains Britain's desire to continue control and to assimilate those under formal rule. In *My Brother*, Kincaid displays the dominating colonizer who chooses to remain in control of a declared dependent state when she writes, "My mother loves her children, I want to say, in her way! And that is very true; she loves us in *her* way. It never has occurred to her that her way of loving us might not be the best thing for us" (*My Brother* 16). This is one of the reasons why Kincaid leaves her home of eighteen years to pursue an education; it is a form of rebellion. While her mother desired to oppress her in an effort to remind her of her shortcomings, Kincaid exposes her mother's dirty secrets (marrying a womanizer, who could not help support them and having more children to keep her husband, knowing they could not afford more children). In her memoir, Kincaid reflects on why she left her master-puppeteer: "It was then [when] I decided that only people in Antigua died, that people living in other places did not die and as soon as I could, I would move somewhere else, to those places where the people living did not die" (*My Brother* 27). Kincaid describes the American spirit as a once colonized county that broke away from the British and remained independent. Although Antigua is independent like many other British territories in the Caribbean, it still has the British Queen on its money and the British influence in its culture as well as its religion. The Antiguan people desired to grow up and away from their long-time oppressors despite how much they had seemed to be a helpful crutch. Kincaid desired her brother Devon, who was dying of AIDS, to live life and not die in death. She wanted him to accept his own misfortunes and learn how to live responsibly and let go of his mother's spoiling him:

> I told him then, It is hard for us to leave our mother, but you are thirty years old, you are a grown man, you must leave; this one thing you should do before you die, leave her, find your own house as soon as you are well enough, find a job, support yourself, do this before you die. He said he understood what I was saying, he said that he had been thinking along the same lines. Earlier that day, my mother had told me of a plan she and he had to build another little room, right next to her bedroom, for him to live in. I did not say, You can't afford to do that, save that money

for a time when it might be needed for medicine, taxi fares to the hospital, just save that money. (*My Brother* 78–79)

In Kincaid's plea to Devon, she makes him see how his colonized thinking is not rational in terms of what is right for him. His mother's desire to add a room to her house was a disservice, because her son would soon die from AIDS. She sought to capitalize on the opportunity as a controlling parent.

In *Lucy*, Lucy leaves home to escape an overbearing mother and educate herself in the United States. To create a statement to her mother's desire to keep Lucy in her eye's view, Lucy decides to reject the mother and to end "the relationship by refusing to open her letters, which is also her rejection of the colonial language and colonialism as a whole. . . . Her decision not to open the letters is also her attempt to silence the mother-master" (Alexander 47). When Kincaid finally removes herself, she admits to being happy. She was free from the master's strings and "in a place where no one knew much about [her]," and she was free living out a life she had always dreamt (*Lucy* 158). She was away from the colonized countries, canons, ideals, and religion that her (mother) colonizers had placed upon her. In many of her works she writes about how women break free from oppressive situations and claim their maturity in a world where adults lack responsibility. Her father, brothers, mother were all culprits to their own family's oppressive state. Kincaid uses these situations to explain that although adults may claim to know everything, they can still be in such a child-like state that the child is the adult and sometimes the adult is the child. In Kincaid's case, her female characters experienced the joy of getting their life back. She conveys this reclamation of identity, fostering their maturity in this statement: "I was transformed from failure to triumph. It was the moment I knew who I was" (*Lucy* 152). Kincaid's triumph was a call to all that are in colonized areas to reclaim their culture, their language, their education, their resources, and their wealth that had been stripped for so many years back.

EDUCATED: IGNORANT

Xuela's stepmother not only disapproved of her cleanliness but also her education. Kincaid conveys her stepmother's attitudes towards women furthering their education: "No one told me what I should do with myself after I was finished with school. It was a great sacrifice that I should go to school, because as his wife often pointed out, I would have been more useful at home" (*Autobiography* 40). Although Xuela's father sought to bring his daughter in conformity with colonized society by giving her books to read on religious piety, she often questioned what these books about John Wesley had in common with her (*Autobiography* 40). She often questioned her father's motives for using her education to set religious standards for her, standards that her father often hypocritically disavowed.

Religion forced upon them in the form of education not only built restrictions on women but also oppressed them through inflicting their political ideals. In *Annie John*, Kincaid demonstrates how teachers value British influence and not their own Caribbean values. In Kincaid's school students read British literature and learned European History, but educators neglected the history of their own country. By desiring to sit up in front, Annie conveys the colonizer's desire to be accepted into the status quo of society: "I hated to be seated so far away from the teacher; because I was sure I would miss something she said. But, even worse, if I was out of my teacher's sight all the time, how could she see my industriousness and quickness at learning things?" (*Annie John* 37). Annie tried so hard to impress her teachers—who were under the colonized way of thinking—that she did not realize later that her teachers taught students a narrow-sided view of their world. Neglecting their Antiguan heritage and values, these students grow up with low self-esteem because their teachers leave the mother tongue out of the classroom, instill colonized religion in school, teach table manners, and set aside a break for tea-time (a British pastime). The propaganda surrounding the school system was taking over students' creativity and their desire to learn about their own history. It was in Annie John's adolescent years that she sought to educate herself on her history. She demanded to discover and learn information that was not encouraged at her school. As a result of her academic deprivation, she rebelled against the history lessons in school by defacing her history book (*Annie John* 82), and she was constantly bombarded with propaganda that encouraged the young girls at her school to adopt submissive and canonized roles for their gender.

This encouragement of borrowing and assimilating culture is observed in Kincaid's *Autobiography of My Mother* as Xuela begins school:

> My teacher was a woman who had been trained by Methodist missionaries; she was of the African people, that I could see, and she found in this a source of humiliation and self-loathing, and she wore despair like an article of clothing. . . . She did not love us; and we did not love her; we did not love one another, not then, not ever. . . . I was of the African people, but not exclusively. My mother was a Carib woman, and when they looked at me this is what they saw: The Carib people had been defeated and then exterminated, thrown away like the weeds in a garden; the African people had been defeated but survived. When they looked at me, they saw only the Carib people. (*Autobiography* 15)

Accepting the mother tongue symbolizes the embracing of one's heritage. She speaks *patois* to herself in order to remember her mother tongue. This language is the only connection she has with her culture, a culture that she cannot develop without immersion into connected familiar bonds:

> We spoke English in school—proper English, not patois—and among ourselves we spoke French patois, a language that was not considered proper at all, a language that a person from France could not speak and could only with difficulty understand. I spoke to myself because I grew to like the sound of my own voice. (*Autobiography* 16)

Kincaid manages to show readers that despite the fact that she was taught in a "good school," the institution may not be teaching the most valuable precepts for identity development. A loss of one's heritage can make a person ignorant of one's history. Kincaid, as her many characters, always had to choose between her mother's ethnic heritage, which was never dominant, and the British (foreign) heritage, which she refuses to assimilate.

LADY: SLUT

Sexuality is a recurring symbol in Kincaid's works. According to Isabel Hoving, Kincaid attempts to dispel all colonized beliefs on being sexual. Hoving supports this theory by stating that "Kincaid evokes the uneasy, loud, hard, tactile and smelly presence of a self-conscious woman. . . . Her body functions not as spectacle but as the fragmented site of a sensual communication with the self, often opening itself to sexual pleasures induced by others" (Hoving 227). Sexuality from the colonizer's viewpoint is that sex is only for bearing children; it is a dirty act, and whatever is conducted between couples should be done in the confines of their bedrooms. Although early colonized thinking reflected conservative "Christian and God-fearing ideals," there were strict conservatives who were using sexuality to appease their natural, lustful desires; this is one of the reasons why Kincaid had a problem with conforming to a model set by those who engage in hypocrisy. She experienced lifestyle contradictions as she was growing up in a colonized society, and she portrayed this conflict in her paternal characters. Her main characters, for example, used exploitative situations that take away their innocence, and in turn they change these situations into positive ones. The canon set for her to be a conservative young lady was not the role she intended. Instead, Annie John, Lucy, Xuela, and the author Kincaid are women who break away from the colonized rationale and make their own structure. Her characters always embrace their sexuality and learn how to find self in terms of what pleases them. Kincaid at the time was not inhibited, because she felt being sexual was an honest feeling. She was not untrue to herself and did not pretend to be a canonized individual with "fallen from grace" convictions. Some examples of the sexual rebellion from the canon can be seen throughout her novels.

Throughout her childhood, Annie John was told that she was on her way to becoming a slut, and finally she snapped. She pointed the finger at the colonizer who constantly accused her of growing into the person she was. She condemned her mother's actions. How could her mother follow the colonizer's way of thinking when it was contradictory? Now a woman, Annie John is scared of the childhood scolding from her mother that caused her to rebel from her standardized notions:

> [My mother] went on to say that, after all the years she had spent drumming into me the proper way to conduct myself when speaking to young men, it had pained her to see me behave in the manner of a slut in the street and that just to see me had caused her to feel shame. . . . The word "slut" (in patois) was repeated over and over, until suddenly I felt as if I were drowning in a well but instead of the well being filled with water it was filled with the word "slut," and it was pouring in through my eyes, my ears, my nostrils, my mouth. As if to save myself, I turned to her and said, "Well, like father, like son, like mother like daughter." (*Annie John* 102)

Out of rage, Annie recognized her mother's mistakes. She pointed out how her unfaithful mother married a womanizer, so how could she accept this treatment from her mother, who was a hypocrite? Annie's mother tried to make her into the conservative colonized woman she was not. She could not make Annie into something her mother never was. Annie's mother has low self-esteem about how her life unraveled; and so out of love, she means well, but she holds the canon strings so tight that it causes Annie to rebel and lose face with her mother's intention: "Why, I wonder, didn't I see the hypocrite in my mother when, over the years, she said that she loved me and could hardly live without me, while at the same time proposing and arranging separation after separation . . ." (*Annie John* 133). Parallel to Annie John, Lucy adopts this forbidden fate as a natural human trait when she introduces Mariah:

> I reminded her that my whole upbringing had been devoted to preventing me from becoming a slut; I then gave a brief description of my personal life, offering each detail as evidence

that my upbringing had been a failure and that, in fact, life as a slut was quite enjoyable, thank you very much. I would not come home now, I said. (*Lucy* 127–28)

It was in the United States, a country where citizens are independent from government, religion and expression, that Lucy finds her acceptance of sexual desires. No strings could ever pull her away, ridicule her, or make her ashamed. She was tired of hypocrisy establishing criteria that they too could not monitor.

It was hypocrisy that gave Xuela's father the sadistic notion to make her a sex slave. Although Xuela knew money was exchanged for her, she did not realize what she was actually being used for. Her father, whose love and approval she longed for, represents the "colonial presence, a ruthless capitalist, exploiter of the villagers, and incapable of love. He trades his daughter with a business associate as a servant and to be used for sex" (Louis 206). She became pregnant as a result of the affairs with her employer, Mr. Roseau. When Xuela told Mrs. Roseau about her pregnancy, Mrs. Roseau was delighted and wanted to keep Xuela's child. But as a sign of slave rebellion, Xuela had an abortion, wishing her child in a better place than in the capitalistic (slavery) system the child was consummated under. As Xuela grows older, she realizes that the world is full of capitalists and there was no way she was going to bring a child into the world. She would have sex only to satisfy herself, but not to please a man or to bear children. This action was an expression of a woman's choice in a colonized society. Xuela chose to be sexual, not caring about the results. She has no mental, physical, or spiritual connections to anyone or anything. She chooses to enjoy all those things that were considered sexual—her body, which is powerful. All these things colonizers claimed to be sinful, when in actuality many of the colonizers capitalized on women who had lustful feelings and devoured those who were under their puppet strings.

ESCAPE: FREE

Kincaid sought to write about the binary oppositions to demonstrate how confusing two different sides can mean the same when used in the canon. As a result of colonizers' destruction and colonized standards throughout the Caribbean islands, many of the inhabitants grew up in a society where women are taught that they are evil, inferior, and unattractive. Although Kincaid and others in similar cultural institutions escape, are they ever free when surrounded by family or friends who still accept or adopt the notions of the slave country? Kincaid often works to convey the common phrase, "You can take the girl out of the island, but you can't take the island out of the girl." Kincaid's pleadings to her mother, brother, and father to gain independence were not only symbolic but a cry for their own freedom. She can not truly become a free person until she rejects everyone who is still living as a slave under the colonizer's whip. Kincaid remembers that once slaves leave the plantation, they can never go back—they can only hope that those still living under the notions that a master is kind to them will stumble across true freedom.

Kincaid explains her difficult childhood not only to expose bad parenting but also to reflect a country's lack of developing its "daughters" into proud Antiguan citizens—not British. In each of her novels, Kincaid dispels all the binaries she is forced to conform to as a child. In adulthood, she educated herself into understanding that freedom is through literacy. With literacy, those in chains learn the advantages of having the privilege to express themselves without ridicule or injustice. Although Kincaid and her characters are at constant battle with binary oppositions, each manages to convey opposing views of a backward, colonized society and break the never-ending chains of that society.

Notes

1. See Jacques Derrida, *Grammatology*.
2. Female characters reject matriarchal maternal roles and bonds forced upon them at early ages (Davies 124).

Works Cited

Alexander, Simone A. J. *Mother Imagery: In the Novels of Afro-Caribbean Women*. Columbia: U Missouri P, 2001. 5–95.

Covi, Giovanna. "Jamaica Kincaid and the Resistance to Canons." *Modern Critical Views: Jamaica Kincaid*. Ed. Harold Bloom. Philadelphia: Chelsea House, 1998. 3–12.

Davies, Carole B. *Black Women, Writing and Identity: Migrations of the Subject*. New York: Routledge, 1994. 113–29.

Deena, Seodial. *Canonization, Colonization, Decolonization*. New York: Peter Lang, 2001.

Derrida, Jacques. *Of Grammatology*. Trans. Gayatri Chakravorty Spivak. Baltimore: Johns Hopkins UP, 1974.

Hoving, Isabel. *In Praise of New Travelers: Reading Caribbean Migrant Women's Writing*. Stanford: Stanford UP, 2001. 184–237.

James, Louis. *Caribbean Literature in English*. New York: Longman, 1999. 205–06.

Kincaid, Jamaica. *Annie John*. New York: Farrar, 1983.

———. "Girl." *At The Bottom of The River*. New York: Farrar, 1983.

———. *Lucy*. New York: Farrar, 1990.

———. *My Brother*. New York: Farrar, 1997.

———. *Autobiography of My Mother*. New York: Farrar, 1996. (Referred to in the text as *Autobiography*.)

KEZIA PAGE

"What If He Did Not Have a Sister [Who Lived in the United States]?": Jamaica Kincaid's My Brother as Remittance Text

In a version of this article presented at a West Indian literature conference in 1998, the title invoked Western Union, a well known remittance service used in the Caribbean and internationally, as material cultural evidence of the active interchange between Caribbean migrant and diaspora communities and their communities at home.[1] Western Union and its many other competitors offer a service that involves transferring money from migrant and diaspora communities, typically in North America and Great Britain, to the Caribbean. This service not only signifies the relationship between Caribbean people in host and home countries, but also implicates the direction of this exchange beyond the economic realm and asks us to explore similar exchanges in other aspects of Caribbean culture. Jamaica Kincaid's *My Brother* examines aspects of this relationship. Kincaid's nonfiction AIDS elegy is very much concerned with the difference in location between the Caribbean and the host countries where Caribbean people live. In *My Brother* Kincaid describes how she remits medicine and money to help her sick brother in Antigua. The dynamic she portrays of a poor, ailing, dependent at home relying on the relatively successful provider abroad, is for the most part the dynamic of remittance culture. The spirit of this dynamic is underscored in the question Kincaid wants to ask her brother's doctor; it is the question that now titles this piece: "I wanted to ask him, if there was no medicine available, if people

From *Small Axe* 21 (October 2006). © 2006 by *Small Axe*.

suffering did not have a sister who lived in the United States . . . what would happen then?"[2]

In this article I focalize Kincaid's text to argue that monetary remittances or unilateral transfers to the Caribbean mirror other cultural transactions, such as literary remittances, which are themselves fraught with problematic social and political implications. Among the dynamics invoked are the tensions between margin and center that are crucially linked to postcolonial theorizing of regions such as the Caribbean, which as independent subjects remain peripheral, even as they inspire and authenticate Caribbean diaspora center discourse.

THEORIZING THE REMITTANCE TEXT

The provenance of the concept of the remittance text as analogue is clear when we consider in real terms the significance of economic remittances to the Caribbean. Remittances represent a significant means of foreign exchange earnings or inflows to Caribbean nations. In Jamaica alone total inflows have climbed from US$508.8 million in 1994 to more than US$1.2 billion in 2002. These figures are noteworthy not just as they signify the intensity of the relationship between Caribbean diaspora and home communities but also as they impact other key economic indicators. For example in 1997 remittances constituted 9.1 percent of the Gross Domestic Product (GDP) of Jamaica; by 2002 remittances totaled 15.3 percent of the GDP. Indeed, remittance inflows to the Caribbean including Jamaica and the Dominican Republic almost doubled between 1997 and 2002. In 1997 the figure was more than US$3.1 billion and by 2002 it was nearly US$6 billion.[3]

This information is helpful in understanding the volume and significance of remittances to home economies. These statistics emphasize the extent of the influence transnational communities maintain outside of their original home spaces. However, much of the discussion about remittances is not simply centered on the volume of monetary and nonmonetary remittances sent to the Caribbean; instead it involves a debate on the effect of these unilateral transfers on the receiving home economy. Succinctly, the debate hinges on whether remittances hinder or help development, what Sharon Stanton Russell terms the "consumption versus investment" debate.[4] Of course remittances are more than staggering statistics; they are evidence of the imbricated interactions between home and diaspora communities.

Remittances represent a facet of the ongoing relationship between Caribbean diaspora communities and communities at home in the Caribbean. Indeed the concept of the remittance, money sent by post and the act of sending money, and other nonmonetary transfers that engage this sender–receiver dynamic, may be part of what James Clifford terms diasporist discourse. He argues: "Diasporic discourses reflect the sense of being part of an ongoing transnational network that includes the homeland not as something simply left behind but as a place of attachment in a contrapuntal modernity."[5] This attachment for Caribbean migrants is closely associated to relatives remaining in the Caribbean. George Lamming labels familial relations that are maintained across nations as "transnational families" and the kind of interdependence fostered as "transnational households."[6] He cites a specific example of how this might function: "They have created the phenomenon of the transnational family which does not allow a funeral in Barbados to take place for over a week after the death since the cortege would be incomplete until relatives have arrived from Jamaica, Trinidad, Guyana, Toronto, Birmingham, Brooklyn."[7] In the same vein Belinda Edmondson distinguishes between exile and nationalism, and immigration and nationalism, by suggesting that the migrant is concerned chiefly with earning a living to support family members back home, while the exile is "preoccupied by the meaning of the native land."[8] Both Lamming and Edmondson theorize the Caribbean migrant experience as active and interactive with the region itself. The remittance text and culture expose the politics of these interactions.

Fernando Lozano Ascencio defines remittances by adding a social dimension to the concept that is useful in the Caribbean context: "Remittances are a portion of the income of international migrants with temporary or permanent residence in the country where they work, and that is transferred from the country of destination to the country of origin. These remittances may be monetary or non monetary."[9] This sending of cash and goods to relatives at home to maintain social networks is what Ascencio terms unrequited or unilateral transfers. This simply means that remittances are not payment for services or goods. Ascencio further delineates what is meant by monetary and nonmonetary remittances, the former denoting cash, money orders, and the like. Nonmonetary remittances are defined thus: "Within this second type there are three subgroups: consumer goods, such as clothing, appliances, televisions, gifts, etc, capital goods, such as, tools, light machinery, vehicles, and the skills and technological knowledge acquired by migrants during their stay."[10] These categories add a human dimension to the transfers conducted by migrant communities to home communities. The last category, which includes skills and technological knowledge or human capital acquired in the host country, begins to more accurately describe the culture of transfers and remittances that Caribbean migrants have maintained with their home countries.

In sum then remittances not only represent pure economic activity but complicated social and cultural networks that have helped define migrant and home communities in the wake of mass migrations out of the Caribbean.

On the economic level the remittance is important to Caribbean society, the home economy, and thus political relations; on the literary and cultural level a remittance text is a way of constructing home in one's mind, preserving memories either by inventing new ones, or calling up old ones. This article questions the benefits and effects of the literary remittance.

From the given facts on migration rates evidenced in the volume of remittances sent to the Caribbean, many inferences can be drawn about the impact on Caribbean national economies and the social climate. The two areas of health and education are directly affected by high migration rates, because there is a depletion of skilled labor. The absence of mothers also disrupts nuclear and extended families and other elements of the social milieu of a country. Generally, while remittances may appear to benefit or improve economies they have adverse effects on the social climate of a nation. It would be incorrect to suggest that this form of self and familial maintenance is at its core entirely unhealthy for the development of a nation. It is clear, however, that the help that remittances provide, as they are used, is short-term. Myron Weiner suggests that remittances may not be as useful as they appear. He advises that remittances are wastefully spent on consumer goods rather than productively invested; they nurture a consumer mentality, worsen imports, and result in a maldistribution of income and increase dependence.[11]

This dependence is further contextualized in James Clifford's discussion of diasporic communities. Clifford explains the extent of the communication and relationship between home and diaspora communities and describes the setting where this dependence functions. His discussion and definition of diasporic communities involves the existence of more and more communication between migrant communities and those in the home space:

> Diasporic forms of longing, memory and (dis)identification are shared by a broad spectrum of minority and migrant populations. And dispersed peoples, once separated from homeland by vast oceans and political barriers, increasingly find themselves in border relations with the old country thanks to to-and-fro made possible by modern technologies of transport and communication, and labor migration.[12]

Communication between those at home and those in diaspora is important both ways. This includes forms of cultural communication, specifically how home and the memory of it is important to self-construction. The model of the remittance suggests that though the transfers are unilateral, the effects are bilateral. Hence, the problem with constructing self goes both ways. That is, a large community in diaspora must also have an effect on the self-construction of those at home. The concept of the remittance provides insight into this two-way relationship, particularly with countries with large numbers of their own living abroad. Those at home are therefore as much a part of the equation as those abroad.

THE CONCEPT OF THE REMITTANCE TEXT

Does literature take part in these pragmatic socioeconomic paradigms? Are the connections made between the concept of the remittance and what I am terming the remittance text useful or even probable? When these connections are made, how do they enhance our reading of the literature in the context of Caribbean and diaspora communities? Theorizing remittance texts involves making a parallel between the economic concept of the remittance (money sent by post and the act of sending money) and the migrant or diaspora text written about the homeland or place of origin. They function similarly as a means of preserving home from abroad. On the economic level the remittance plays an important part in Caribbean society, the home economy, and thus political relations; on the literary level a remittance text is a way of constructing home in one's mind, preserving memories either by re-inventing new ones, or calling up old ones. Hence, there is a distinct and workable relationship between the monetary and the literary remittance; both are a form of communication and mediation between home and abroad.

Theorizing the remittance text involves concentrating on a subset of Caribbean migrant and diaspora literature as well as understanding the literature within the broader context of the Caribbean migrant experience. As evidenced in the socioeconomic facts already stated, remittances perform a major part in the definition of new Caribbean communities where record numbers of people have emigrated to the United States and Europe, and where even more have been exposed to alternate ways of life through "modern technologies" as Clifford terms them. The remittance text therefore makes its debut in post-independence Caribbean societies, just about the time when local governments are beginning to feel the effects of the raw deal of colonialism. The immediate effects of the end of colonialism and the beginning of what we term postcolonialism left newly independent Caribbean societies to grapple with masses of uneducated people, insufficient infrastructure, and too few jobs. At this juncture Caribbean people begin another wave of mass exodus in search of better opportunities.

Caribbean literary culture is facing again what Caribbean societies have faced during various waves of migration. Many of our writers and critics live and work outside of the region. Remittance texts, in theory, that is texts written abroad and sent home (as Caribbean literature), are much more frequent. Some Caribbeanists see this moment in Caribbean literary history as positive, as a way of actively incorporating the Caribbean diaspora in its broadest sense. These readings celebrate migration and diaspora instead of understanding them as the colonial exile of Lamming, Sam Selvon, and to a lesser degree V. S. Naipaul. The discourse has evolved, however, from postcolonial celebration and into what is for some a neocolonial guardedness. Can the Caribbean region sustain the dialectic when the successful manipulation of borders for some implies that we ignore the material constraints of movement and fluidity for the majority of others? I suggest that the sociocultural indignation witnessed in Devon's reaction to Kincaid in *My Brother* can be understood as an indirect response to the presentation of the Caribbean by its nationals and former nationals writing abroad. Though transnational networks are maintained between sender and host communities, to imply that the migrant or the diaspora version of home always remains the same as the homeland's version of itself, is to suggest that identity remains static even with crossing borders. It is to suggest that frequent visits to the Caribbean, telephone calls, remittances, and the Caribbean flavor that a few tolerant cities in North America and Britain take on constitutes a world without borders, a world where the first world and its values are always accepted. A study of the remittance text, therefore, facilitates the perspective of both the senders and the receivers.

JAMAICA KINCAID'S *MY BROTHER*

My Brother is Jamaica Kincaid's second nonfiction book. The narrative of Devon Drew's struggle with and eventual succumbing to the AIDS virus is also the story of Kincaid's (a migrant's) relationship with her birth home and family. As with Kincaid's first nonfiction piece, *A Small Place*, the paradigm of woman and nation is crucial to the understanding of Kincaid and her work.[13] Kincaid identifies herself as writer/remitter and sister in "foreign." On one level she is the remitter of medicines and money to sustain her brother while he suffers in a hospital in Antigua with neither, and on another level she is the remitter of memories and words through her text *My Brother*.

It is from this literary position that I choose to begin. Kincaid says when she heard of her brother's sickness she knew she would write about it: "I became a writer out of desperation, so when I first heard my brother was dying I was familiar with the act of saving myself: I would write about him. I would write about his dying."[14] Though this statement comes toward the end of the text, it helps us clarify the nature of this literary piece. Kincaid locates her writing as a kind of emotional response or working through of difficult situations; she also sites it historically as an economic response—a way of escape in desperate situations. *My Brother* clearly participates in a kind of literary economy, one that not only sustains the home economy, but also the remitter or the writer. Still *My Brother* functions in at least three other forms: as nonfiction, as "old time story," and as elegy, but always in communication with migrant and home community—always as a remittance text.

In *My Brother* Kincaid seems somewhat self-conscious about the form of the text. Early in the second half of the text, after Devon's death, she clarifies the form of the text: "What I am writing now is not a journal; a journal is a daily account, an immediate account of what occurs during a certain time. For a long time after my brother died I could not write about him, I could not think about him in a purposeful way."[15] Kincaid is very aware of the form *My Brother* takes. She is clearly writing the story, as she remembers it, of her brother. She explains: "I would write about him. I would write about his dying."[16] So for all intents and purposes *My Brother* is nonfiction. From the photograph of Devon Drew on the jacket cover, to the names mentioned in the text, to the events chronicled, we can assume that these are Kincaid's recollections of the dying and death of her brother.

Reading *My Brother* as nonfiction allows us to examine some of the fundamental themes and concerns crucial to understanding the politics of the text. Since Kincaid tells a true story using real names and real experiences it seems fair that we would add the expectation of truth. Her peaceful, pastoral Vermont world is disturbed by the news that her brother, Devon Drew, is in the hospital dying of the AIDS virus. Kincaid travels to Antigua to visit him and finds her youngest brother in terrible shape. The stigma attached to AIDS in Antigua, along with poverty and a neglectful government, prevents Devon from being treated properly and effectively. Kincaid returns to the US and begins remitting AZT, an expensive drug cocktail used to treat AIDS patients. To her and her mother's reward and relief, Devon improves and is released from the hospital. He returns to a careless, promiscuous lifestyle, incurring the disapproval of his sister. This is cut short when he stops responding to the medicine and dies. Subsequent to Devon's passing Kincaid is informed that her brother was a homosexual. She closes the text lamenting his loss and the fact that she did not know him.

My Brother is Kincaid's version of Devon's life and death. She admits to the distance that characterizes their relationship; she has not seen him for a long time. Kincaid shares with the reader her surprise when she realizes that she loves this brother whom she hardly knows and hardly tries to understand. The dynamics of their relationship are also presented straightforwardly. Devon is the poor, dying brother with nothing but needs; Kincaid is the sister in "foreign," with a nice family and new name. She sends the medicine that is too expensive to be stocked in Antigua. Devon's carelessness is in opposition to Kincaid's carefulness; Devon's fast-paced Antiguan Creole is unintelligible to Kincaid, as her "funny talk" is unintelligible to him. For all intents and purposes they are strangers to each other, though still blood relations. How does this impact our reading of Kincaid's representation of her family? Is this representation as a result of her idiosyncrasies or are they otherwise motivated?

Kincaid, in a 1991 interview with Allan Vorda, explains why she changed her name. Not only does she dislike the name that her mother gave her, Elaine Potter Richardson, she also wished to maintain her anonymity as a writer.

> I wanted to write and I didn't know how. I thought if I changed my name and I wrote and it was bad, then no one would know. I fully expected it to be bad, by the way, and never to be published, or heard from again. So I thought they'd never get to laugh at it because they wouldn't know it was me.[17]

Twenty-four years after her renaming, when *My Brother* is published, Kincaid is a prolific and prominent writer. Her concerns are no longer about anonymity; in fact the literary fodder that is her family's life and her relationship with Antigua is respected and received as such. However, Kincaid's telling of Devon's story is intrusive on the deterioration and pain of his diseased body, yet we know that he does not have the option of anonymity. The reader is given the intricacies of his sickness from early in the narrative. She first speaks of this when she describes her mother's dedication to her ailing brother. Kincaid's mother notices a sore on his penis; this sore is so embarrassing that Devon and his mother have a very limited exchange about it. Still, this specific aspect of his pain is detailed in the text. Similarly, closer to his death a delirious Devon exposes his penis, the symbol of his life (albeit irresponsibly promiscuous) to his sister:

> [H]e suddenly threw the sheets away from himself, tore his pajama bottoms away from his waist, revealing his penis, and then grabbed his penis in his hand and held it up, and his penis looked like a bruised flower that had been cut short on the stem; it was covered with sores and on the sores was a white substance, almost creamy, almost floury, a fungus.[18]

We are also given detailed descriptions of the deterioration of Devon's body because of the effects of AIDS, and with these little regard is shown for his pride or his privacy.

Underlying these descriptions is the dichotomy between Antigua and Vermont. Antigua is the location where Kincaid's brother lies sick and dying; Vermont is where the life-prolonging medicines are found. Vermont is where Kincaid's healthy, loving family lives; in Antigua there is poverty, sickness, and a dysfunctional family. This dichotomy and the intrusive nature of Kincaid's nonfiction are fueled by her distance, and a kind of absence of respect for familial privacy for the family she had not visited for more than twenty years. Antigua at arm's length is configured as a dilapidated old colony run by thieves and populated by poor irresponsible black people.

Later in the interview with Vorda, Kincaid responds to a question regarding Antigua's reaction to *A Small Place*.[19] Her answer captures a careless ambivalence also evidenced in *My Brother*. Kincaid suggests that the reaction to *A Small Place* would be violent. She expresses her fear of being shot and killed. So on one level she recognizes the gravity of her criticisms, just as she must be conscious that some of her revelations about her brother's illness and the rest of her family might be intrusive, if read as nonfiction. Yet in this same answer she reveals something quite private about her mother's politics:

> I wouldn't be surprised if they had henchmen who would do it because politics in the West Indies is very tribal. People take their colors very seriously. They divide themselves into people who wear red and people who wear blue. My mother is a blue. I'm nothing. When we were growing up we were reds. Then my mother joined the party that had broken away from the reds, and they are blue. She takes it so seriously.[20]

Kincaid conveys the ludicrous nature of political tribalism. Nevertheless she reveals her mother's allegiances, even though her mother is not protected by distance as Kincaid is. Similarly, Kincaid understands the stigmas attached to homosexuality in Antigua, yet she reveals her brother's sexual persuasion as though it might mean to everyone what it means to her.[21] Indeed the politics of the remitter are much different from the politics of the text recipients in Antigua.

My Brother as nonfiction or "factual/true cultural remittance" is sent home bearing an image of Antigua that is in tandem with first world perceptions of the Caribbean. Kincaid's portrayal of her relationship with Devon is in broader terms a version of the relationship between Antigua and the US. The terms of the remittance erase notions of cultural equality and instead enforce relations of third world dependency. The other side of the dichotomy presents Vermont or the US as the cultural superior to Antigua or the Caribbean. There is no political tribalism in Vermont, there family relationships are positive, and in Vermont the almighty dollar is able to purchase the medicine that will postpone Devon's death from the poor, promiscuous third world.

Sarah Brophy underlines another aspect of the differences between the "first world" of North America and the "third world" of the Caribbean as it relates to Kincaid's reaction to Devon's suffering from AIDS. Brophy compares the disparity between Kincaid's and Devon's reactions to his lifestyle and the results of his lifestyle. Brophy cites statistics from the Joint United Nations Programme on HIV/AIDS, which puts the rate of HIV infection in the Caribbean region second only to sub-Saharan Africa.[22] Brophy suggests that this alarming rate in the Caribbean is connected to "neocolonial economic and social factors: poverty, intravenous drug use, the stigmatization of homosexuality, and economic reliance on tourism."[23] Here, as in the above example of political tribalism in the Caribbean, Kincaid is aware, and very personally so, of the social inequalities that characterize her old world—the world of her brother—and the new world of her privilege. Her awareness is previously, as in *A Small Place*, spitfire venom at the oblivious tourist who perpetuates poverty and underdevelopment. However, as Brophy points out, in *My Brother* Kincaid seems strangely complicit.

> The power of the sadness that Devon inspires moves the memoir back and forth between, on the one hand, satisfaction with the sufficiency of empathy and help and, on the other, an emergent and troubling recognition of how much distance there is between brother and sister along with the way their lives are implicated in and mirror each other's.[24]

Reading Devon as a mirror of Kincaid encourages a parallel reading of Antigua and Vermont. Kincaid's distance is not simply bridged by her visits and her remittances; in fact, it is in these contexts that she seems most distant and different. Part of the mourning of the text is exactly these differences; they are the self-reflexive moments in the text when Kincaid sees herself as more of an insider than an outsider.

My Brother is also what Mrs. Drew calls "old time story." By this she means a story that to her is better left in the past, or which should be forgotten, especially one with a bad ending. Kincaid recounts an episode in which she shares a memory with her mother that Mrs. Drew doesn't want to think about: "If I should bring it up, she says it is an old story ('e' a' ole time 'tory; you lub ole-time 'tory, me a warn you'), and for my mother an old story is a bad story, a story with an ending she does not like."[25] Kincaid's memory and method of sharing stories is objectionable to her family members. It seems that her relationship to the past is different from theirs, though equally significant.[26] Perhaps her life is distant enough that she is able to take these memories lightly or is able to transform them into fodder for her work.

But what are the ramifications of Kincaid's perspective (what her mother calls old time story) in a nonfiction, factual piece about her brother's illness, her family, and birth country? Kincaid's mother treats this part of her daughter with suspicion. After reminding her mother about an incident when Devon was a newborn baby and red ants almost killed him, Kincaid describes her mother's reaction: "Her eyes narrowing in suspicion, she said, 'what a memory you have!'"[27] Later in the text Kincaid describes the history of her suspicious memory.

> When I was a child, I would hear her recount events that we both had witnessed and she would leave out small details; when I filled them in, she would look at me with wonder and pleasure and praise me for my extraordinary memory. This praise made an everlasting mark and nothing anyone could do made me lose this ability to remember, however selectively I remember. As I grew up, my mother came to hate this about me, because I would remember things that she wanted everyone to forget.[28]

Kincaid's memories are met with resistance. There are no questions about their truth-value; however these conflicted recountings are mistrusted by her family members and become cause for concern.[29] Baby Devon's unfortunate experience with the ants, the burning of young Kincaid's books, and Devon's conviction, arrest, and release are all considered old time story and become part of the dispute about remembering and forgetting.

Kincaid's construction of familial identity seems to exist outside of communal memory; that is, communal remembering and forgetting. Kincaid's version is in tandem with her self-construction as outsider and insider, impatient and dissatisfied with her birth home. Mrs. Drew's version is a rendering physically closer, understandably sensitive to a past that is very similar to her present experience. Kincaid's intrusions and her proud recounting of old time story seem acute in the context of her self-imposed distance. From a distance it becomes easier to remember and tell what others at home try to forget.

My Brother is also an elegy. It mourns the dying and death of Devon Drew and at the same time mourns Kincaid's loss of country, home, and language. Many of the metaphors used in *My Brother* betray a kind of decay. The text opens with Kincaid seeing Devon Drew sick on a bed in the Holberton Hospital in Antigua. She immediately thinks about his birth and parallels this event with two other deaths, that of the six-year-old child of her mother's friend and another older neighbor who dies of a heart attack. Devon's dying conjures memories of his birth, which for Kincaid is associated with dying. Here she begins the lament, which by the association of his birth with death colors her brother's life.

The descriptions of the effects of the AIDS virus on Devon's body, and later the effects of disease on other bodies, set the tone of the text to a steady lament not just of death, but dying. Kincaid describes his darkened skin, scarlet lips with gold crusted sores, his frailty, the carpet of thrush on his tongue and tonsils, the sore on his penis, the yellow liquid oozing from his anus, and finally a smell that only disappears when Devon dies. In the seminar she attends conducted by Dr. Ramsey, Kincaid uses more metaphors of disease and decay. The fact that the decay seems to center around reproductive organs indicates a kind of looming barrenness consistent with Kincaid's perception of Devon's life, but also implicated in her portrayal of Antigua.

Parallel to Devon's dying is Kincaid's sense of loss of country. She chronicles the changes in Antigua, the deterioration of a post-British colony left to its own devices. The state of the Holberton Hospital begins her descriptions of the decline of civic buildings and national monuments. Her detailed description of the dirt, rust, and broken fixtures in Devon's room speaks to the general decay in Antigua. Devon's hospital room can be read as a metonym for what Kincaid sees as a crumbling Antigua.[30] She criticizes the health and education systems, and summarizes their decay in an apostrophe of loss, "In Antigua itself nothing is made."[31] This to me is Kincaid's way of saying that she no longer sees the virtues in her island home. Marie-Helene Laforest suggests that Kincaid straddles both worlds only through maintaining the Caribbean thematic in her literary pieces.[32]

Kincaid's loss is also evident in her loss of language. She explains from very early in the text that she has difficulty understanding the locals: "I had lived away from my home for so long that I no longer understood readily the kind of English he spoke and always had to have him repeat himself to me; and I no longer spoke the kind of English he spoke."[33] Kincaid's "no longer" here reads as a conscious decision to forget or not to speak the nation language that she once spoke, a language that seems necessary to effectively communicate with her family.[34] In turn she places the nation language she uses in parentheses, and provides an English translation. Setting the Antiguan Creole off from the rest of the text suggests that in her mind English and nation language are not the same. Her use of parentheses clearly indicates who her audience is, and who it is not. Kincaid even in this respect configures the Caribbean as a place she has lost. The politics of the parentheses are numerous. Kriszner and Mandell, in a comprehensive text on grammar and punctuation, explain that "parentheses may be used to set off interruptions within a sentence. Parentheses, however, indicate that the enclosed material is of secondary importance."[35] Kincaid seems to be suggesting that the language of her brother is not legitimate enough to exist in the text on its own, that it is secondary to her English and the English of her readers. She frames his speech in the same way that she frames Antigua—as a place which doesn't have enough, as a place which is not enough.

Kincaid's commentary on the death of her language continues a theme evident in each approach to reading *My Brother—nonfiction, old time story, elegy, and remittance text.* From each of these Kincaid's text reveals her preoccupation with difference. To articulate this difference and loss she uses language, which her brother deems "funny." Kincaid's mourning of her brother begins before his death because of her coming to terms with their unchangeable differences. The similarities shared between Kincaid and her siblings are still not enough to bridge the gulf that separates them. For example all four of them unite to hate their mother, yet there is nothing more than this temporary convergence, which does not bloom into a productive relationship among them. On the other hand, however, it is the difference between Devon and Kincaid that facilitates her being in a position to help him when he gets sick. For though she and her mother are healthy, and both she and her mother care whether Devon lives or dies, her mother does not have access to AZT. Kincaid is the only one who can take up this aspect of responsibility.

The theme of loss is how the author reckons with her inability to recapture or save home or Antigua and her dying brother Devon. Inscribed on her brother's body are the wasted years of youth, a young nation independent but with really very little choice to improve and develop. Kincaid's multiple descriptions of Devon's dying, stinking body parallel the deterioration and dilapidation that for her characterizes Antigua. This image of Antigua ignores her brother's perspective about his own sickness as a way of censuring his carelessness. Equally it ignores her mother's perspective as a way of censuring what Kincaid sees as the untimeliness of the latter's devotion.[36] These counter perspectives to Devon's body and his illness can be read as counter perspectives to the perception of Antigua as nation. Kincaid's anxiety about her wasted island and her brother's wasted life reduce the validity of Devon's self-image as well as the possibility that viable local opinions exist. Similarly, in her fleeting dismissals which betray loss ("In a place like Antigua" where nothing is made and "I can't do what you are suggesting—take this strange, careless person into the hard-earned order of my life") she chooses to write both epitaphs.[37] When she first views Devon's corpse she suggests that the body does not look like her brother. His hair is uncombed and his face unshaven. Both his eyes and mouth are wide open as if he didn't expect what overcame him. Yet at the funeral service, the prepared-for-burial corpse with eyes sewn shut, mouth clamped shut, hair combed, and face clean and shaven Devon still does not look like himself. Kincaid underscores how unreal his corpse seems to her when she suggests that instead of looking like the dead, Devon looks like an advertisement for the dead.[38] The image of Devon, his body without his regular features, himself—but not himself, reads almost like the image of an island/home flashed across the television screen. It is a place that looks like home, the view of the coast and the rolling hills are familiar, but the features are too calmed, too devoid of the intense color to which one is accustomed. Kincaid's loss of brother and country involves the sad recollection of lives that could never really be what she hoped them to be. Devon and Antigua, present mostly in her literary re-visits and re-memories, seem always to be compared to her immediate family and Vermont. Sadly, they are never enough.

My Brother functions as a remittance text on two levels. One, it tells the story of the author maintaining her family, specifically her sick brother, with cash and kind from abroad. Two, My Brother is written outside of the geographical location of the Caribbean, outside of Antigua, then sent home to Antigua. Undoubtedly, this involves a remembering and representation of home from "foreign" eyes. Kincaid's decision to call on memories and revisit Antigua is indeed a form (however warped) of preserving home from the outside. Even though this act of nonfiction may be construed as much more self-centered than a monetary remittance, it does play its part in a cultural economy.

On the first level Kincaid herself underscores the importance and necessity of the remittance. She constructs her brother, and by extension Antigua, to be in need and to be dependent on her. In a kind of mourning for her country she expresses the lack of necessities and then foregrounds her role as provider and sender. Here I foreground the quotation from which the title of this article is taken:

> I wanted to ask him, if there was no medicine available, if the people suffering did not have a sister who lived in the United States and this sister could call up a doctor who would write a prescription for some medication that might be of help what would happen then?[39]

Kincaid is very conscious of her role as remitter, provider, and foreign big sister. Her articulation of difference and loss is also an articulation of privilege. Her remittance is something her brother can not do without.

Kincaid's work is called Caribbean literature not only because she is from Antigua, but also because Kincaid's texts are all set in her memory of home and in many ways reflect her own experience as a Caribbean native and migrant. As is evident above, Kincaid associates herself as a part of the conflicted colonial past and postcolonial present of the Caribbean. She wants her children to know their grandmother, and she wants them to know where she is from. The text sent home is particularly strange then with her nation language put in parentheses, and Caribbean life and society portrayed as on the periphery of Western civilization, in contrast to

Vermont, which functions as a bastion. Maria Helena Lima takes to task Kincaid's movements toward "center discourse":

> The longer Kincaid feels like an American, the harder it will become for her to continue to "express the voice of the decolonized subject [. . .] journeying back and forth between empires and colonies of the past and the present," as Giovanna Covi posits, "always refusing to adopt the language of either the vanquished or the victors" (60). It will be more difficult for her protagonist (and for Kincaid) not to acknowledge *both* in herself and do away with the binary altogether—at least in her writing.[40]

Lima with Giovanna Covi argues that Kincaid herself recognizes the difficulties of maintaining middle ground in the them/us binary. In pieces like *My Brother* the middle ground is shifting and unstable.

The strangeness of Kincaid's text cannot be explained simply as poetic license; Kincaid's rare moments of solidarity with Antigua do not represent her real opinions of the place. The long-term effects of these remittances are illusory. Devon can be read as representative of Antigua and the larger Caribbean. His sick body is a metaphor for the diseased economies and politics of the region. Kincaid's remittances of AZT sent to help curb the effects of AIDS become an interesting way of evaluating the effects of this kind of remittance of the Caribbean. The effect of the remitted AZT is illusory; it provides a temporary feeling and appearance of health. This appearance is clearly more dangerous than it is helpful, for it is Devon's illusion of health that fuels his deception and the infection of healthy members of his community. The remittance then is eventually quite destructive, for the illusion of health becomes a license for Devon to return to his promiscuous lifestyle. Kincaid records his behavior with disgust: "He said he did not believe he had the HIV virus anymore and he demanded that Dr. Ramsey test him again."[41] The facade of health is enough for Devon to forget the extent of his sickness. The long-term effects of the remittance are indeed more destructive than they are helpful. While they ameliorate some of the immediate problems, they are unable to solve any long-term concerns.

Remittance texts represent the fusing of a very active socioeconomic concept in migrant or diaspora and home communities and the literature that reflects these communities. These texts recognize a crucial perspective that has begun to be marginalized and silenced—the Caribbean perspective in the Caribbean. The voices of Devon and Mrs. Drew cannot only be read as the voices of useless tradition, ignorance, and poverty; they are still the voices of Caribbean people. They are not as receivers of remittances, secondary or less important; on the contrary they are important to an understanding of the full experience.

Notes

1. Kezia Page, "'Send It Western Union!' Jamaica Kincaid's *My Brother* as a Remittance Text" (paper presented at West Indian Literature Conference, University of the West Indies, Mona, April 7, 1998).

2. Jamaica Kincaid, *My Brother* (New York: Farrar, Straus, and Giroux, 1997), 36.

3. Elaine Hayle, "Remittances: The Jamaican Experience," unpublished presentation based on Bank of Jamaica figures, Kingston, March 2004.

4. Sharon Stanton Russell, "Migration, Remittances and Development," in *Migration and Public Policy*, ed. Vaughan Robinson (Northhampton: Edward Elgar Collection, 1999), 271.

5. James Clifford, *Routes: Travel and Translation in the Late Twentieth Century* (Cambridge: Harvard University Press, 1997), 256.

6. George Lamming, *Coming, Coming, Coming Home: Conversations 2* (St. Martin: House of Nehesi Publishers, 1995), 32.

7. Ibid.

8. Belinda Edmondson, *Making Men: Gender, Literary Authority, and Women's Writing in Caribbean Narrative* (Durham: Duke University Press, 1999), 141.

9. Fernando L. Ascencio, *Bringing It Back Home: Remittances to Mexico from Migrant Workers in the United States*, trans. Anibal Yanez (San Diego: Center for U.S.-Mexican Studies University of California, 1993), 5.

10. Ibid., 8.

11. Myron Weiner, "International Emigration and the Third World" in *Population in an Interacting World*, ed. William Alonso (Cambridge: Harvard University Press, 1987), 192.

12. Clifford, *Routes*, 247.

13. I parallel Kincaid's fixation on the paradigm of woman and nation with her fixation on her relationship with her mother. Where Kincaid explores one relationship she explores the other. Both modes of exploration are concerned with a strange dynamic of love and hatred, expectation and disappointment.

14. In an interview with Kay Bonetti Kincaid recounts how she began writing the "Talk of the Town" column in the *New Yorker*. She describes how George Trow befriended her and how she became his "sassy black friend." Writing the "Talk of the Town" became a bread and butter issue for Kincaid. She explains, "I was so grateful, because I was very poor. Sometimes the only meal I ate was those little cocktail things." See Kay Bonetti, "An Interview with Jamaica Kincaid," *The Missouri Review* 15, no. 2 (1992): 135. Kincaid makes it clear that her work at the *New Yorker*, or her writing, literally saved her life.

15. Kincaid, *My Brother*, 91.

16. Kincaid, *My Brother*, 196.

17. Allan Vorda, "An Interview with Jamaica Kincaid," *Mississippi Review* 20, no. 1–2 (1991): 14.

18. Kincaid, *My Brother*, 91.

19. *A Small Place* is Kincaid's 1988 nonfiction piece that, among other things, passionately explores the ill effects of neocolonialism on Antigua. Her criticism of tourists and the long-term adverse effects on an economy like Antigua's in many ways positions itself as much more caustic than *My Brother* in relation to first world visitors.

20. Vorda, "Interview with Kincaid," 21–22.

21. I am not suggesting that Kincaid keep these facts about her family secret; however I am arguing that her revelation of these private things projects a marked difference between what Kincaid views as sensitive information and what her family views as sensitive information. I am also suggesting that these differences are a result of their different locations.

22. Sarah Brophy, "Angels in Antigua: The Diasporic Melancholy in Jamaica Kincaid's *My Brother,*" *PMLA* 117 (2002): 266.

23. Ibid.

24. Ibid., 267.

25. Kincaid, *My Brother*, 25.

26. Louise Bernard argues that "Kincaid's invocation of memory is positioned as defiance, first against the constraints of a colonial history that sought to silence her and all who look like her, and second against her nemesis, the mother," in "Countermemory and Return: Reclamation of the (Postmodern) Self in Jamaica Kincaid's *The Autobiography of My Mother* and *My Brother,*" *Modern Fiction Studies*, 48, no. 1 (2002): 124. Bernard's perspective on Kincaid's memory or "old time story" suggests that it exists outside of communal memory because it functions as resistance.

27. Kincaid, *My Brother*, 6.

28. Ibid., 75.

29. Though *My Brother* is a personal narrative, by virtue of the title and Kincaid's explanation of why she writes this nonfiction piece—"I would write about him. I would write about his dying"—the reader expects that Kincaid's expressions of loss and partial reconciliation are to be read in the same way the factual retelling of Devon's story is read. The mistrust Kincaid's memory encounters, and by extension the mistrust the text encounters, are not concerns over legitimacy, but rather how her family members in Antigua view the perceptions of an estranged member in Vermont. If Kincaid's expressions of loss are legitimate, then her mother's mistrust of her expressions are legitimate.

30. Sandra Paquet makes a similar connection between Devon's disease and devastation and the disease and dilapidation of Antigua, stating: "Despite the recurring cycle of rejection, her troubled relationship with her mother and with Antigua endures in the elegiac rhythms of identification and dissociation that characterize the abjection of this mourner's relationship to the dead, the past, and her native place." See Sandra Paquet, *Caribbean Autobiography: Cultural Identity and Self-Representation* (Madison: University of Wisconsin Press, 2002), 249. Kincaid's mourning and conflicted feelings towards her brother are directly parallel to her emotional response to the island of her birth.

31. This statement by Kincaid is resonant of V. S. Naipaul's notorious criticism of the West Indies in *The Middle Passage* (London: Picador, 1962), 25. Naipaul argues thus, "The history of the islands can never be satisfactorily told. Brutality is not the only difficulty. History is built around achievement and creation; and nothing was created in the West Indies." Naipaul's nothing and Kincaid's nothing are punctuated by a sense of loss. Both nothings are used against the backdrop of history, and with the ambivalence of the end of colonial domination.

32. Marie-Helene Laforest, *Diasporic Encounters: Remapping the Caribbean* (Napoli: Liguori, 2000), 217.

33. Kincaid, *My Brother*, 8.

34. Nation language is a term coined by Kamau Brathwaite to refer to "the kind of English spoken by the people who were brought to the Caribbean, not the official English now, but the language of slaves and labourers, the servants who were brought in by the

conquistadors." See Kamau Brathwaite, "History of the Voice," in *Roots* (Ann Arbor: University of Michigan Press, 1993 [published previously in 1979 and 1981]), 260.

35. Laurie Kriszner and Stephen Mandell, *The Holt Handbook* (Fort Worth: Harcourt Brace College Publishers, 1995), 524.

36. In *My Brother* Kincaid suggests that her mother's love for her children is somehow warped. She cites the fact that Devon will return to their mother's house when he is discharged from the hospital so that Mrs. Drew can care for him as the "extraordinary ability of her love for her children to turn into a weapon for their destruction" (53). Kincaid argues that her mother's love is only evident when her children are in desperate need of her care and that in other circumstances it is destructive (28).

37. Ibid., 49.

38. Ibid., 181.

39. Ibid., 36.

40. Maria Helena Lima, "Imaginary Homelands in Jamaica Kincaid's Narratives of Development," *Callaloo* 25, no. 3 (2002): 861.

41. Kincaid, *My Brother*, 68.

Chronology

1949	Born on May 25 as Elaine Potter Richardson in St. John's, Antigua, in the Caribbean.
	Mother is Annie Richardson Drew, a homemaker and political activist. Father is Frederick Potter, employed at the Mill Reef Club. Stepfather is David Drew, a cabinetmaker and carpenter.
1952	Mother teaches her to read and enrolls her in the Moravian School at age three.
1956	Attends the Antiguan Girls School. Apprenticed to a seamstress. Attends Princess Margaret School.
1958	Joseph Drew, her first brother, is born.
1959	Dalma Drew, her second brother, is born.
1961	Devon Drew, her third brother, is born.
1965	Leaves Antigua for the United States shortly after her sixteenth birthday.
1969–70	Studies photography at the New School for Social Research in New York City and at Franconia College in New Hampshire.
1973	Changes name to Jamaica Kincaid. Publishes "When I Was Seventeen."
1976	Becomes *New Yorker* magazine staff writer.

1978	Writes "Girl," her first fiction, which later gets published in the *New Yorker* and in the collection *At the Bottom of the River*.
1979	Marries Allen Shawn, a composer and teacher at Bennington College and the son of William Shawn, editor of the *New Yorker*. They later have two children, Annie and Harold.
1983	Wins the Morton Dauwen Zabel Award of the American Academy and Institute of Arts and Letters for *At the Bottom of the River*.
1985	Publishes *Annie John*.
1986	Publishes *Annie, Gwen, Lilly, Pam and Tulip* along with Eric Fischl.
1988	Publishes *A Small Place*. Receives a Guggenheim Fellowship.
1990	Publishes *Lucy*.
1996	Resigns from the *New Yorker*, citing creative differences with new editor, Tina Brown. Publishes *The Autobiography of My Mother*, a National Book Critics Circle Award finalist for fiction and a PEN Faulkner Award finalist.
1997	Publishes *My Brother*.
1998	Publishes, along with Lynn Geesaman, *Poetics of Place*. Editor of *My Favorite Plant: Writers and Gardeners on the Plants They Love*.
1999	Publishes *My Garden (Book)*.
2000	Publishes *Talk Stories*.
2002	*Mr. Potter* is published.
2005	Publishes *Among Flowers: A Walk in the Himalaya*. Editor of *The Best American Travel Writing 2005*.

Contributors

HAROLD BLOOM is Sterling Professor of the Humanities at Yale University. He is the author of 30 books, including *Shelley's Mythmaking*, *The Visionary Company*, *Blake's Apocalypse*, *Yeats*, *A Map of Misreading*, *Kabbalah and Criticism*, *Agon: Toward a Theory of Revisionism*, *The American Religion*, *The Western Canon*, and *Omens of Millennium: The Gnosis of Angels, Dreams, and Resurrection*. *The Anxiety of Influence* sets forth Professor Bloom's provocative theory of the literary relationships between the great writers and their predecessors. His most recent books include *Shakespeare: The Invention of the Human*, a 1998 National Book Award finalist, *How to Read and Why*, *Genius: A Mosaic of One Hundred Exemplary Creative Minds*, *Hamlet: Poem Unlimited*, *Where Shall Wisdom Be Found?*, and *Jesus and Yahweh: The Names Divine*. In 1999, Professor Bloom received the prestigious American Academy of Arts and Letters Gold Medal for Criticism. He has also received the International Prize of Catalonia, the Alfonso Reyes Prize of Mexico, and the Hans Christian Andersen Bicentennial Prize of Denmark.

MOIRA FERGUSON teaches English at the University of Missouri, Kansas City. She is the author of *Nine Black Women: An Anthology of Nineteenth Century Writers from the United States, Canada, Bermuda and the Caribbean*.

MERLE HODGE is a lecturer in the Department of Language and Linguistics at the University of the West Indies in Trinidad. She has published two novels as well as numerous short stories and is on the editorial board of *Caribbean Review of Gender Studies*.

ANTONIA MACDONALD-SMYTHE is associate dean at the School of Arts and Sciences, St. George's University, Grenada, West Indies. She has written numerous pieces on Jamaica Kincaid and authored the book *Making Homes in the West Indies: Constructions of Subjectivity in the Writings of Michelle Cliff and Jamaica Kincaid.*

LAURA NIESEN DE ABRUNA has taught at Ithaca College. Her work focuses on Anglophone Caribbean women writers and has appeared in *Modern Fiction Studies* and *World Literature Written in English.*

K. B. CONAL BYRNE has been the film critic for the *Atlanta Press*. He has published in the *Romance Review, Hispanófila*, and the *Irish Literary Journal.*

IRLINE FRANÇOIS teaches in the Women's Studies Program at Goucher College. Her research focuses on contemporary Caribbean literature, Latin American women's social movements, and international feminist theory.

RAMÓN E. SOTO-CRESPO teaches at the State University of New York, Buffalo. He is the author of essays on Caribbean literature and a book manuscript, "Caribbean Troubles: Queer Writing, Nationhood, and the Diaspora, 1959–1997."

MARIA HELENA LIMA teaches at the State University of New York, Geneseo. She coauthored *Women Righting: Afro-Brazilian Women's Short Fiction.*

ELIZABETH J. WEST teaches at Georgia State University. Her work has appeared in publications such as *Oxford Companion to African American Literature, MELUS*, and *South Atlantic Review.*

J. BROOKS BOUSON teaches English at Loyola University Chicago. Among her published work is *Quiet As It's Kept: Shame, Trauma, and Race in the Novels of Toni Morrison.*

COLENA GARDNER-CORBETT has taught at Johnson C. Smith University in Charlotte, North Carolina. She writes poetry and short stories.

KEZIA PAGE teaches English at Colgate University. Her writing has been published in the *Journal of West Indian Literature* and *Anthurium.*

Bibliography

Anatol, Giselle Liza. "Speaking in (M)Other Tongues: The Role of Language in Jamaica Kincaid's *The Autobiography of My Mother*." *Callaloo* 25, no. 3 (Summer 2002): 938–53.

Bernard, Louise. "Countermemory and Return: Reclamation of the (Postmodern) Self in Jamaica Kincaid's *The Autobiography of My Mother* and *My Brother*." *Modern Fiction Studies* 48, no. 1 (Spring 2002): 113–38.

Berrian, Brenda F. "Snapshots of Childhood Life in Jamaica Kincaid's Fiction." In *Arms Akimbo: Africana Women in Contemporary Literature*, edited by Janice Lee Liddell and Belinda Yakini Kemp, 103–16. Gainesville: University Press of Florida, 1999.

Birbalsingh, Frank. *Jamaica Kincaid: From Antigua to America*. New York: St. Martin's, 1996.

Braziel, Jana Evans. "Alterbiographic Transmutations of Genre in Jamaica Kincaid's 'Biography of a Dress' and *Autobiography of My Mother*." *A/B: Auto/Biography Studies* 18, no. 1 (Summer 2003): 85–104.

———. "Jamaica Kincaid's 'In the Night': Jablesse, Obeah, and Diasporic Alterrains in *At the Bottom of the River*." *Journal x* 6, no. 1 (Autumn 2001): 79–104.

Broeck, Sabine. "When Light Becomes White: Reading Enlightenment through Jamaica Kincaid's Writing." *Callaloo* 25, no. 3 (Summer 2002): 821–43.

Brophy, Sarah. "Angels in Antigua: The Diasporic of Melancholy in Jamaica Kincaid's *My Brother*." *PMLA: Publications of the Modern Language Association of America* 117, no. 2 (March 2002): 265–77.

Byerman, K. E. "Anger in *A Small Place*: Jamaica Kincaid's Cultural Critique of Antigua." *College Literature* 22, no. 1 (1995): 91–102.

Caton, Louis F. "Romantic Struggles: The Bildungsroman and Mother–Daughter Bonding in Jamaica Kincaid's *Annie John*." *MELUS* 21, no. 3 (1996): 126–143.

Chick, Nancy. "The Broken Clock: Time, Identity, and Autobiography in Jamaica Kincaid's *Lucy*." *CLA Journal* 40, no. 1 (1996): 90–104.

Collett, Anne. "Boots and Bare-Feet in Jamaica Kincaid's 'Garden (Book).'" *Wasafiri* 48 (Summer 2006): 58–63.

———. "A Snake in the Garden of the *New Yorker*? An Analysis of the Disruptive Function of Jamaica Kincaid's Gardening Column." *Missions of Interdependence: A Literary Directory*, edited by Gerhard Stilz, 95–106. Amsterdam, Netherlands: Rodopi, 2002.

Cousineau, Diane. "Women and Autobiography: Is There Life Beyond the Looking Glass?" *Caliban* 31 (1994): 97–105.

Covi, Giovanna. "Alterity: Jamaica Kincaid's Resistance." In *Resisting Alterities: Wilson Harris and Other Avatars of Otherness*, edited by Marco Fazzini, 197–208. Amsterdam, Netherlands: Rodopi, 2004.

———. *Jamaica Kincaid's Prismatic Subjects: Making Sense of Being in the World*. London, England: Mango, 2003.

Cudjoe, Selwyn R., ed. *Caribbean Women Writers: Essays from the First International Conference*. Wellesley, Mass.: Calaloux Publications, 1990.

Dance, Daryl Cumber. *Fifty Caribbean Writers: A Bio-bibliographical and Critical Sourcebook*. Westport, Conn.: Greenwood Press, 1986.

Davidson, Diana. "Writing AIDS in Antigua: Tensions between Public and Private Activisms in Jamaica Kincaid's *My Brother*." *Journal of Commonwealth and Postcolonial Studies* 10, no. 1 (Spring 2003): 121–44.

Donnell, Alison. "When Daughters Defy: Jamaica Kincaid's Fiction." *Women: A Cultural Review* 4, no. 1 (1993): 18–26.

———. "When Writing the Other Is Being True to the Self: Jamaica Kincaid's *The Autobiography of My Mother*." In *Women's Lives into Print: The Theory, Practice and Writing of Feminist Auto/Biography*, edited by Pauline Polkey, 123–36. New York; London, England: St. Martin's; Macmillan, 1999.

Dutton, Wendy. "Merge and Separate: Jamaica Kincaid's Fiction." *World Literature Today* 63 (Summer 1989): 406–10.

Ferguson, Moira. *Jamaica Kincaid: Where the Land Meets the Body.* Charlottesville: University Press of Virginia, 1994.

———. "A Lot of Memory: An Interview with Jamaica Kincaid." *Kenyon Review* 16, no. 1 (Winter 1994): 163–88.

———. "*Lucy* and the Mark of the Colonizer." *Modern Fiction Studies* 39, no. 2 (1993): 237–259.

Garis, Leslie. "Through West Indian Eyes." *New York Times Magazine* (October 7, 1990): 42.

Gauch, Suzanne. "*A Small Place*: Some Perspectives on the Ordinary." *Callaloo* 25, no. 3 (Summer 2002): 910–19.

Gilkes, Michael. "The Madonna Pool: Woman as 'Muse of Identity.'" *Journal of West Indian Literature* 1, no. 2 (June 1987): 1–19.

Grayson, Erik. "The Most Important Meal: Food and Meaning in Jamaica Kincaids's *Lucy*." *Journal of the Georgia Philological Association* 1 (December 2006): 212–27.

Gregg, Veronica Marie. "How Jamaica Kincaid Writes the Autobiography of Her Mother." *Callaloo* 25, no. 3 (Summer 2002): 920–37.

Harkins, Patricia. "Family Magic: Invisibility in Jamaica Kincaid's *Lucy*." *Journal of the Fantastic in the Arts* 4, no. 3 (1991): 53–68.

Higonnet, Margaret. *Borderwork.* Ithaca, N.Y.: Cornell University Press, 1994.

Holcomb, Gary E. "Travels of a Transnational Slut: Sexual Migration in Kincaid's *Lucy*." *Critique* 44, no. 3 (Spring 2003): 295–312.

Holcomb, Gary; and Holcomb, Kimberly S. "'I Made Him': Sadomasochism in Kincaid's *The Autobiography of My Mother*." *Callaloo* 25, no. 3 (Summer 2002): 969–76.

Insanally, Annette. "Contemporary Female Writing in the Caribbean." In *The Caribbean Novel in Comparison: Proceedings of the Ninth Conference of Hispanists*, edited by Ena V. Thomas, 115–141. St. Augustine, Trinidad: University of the West Indies, Department of French and Spanish Literatures, 1986.

Ippolito, Emilia. "Room as a Catalyst of Differences: In Search of Autonomous Subjectivity in the Caribbean (Con)Text of Jamaica Kincaid." In *Borderlands: Negotiating Boundaries in Post-Colonial Writing*, edited by Monika Reif-Hülser, 145–54. Amsterdam, Netherlands: Rodopi, 1999.

Joseph, Betty. "Gendering Time in Globalization: The Belatedness of the Other Woman and Jamaica Kincaid's *Lucy*." *Tulsa Studies in Women's Literature* 21, no. 1 (Spring 2002): 67–83.

Lang-Peralta, Linda, ed. *Jamaica Kincaid and Caribbean Double Crossings*. Newark: University of Delaware Press, 2006.

Ledent, Benedicte. "Voyages into Otherness: *Cambridge* and *Lucy*." *Kunapipi* 14, no. 2 (1993): 53–63.

Lenz, Brooke. "Postcolonial Fiction and the Outsider Within: Toward a Literary Practice of Feminist Standpoint Theory." *NWSA Journal: National Women's Studies Association Journal* 16, no. 2 (Summer 2004): 98–120.

Louis, James. "Reflections, and the Bottom of the River: The Transformation of Caribbean Experience in the Fiction of Jamaica Kincaid." *Wasafiri* 89 (Winter 1988): 15–17.

Mahlis, Kristen. "Gender and Exile: Jamaica Kincaid's *Lucy*." *Modern Fiction Studies* 44 (1998): 164–83.

Mangum, Bryant. "Jamica Kincaid." In *Fifty Caribbean Writers: a Bio-bibliographical Critical Source Book*, edited by Daryl Cumber Dance, 255–63. New York: Greenwood Press, 1986.

Matos, Nicole C. "'The Difference between the Two Bundles': Body and Cloth in the Works of Jamaica Kincaid." *Callaloo* 25, no. 3 (Summer 2002): 844–56.

Melbourne, Lucy. "'Young Lady' or 'Slut': Identity and Voice in Jamaica Kincaid's *Annie John* (1983)." In *Women in Literature: Reading through the Lens of Gender*, edited by Jerilyn Fisher and Ellen S. Silber, 15–17. Westport, CT: Greenwood, 2003.

Mitchell, Rick. "Caribbean Cruising: Sex, Death, and Memories of (Congo) Darkness." *Atenea* 23, no. 2 (December 2003): 9–23.

Morris, Kathryn E. "Jamaica Kincaid's Voracious Bodies: Engendering a Carib(bean) Woman." *Callaloo* 25, no. 3 (Summer 2002): 954–68.

Muirhead, Pamela Buchanan. "An Interview with Jamaica Kincaid." *Clockwatch Review* 9.1 and 2 (1994–1995): 39–48.

Murdoch, Adlai H. "The Novels of Jamaica Kincaid: Figures of Exile, Narratives of Dreams." *Clockwatch Review* 9.1 and 2 (1994–1995): 141–54.

Murray, Melanie A. "Shifting Identities and Locations in Jamaica Kincaid's *My Garden (Book)* and *A Small Place*." *World Literature Written in English* 39, no. 1 (2001): 116–26.

Narain, Denise deCaires. "Moving Worlds with Words: The Postcolonial Woman-as-Writer in Jamaica Kincaid's Fiction." *Moving Worlds: A Journal of Transcultural Writings* 3, no. 2 (2003): 70–83.

Natov, Roni. "Mothers and Daughters: Jamaica Kincaid's Pre-Oedipal Narrative." *Children's Literature* 18 (1990): 1–16.

O'Brien, Susie. "New Postnational Narratives, Old American Dreams; Or, the Problem with Coming-of-Age Stories." In *Postcolonial America*, edited by Richard C. King, 65–80. Urbana: University of Illinois Press, 2000.

Paravisini-Gebert, Lizabeth. *Jamaica Kincaid: A Critical Companion.* Westport: Greenwood Press, 1999.

Scott, Helen. "'Dem Tief, Dem a Dam Tief': Jamaica Kincaid's Literature of Protest." *Callaloo* 25, no. 3 (Summer 2002): 977–89.

Sharrad, Paul. "Cloth and Self-Definition in Jamaica Kincaid's *The Autobiography of My Mother.*" *Kunapipi* 26, no. 1 (2004): 54–65.

Shima, Alan. "No Beginning, No End: The Legacy of Absence in Jamaica Kincaid's *The Autobiography of My Mother.*" *Kunapipi* 26, no. 2 (2004): 61–73.

Sicherman, Carol. "Escape from the Mother/Land in Jamaica Kincaid's *Annie John.*" *Commonwealth Novel in English* 9–10 (Spring–Fall 2001): 180–96.

Simmons, Diane. "Coming-of-Age in the Snare of History: Jamaica Kincaid's *The Autobiography of My Mother.*" *The Girl: Construction of the Girl in Contemporary Fiction by Women*, edited by Ruth O. Saxton, 107–18. New York: St. Martin's, 1998.

———. *Jamaica Kincaid.* New York: Twayne, 1994.

———. "The Mother Mirror in Jamaica Kincaid's *Annie John* and Gertrude Stein's *The Good Anna.*" In *The Anna Book: Searching for Anna in Literary History*, edited by Mickey Pearlman, 99–104. Westport, Conn.: Greenwood Press, 1992.

———. "The Rhythm of Reality in the Work of Jamaica Kincaid." *World Literature Today* 68, no. 3 (1994): 466–472.

Smith, Ian. "Misusing Canonical Intertexts: Jamaica Kincaid, Wordsworth and Colonialism's 'absent things.'" *Callaloo* 25, no. 3 (Summer 2002): 801–20.

Tapping, Craig. "Children and History in the Caribbean Novel: George Lamming's *In the Castle of My Skin* and Jamaica Kincaid's *Annie John.*" *Kunapipi* 9 (1989): 51–59.

Tiffin, Helen. "Decolonization and Audience: Erna Brodber's *Myal* and Jamaica Kincaid's *A Small Place*." *Span* 30 (1990): 27–38.

Yost, David. "A Tale of Three Lucys: Wordsworth and Brontë in Kincaid's Antiguan Villette." *MELUS* 31, no. 2 (Summer 2006): 141–56.

Acknowledgments

Moira Ferguson, "A Small Place: Glossing Annie John's Rebellion," *Colonialism and Gender Relations from Mary Wollstonecraft to Jamaica Kincaid, East Caribbean Connections,* Columbia University Press, 1993. Copyright © 1993 Columbia University Press. Reprinted by permission.

Merle Hodge, "Caribbean Writers and Caribbean Language: A Study of Jamaica Kincaid's *Annie John,*" *Winds of Change: The Transforming Voices of Caribbean Women Writers and Scholars,* Peter Lang, 1998. Reprinted by permission.

Antonia MacDonald-Smythe, "Authorizing the Slut in Jamaica Kincaid's At the Bottom of the River, MaComère, vol. 2, 1999.

Laura Niesen de Abruna, "Jamaica Kincaid's Writing and the Maternal-Colonial Matrix," Caribbean Women Writers: Fiction in English, New York: St. Martin's, 1999.

K. B. Conal Byrne, "Under English, Obeah English: Jamaica Kincaid's New Language," CLA Journal, vol. XLIII, no. 3, March 2000.

Irline François, "The Daffodil Gap: Jamaica Kincaid's *Lucy,*" *MaComère,* 1999. Used by permission of Irline François.

Ramón E. Soto-Crespo, *Contemporary Literature,* Vol 43, No 2 (Summer 2002). Copyright 2002 by the Board of Regents of the University of Wisconsin System. Reproduced by permission.

Maria Helena Lima, Imaginary Homelands in Jamaica Kincaid's Narratives of Development. *Callaloo* 25:3 (2002), 857–867. © Charles H. Rowell.

Elizabeth J. West, In the Beginning There Was Death: Spiritual Desolation and the Search for Self in Jamaica Kincaid's *Autobiography of My Mother*. *South Central Review* 20:2/4 (2003), 2-23, © South Central Review. Reprinted by permission of The Johns Hopkins University Press

J. Brooks Bouson, "Like Him and His Own Father before Him, I Have a Line Drawn through Me': Imagining the Life of the Absent Father in Mr. Potter," Jamaica Kincaid: Writing Memory, Writing Back to the Mother, Albany: State University of New York Press, 2005.

Colena Gardner-Corbett, "Escaping the Colonizer's Whip: The Binary Discipline," CLA Journal, vol. XLIX, no. 1, September 2005.

Kezia Page, "What If He Did Not Have a Sister [Who Lived in the United States]?": Jamaica Kincaid's *My Brother* as Remittance Text, *Small Axe*, 2006. Copyright © 2006 Indiana University Press. Reproduced by permission.

Index